THE
BHAGAVAD GITA

The Oxford Centre for Hindu Studies
Mandala Publishing Series

THE
BHAGAVAD GITA

A New Translation and Study Guide

Dr. Nicholas Sutton

MANDALA
PUBLISHING

San Rafael, California

CONTENTS

CONTENTS

PREFACE

In this book, I have undertaken a detailed study of the Bhagavad-gita and the principal ideas it presents to its readers. As the Gita is a relatively short work of 18 chapters and 700 verses, it might seem that this is a far easier task than would be the case for a longer text such as the *Mahabharata* or the *Ramayana*. I have not, however, attempted a verse by verse consideration of the Bhagavad-gita and have chosen instead to adopt a thematic approach aimed at establishing and exploring the main themes of the discourse and the principal ideas presented in each chapter.

The Bhagavad-gita appears as a section of the *Bhishma-parvan*, the sixth book of the *Mahabharata*, at the point just prior to the 18-day battle at Kurukshetra. In this conflict the hopes of the Pandava faction rest largely on the martial prowess of Arjuna, the third of the five Pandava brothers. At the start of the Bhagavad-gita, however, we find the hero disconsolate and unwilling to wage war against his own family members. It is at this point that Krishna, his cousin and charioteer, begins to offer instruction to Arjuna. The initial intention of the discourse is to persuade Arjuna that waging war is not necessarily an act of wickedness, but the full treatise goes far beyond this initial thesis, developing into a thoroughgoing exposition of belief and practice that has had an immeasurable influence on the formation of Hindu religious doctrines.

I will consider the Bhagavad-gita chapter by chapter and try to establish the main ideas it pursues in its teachings, thereby seeking to identify the full significance of this famous scripture. At certain points, attention will be drawn to significant Sanskrit terms, and some use will be made of three traditional commentaries on the Gita, namely those of Shankaracharya, Ramanujacharya, and Madhvacharya. I will also try to expand the discussion so that at certain junctures it will be possible to reflect on the contemporary significance of the teachings and of how they can be of relevance to the modern world.

INTRODUCTION

A BRIEF SYNOPSIS

In the introduction, the position of the Gita within the *Mahabharata* and its status within the Hindu tradition will be considered before looking briefly at some of the views of contemporary scholars. We will then turn our attention to the Gita's opening chapter with a consideration of Arjuna's lamentation, which prompts Krishna to begin his teachings. Moving on to Chapter 2 we begin with a review of Krishna's initial responses to Arjuna's refusal to fight and in particular the way in which he emphasises the eternal nature of the living being. We then move on to concentrate on the idea of *karma-yoga*, which Krishna offers as a direct response to Arjuna's fear of sinful action. This notion is particularly important in Hindu religious thought, as it reveals how a person can simultaneously fulfil his social obligations whilst striving to attain the highest spiritual goals.

In considering Chapter 3 we can look in further detail at Krishna's explanation of *karma-yoga* and then note the progression in the teachings from *karma-yoga*, concluded in Chapter 5, to the explanation of *dhyana* presented in Chapter 6. Here, we find another form of spirituality advocated by the Bhagavad-gita, the process of meditational yoga by which one acquires direct perception of the inner self, the *atman*, a realisation that leads to liberation from the cycle of rebirth.

After this discussion of meditational yoga, we proceed further into the main body of our text, at this point noting how from Chapter 7 onwards the direction of the discourse changes dramatically. The opening six chapters focused on the ways in which an individual could pursue the path of renunciation whilst fulfilling social obligations, but from the beginning of Chapter 7 onwards we now find a switch in emphasis towards providing an understanding of the nature of God and of the power of divine grace. In the middle section (Chapters 7–12) of the Bhagavad-gita, Krishna not only teaches Arjuna about the nature of the Supreme Deity but also reveals that he himself is that Deity. And in response to Arjuna's prayer, he also manifests his divine identity as that which is all things, the unseen presence of God pervading the entire creation.

After the great revelation of the divine in Chapter 11 and the emphasis placed on devotion to God, Chapters 13–16 diversify the Gita's teachings and cover a variety of topics that serve to reinforce the teachings that have gone before. One common theme running through these later chapters is the emphasis on Samkhya ideas, the philosophical system that seeks to define the material manifestation and to establish the distinctive identity of the individual soul in all beings. In our sixth chapter, we will consider the ways in which Krishna employs concepts derived from the Samkhya system to add greater depth to his teachings.

In reviewing the final two chapters of the Gita (17 and 18), we again find a diversity of ideas, including an exploration of the way the *gunas*, the three inherent qualities of matter, can be identified within this world. The Bhagavad-gita ends its teachings by revisiting the main ideas it has presented earlier, finally concluding with a renewed emphasis on the importance of devotion and the power of divine grace in saving the devotee from rebirth.

RECOMMENDED READING

The Bhagavad-gita is widely known and studied both in the West and in India, and innumerable English translations of the text are available. Academics have also paid considerable attention to the Gita, and many books have been published analysing the content and proposing various theses about its sources, date, origin, and structure.

The problems you may encounter with English translations are twofold. Academic renditions of the texts such as those produced by Robert Zaehner, Will Johnson, or Franklin Edgerton tend to be excessively literal. This means that they are very faithful to the literal meaning of the Sanskrit text but often produce a style of English that is difficult to comprehend and rather obscures the intended meaning. Other translations give a version that can be more readily understood but are produced from a particular philosophical or religious perspective. The problem here is that translation cannot be entirely separated from commentary; often, different meanings can be derived from the same words and phrases, and the meaning given in the English version will tend to reflect the translator's own religious orientation.

Here are some reasonable academic translations:

- Edgerton, F. (1997) *The Bhagavad-gita*. Cambridge, Massachusetts, Harvard University Press
- Johnson, W. (2004) *The Bhagavad-gita*. Oxford, Oxford University Press
- Parrinder, G. (1974) *The Bhagavad-gita, a Verse Translation*. London, Sheldon Press
- Zaehner, R. (1973) *The Bhagavad-gita*. Oxford, Oxford University Press
- Juan Mascaro's version, published by Penguin Classics, is still popular and very readable, although some of his translations are rather dubious.

The ISKCON edition with translation and commentary by A. C. Bhaktivedanta Swami Prabhupada is a very accessible version, and the purports shed light on the meaning of the text. One must be aware, however, that the translation and commentary are presented from a specific Vaishnava perspective.

Dr Radhakrishnan's translation is based on an impressive standard of scholarship but is perhaps overly influenced by the commentary of Shankaracharya.

The Ramakrishna Math has recently produced two English versions of the Bhagavad-gita, one with the full commentary of Shankaracharya and one with Ramanuja's commentary. These are very interesting works from the point of view of textual exegesis and the development of Indian religious thought, but of course the translations and commentaries are reflective of the commentators' own religious perspectives and, at times, seem to stretch the meaning of the Sanskrit original for that purpose. The same can be said of the two commentaries produced by Madhvacharya – now very difficult to obtain in English.

Academic scholarship on the Bhagavad-gita has tended to focus on the structure of the text and its relationship to the *Mahabharata*. Some studies have tried to divide the verses and chapters into various strata, which they claim come from different authors, whilst others attempt to demonstrate that the Gita is an interpolation that was added to the *Mahabharata* at a later date. Our principal aim here, however, is to convey an understanding of the meaning of the teachings Krishna offers, and, hence, critical studies of this type are not particularly relevant. Edgerton and Zaehner, however, do provide essays and commentaries on the text in which they discuss the meaning of teachings, and these will be referred to at different times.

KEY CONCEPTS

Dharma

In the Bhagavad-gita, *dharma* means both 'virtuous conduct' and 'the social duties an individual is bound to perform in relation to his *varna*, or social class'. In Chapter 1, Arjuna argues that the death of family elders leads to a decline in family *dharma*, while in Chapter 7 (verse 12), Krishna identifies himself as desire but only when it does not contravene *dharma*. The main reference to *dharma*, however, is in relation to Krishna's insistence that Arjuna must fulfil the *dharma* of his social class, the *kshatriyas*, by waging war against wrongdoers. We first find this instruction in Chapter 2, verses 31–6. Moreover, the *karma-yoga* that Krishna emphasises in the opening chapters of the Gita is based on the idea that *dharma*, or duty, should be performed without desire for personal gain.

In Chapter 18, the concept of *dharma* is revisited with some interesting refinements of the points made earlier. In verses 41–4, the *dharma* of each *varna* is outlined, and in verses 45–6, a link is made between *dharma* and *bhakti*, devotion to God, with dharmic duty represented as a means of worshipping God, who is the creator of *dharma*. It is therefore wrong for an individual to abandon his or her *dharma*; in any case, *dharma* is not just a series of tasks one ought to perform but a part of one's very nature. Hence, for the Gita, *dharma* is descriptive as well as prescriptive. It is not just what a person ought to do; it is a reflection of a person's inner nature (*sva-bhava*) generated as a result of past karma.

Karma

The idea of good and bad fortune in this world being the result of previous actions, or karma, is fundamental to Indian religious thought and is more or less taken for granted in the Bhagavad-gita. Arjuna's reluctance to fight is based in part on his fear of the future results of sinful action; and in Chapter 14, Krishna relates the idea of karma to the influence of the three *gunas* over human action. '*Guna*' can be defined as the quality or characteristic with which action is coloured. Adhering to the ideas found in Yoga philosophy, the Gita refines the doctrine of karma still further by insisting that it is the consciousness of the performer rather than the action itself that is the crucial factor. This, once again', is related to the idea of *karma-yoga*. In Chapter 4, it is explained that actions performed without selfish desire are *akarma*, literally 'non-karma', because they produce no reaction, whilst even a failure to act produces a result if that abstention is based on selfish desire. This idea is taken up again in the first twenty verses or so of Chapter 18. Action, good or bad, produces future results and rebirth in another body, and so one might think that *moksha*, release from rebirth, can be gained only by renouncing all action. The Bhagavad-gita teaches, however, that it is not the action itself that must be renounced but the selfish desire that prompts it. In this way, the performance of dharmic duty becomes compatible with escaping from the cycle of good and bad karma.

Moksha

The Bhagavad-gita is essentially a *moksha-shastra,* as its main purpose is to teach its hearers how to gain release from rebirth. It is anxious to show that the quest for *moksha,* literally 'release' or 'liberation', need not involve giving up dharmic duty, and for this reason it offers the *karma-yoga* as a means of pursuing this highest goal. In Chapter 6, *dhyana-yoga,* the yoga of meditation, is revealed as a spiritual practice that leads to liberation from rebirth. And then in Chapters 7–12, we are shown that *moksha* is in fact a gift of grace granted by Krishna himself to the devotees whom he loves. This is revealed particularly in 7.14, 11.55, 12.6–7, and 18.66. Whilst the Gita offers several different paths to *moksha,* including karma, *dhyana,* and *bhakti,* it does not say a great deal about what *moksha* actually is or the state of existence experienced by one who has transcended rebirth. There are many different phrases used by the Gita to refer to *moksha*, but they do little more than reveal that this is the state in which Krishna exists, that it is joyful, and that is free from any danger of a return to the existence in which rebirth takes place. It is also clear from verses such as 8.15–16, 9.33, and 13.8 that the Gita regards this world as a place of suffering from which one should seek to escape, thereby confirming the first noble truth of the Buddha.

Bhakti and the nature of God

There is a lot that can be written under this heading, as it is a topic the Bhagavad-gita deals with in some detail. In considering 'the nature of God', one might look at the *avatara* verses at the start of Chapter 4 and then the discussions in Chapter 7, Chapter 9, and the opening verses of Chapter 10. One might also consider the significance of the *vishva-rupa*, revealed to Arjuna in Chapter 11. There is substantial evidence to suggest that the Gita regards *bhakti* as the best spiritual path for an aspirant to follow. In following the *karma-yoga* and the *dhyana-yoga* described in the first six chapters, one relies on one's own efforts to transform oneself through higher realisation. It is made clear, however, that Krishna himself grants *moksha* to his devotee as an act of divine grace. This is apparent from verses such as 7.14, 10.11, 12.6–7, and 18.66. Moreover, the Bhagavad-gita provides the foundation for the emotional forms of devotion that are so important in Hinduism today. In Chapter 12, Krishna repeatedly refers to the mood of love that exists between himself and his devotee, using the word *priya*, to make the point.

Yoga

The Bhagavad-gita uses the term yoga for all the paths it recommends, and this allows for a very broad definition. Here, however, it is probably a good idea to confine the discussion to a narrower definition and look at the teachings it provides on the types of yoga similar to those recommended by Patañjali in his *Yoga Sutras*. In Chapter 6 and again in Chapter 8, Krishna instructs Arjuna in techniques of meditation and inward contemplation. The important points to note here are the techniques recommended, the object of meditation and the reasons why this practice is advocated. It is clear that the yoga taught by the Gita is intended to allow realisation of the *atman* within one's own being, and that this realisation is regarded as a means of transcending the unwanted conditions of life in this world. The techniques set forth involve *asana*, withdrawal of the senses from external objects, and the regulation of the mind so that it can be fixed on a single point and maintained in that intense form of contemplation. It is also interesting to note Arjuna's rather negative response to this teaching, which we find in verses 33 and 34 of Chapter 6.

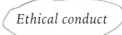

Ethical conduct

Arjuna's initial objection to fighting rests substantially on his view that to do so would be *adharma*, a breach of his ethical code. In teaching *karma-yoga*, Krishna switches the focus away from the action itself towards the motive that prompts a person to perform it. Hence, for Arjuna, killing those who oppose him is acceptable providing his motive is not one of selfish desire. Here also, Krishna reasserts the traditional notion of *varna-dharma,* or duty, according to one's social status, insisting that it is Arjuna's duty to fight because of his social identity as a *kshatriya,* or warrior. The Bhagavad-gita does not give lists of approved or forbidden acts (it is not a book of religious law), but it does provide lists of qualities that one should strive to incorporate into one's own character. In Chapter 13, verses 7–11 describe knowledge in terms of the qualities displayed by a person who possesses knowledge, though these seem to be more applicable to a person who has renounced the world. And in Chapter 16, we are given lists of qualities relating to persons who possess the nature of the gods and to those who possess the nature of the evil *asuras*. Here again, however, we have an interesting twist when, in verse 5, Krishna tells Arjuna that he was born with the qualities of the gods, which of course raises questions as to whether morality is something one strives to achieve or is just something one is born with as a result of previous action.

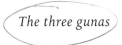

The three gunas

The idea that matter is pervaded by three fundamental qualities (*gunas*) – *sattva*, *rajas*, and *tamas* – is an important element of Samkhya philosophy, and it is one that the Bhagavad-gita makes extensive use of, particularly in its later chapters. Chapter 13 emphasises the division between *prakriti* and *purusha* (matter and spirit), but it is in Chapter 14 that we find an extensive analysis of the way in which these three *gunas* (literally 'strands' or 'qualities') influence and shape the lives of living beings. In Chapter 17 and verses 18–40 of Chapter 18, Krishna uses the *gunas* as the basis for his discussion of different facets of human life including such categories as food, charity, austerity, knowledge, action, and pleasure. He thereby demonstrates how the *gunas* are influential in shaping different areas of human life and also human nature. Ultimately, however, one who seeks *moksha* must go beyond all three *gunas*, even *sattva*, which represents purity and goodness. Verses 25 and 26 of Chapter 14 make it clear that one who seeks the highest goal must become *gunatita*, completely beyond the range of the *gunas*.

CONTEXT

What is the date of the Bhagavad-gita's composition?

As is always the case with ancient Sanskrit literature, it is very difficult to give a precise date of composition, and there are disagreements amongst scholars on this subject. The Hindu tradition regards the Bhagavad-gita as an integral part of the *Mahabharata*, which was composed by Vyasa at the beginning of the present age, the *Kali-yuga*. If this view is accepted, then the Bhagavad-gita is to be dated to sometime around 3000 BC (according to traditional Hindu calculations, the *Kali-yuga* began on 18 February 3102 BC). With one or two notable exceptions, most modern scholars regard the Gita as having been written in the post-Buddhist era. Alf Hiltebeitel suggests a date in the Gupta era, sometime between 150 BC and the year 0, and Robert Minor agrees with this assessment. John Brockington departs somewhat from the conventional view and suggests a later date between the first and third centuries AD (see *The Sanskrit Epics* in Flood (ed.) 2003, p. 147). Contemporary views are summed up rather well by Robert Zaehner when he writes: "As with almost every major religious text from India no firm date can be assigned to the Gita. It seems certain, however, that it was written later than the 'classical' Upanishads with the possible exception of the Maitri and that it is post-Buddhistic. One would probably not be going far wrong if one dated it at some time between the fifth and second centuries BC" (Zaehner, 1973, p. 7).

How does the Bhagavad-gita fit into the Mahabharata?

The Bhagavad-gita appears in the sixth book of *Mahabharata*, the *Bhishma-parvan*, in which its eighteen chapters appear as Chapters 23–40 in the Critical Edition of the text. There is a long tradition, however, of taking the Gita as an almost independent work and the *acharyas* comment upon it as a discrete text in its own right. Modern scholarship has tended to regard the Bhagavad-gita as a work that was composed separately from the *Mahabharata* and then inserted into it at a later date by an editor or redactor of the final version of the text. According to Franklin Edgerton, 'We must think of the Gita primarily as a unit complete in itself, without reference to its surroundings' (Edgerton, 1997, pp. 105–6), and John Brockington seems to take a similar position when he writes, 'One cannot sensibly regard the Bhagavad-gita as both integral to the epic and theologically profound'. (See *The Sanskrit Epics* in Flood (ed.) 2003, p. 146.)

Scholarly views on this subject are divided, however, and others have recognised that the Bhagavad-gita is addressing a philosophical and ethical issue that forms a central theme running throughout the *Mahabharata*. This is the problem of *dharma* and specifically how a person can pursue the goal of liberation from rebirth whilst remaining active in the world. In the *Mahabharata*'s portrayal of Yudhishthira, Arjuna's eldest brother, we see a man who is deeply committed to *dharma* in the form of virtue and who therefore faces repeated crises of conscience in attempting to effectively perform his social duty as a king and a warrior. He loathes the violence, anger, and greed inherent in kingship, and yet he is duty-bound by social *dharma* to act in that capacity. We might also consider a historical context in which followers of ascetic movements such as Buddhism and Jainism were advocating the renunciation of society in pursuit of spiritual perfection. The *Mahabharata* is clearly confronting this tension between social obligations and spiritual inclination, and we can thus see how the Bhagavad-gita adds a contribution to this ongoing discussion that runs throughout the *Mahabharata*.

Hence, I would suggest that the wider context of the *Mahabharata* is indeed very important for an understanding of the Bhagavad-gita, for the Gita is directly responding to fundamental questions about *dharma* that have been posed and considered throughout the *Mahabharata*. Of course it does stand as a work in its own right, but an understanding of the *Mahabharata* will, in my view, contribute significantly to an understanding of the Bhagavad-gita. There are a number of prominent scholars who share this view on the importance of the Gita's context; in his introduction, Robert Zaehner writes, 'Hence it is fair to conclude that the Gita was originally conceived as an integral part of the Epic' (Zaehner, 1973, pp. 6–7), whilst for V. S. Sukthankar, '. . . the Gita is in fact the heart's heart of the *Mahabharata*' (Sukthankar 1957, p. 119).

The question of whether the Bhagavad-gita was a part of the original composition of the *Mahabharata* or whether it was composed independently is one that is almost impossible to answer. It is clear, however, that the Gita is very much aware of its setting within the *Mahabharata* narrative, and it makes effective use of that context in conveying its teachings. Throughout the *Bhishma-parvan* (even after the Bhagavad-gita), we find that Arjuna is reluctant to exert himself fully in fighting against Bhishma, and the Bhagavad-gita uses these misgivings as the starting point for its discourse on *dharma*. And then, in the eleventh chapter, the vision of the *vishva-rupa* is directly related to the *Mahabharata*'s story, for here, we are shown that all the events that will occur at Kurukshetra are subject to the will of the Supreme Deity. Despite their undoubted valour and prowess, the Pandavas will be victorious only because of the will of the Deity. In the vision that Arjuna sees, it is the destruction of the great warriors of the *Mahabharata* –

Bhishma, Drona, and Karna – that reveals the absolute supremacy of the divine will over human endeavour. So whether or not
the Bhagavad-gita was added to the *Mahabharata* at a later date, it
clearly regards itself as a part of the *Mahabharata*'s narrative structure and makes considerable use of its location there in conveying
its principal teachings.

What is the relationship between the Bhagavad-gita and the Upanishads?

The Veda is the large body of Sanskrit texts that comprises India's
earliest scripture and literature. The Upanishads, also known as
Vedanta, or end of the Veda, form an important body of philosophical
texts that comprise one section of the Veda and are therefore defined
as *shruti* (literally, 'that which is heard'); this, in theory at least, gives
them a higher and more authoritative status than any other religious
literature. As a part of the *Mahabharata*, the Bhagavad-gita is referred
to as *smriti* (literally, 'that which is remembered') rather than *shruti*;
however, because its speaker is Krishna, the Supreme Deity himself,
it has considerable status in its own right.

The Bhagavad-gita is well acquainted with the teachings of the
Upanishads and makes considerable use of their ideas. At certain
points, it quotes directly from the Upanishads. For example, in
Chapter 2, where Krishna is pointing out to Arjuna that the soul
is eternal and undying, he draws on material from the Katha Upanishad, which deals with the same subject of the eternal *atman*.
And although the Shvetashvatara Upanishad is a Shaiva text, its
identification of a Deity distinct from the self provides common
ground with the teachings of the Gita in Chapters 13 and 15,
which appear, to some extent, to be based on the Shvetashvatara.
Furthermore, the idea of *karma-yoga* can be recognised in the Isha
Upanishad, and in Chapter 8 of the Gita, we find a discussion
of the Chandogya Upanishad's instruction on the best times to
depart from this world.

To a large extent, the teachings of the Bhagavad-gita are congruent with those of the Upanishads, stressing the presence of the supreme principle within every being and the need to understand the higher nature of the eternal self. There are, however, some notable distinctions. Firstly, unless one accepts Shankaracharya's view that Krishna is the *atman* rather than a separate Deity, the theology of the Bhagavad-gita does not seem to support the Advaitic line of thought pursued throughout most of the Upanishads. In its idea of God, the Gita seems to be closer to the Shvetashvatara Upanishad in establishing three distinct though closely related principles of existence – the Deity, the *atman*, and matter. The Gita, however, goes far beyond any of the Upanishads in arguing that one should not merely know this Deity but also worship him, and even develop a mood of loving devotion. It is this insistence on the importance of *bhakti* that is the principal distinction we can identify between the ideas found in the Bhagavad-gita and Upanishadic thought, though in other areas of its teaching the Gita makes considerable use of the ideas revealed within the Upanishads.

How does modern scholarship view the Bhagavad-gita?

As noted above, much modern scholarship has been devoted to establishing the date of the Bhagavad-gita or considering its relationship to the *Mahabharata*. Some scholars have attempted to divide the Gita itself into different chronological layers, seeking to identify different authors for different sections of the text. In terms of the meaning of the Gita, it is frequently asserted that the teachings it presents are confusing and even contradictory.

One might suggest that the recognition of contradiction within the Bhagavad-gita is culturally rooted in Western perceptions based on notions of either/or, whilst Hindu thought has always appeared to be more comfortable with paradox and different levels of truth. One only has to read the Kena or Isha Upanishad to recognise the prevalence of such patterns of thought. Franklin Edgerton suggests that the perceived illogicalities in the Gita's discourse are due to the fact that it is primarily a text that seeks to convey mystical realisations rather than sequentially logical formulae. In other words, it is less important to follow the logic of its arguments than to personally absorb its truths by means of higher perception. Arvind Sharma, however, rejects this view and suggests that any lack of consistency must be put down to the exigencies of the situation. Krishna is primarily concerned not to purvey a piece of logically reasoned religious philosophy but simply to use any means possible to get Arjuna back into line. Hence, the Bhagavad-gita is dealing not with absolute truths but with very practical arguments that will serve their purpose in the time and place in which they are spoken.

Not all modern scholars share this view of the Gita as being self-contradicting. John Brockington merely says that it is 'not a completely consistent text' (Brockington 1998, p. 57), noting at the same time that it 'holds out the hope of real spiritual progress to those who are nonetheless still very much involved in the affairs of the world' (ibid., p. 56). And on the same subject, Robert Zaehner writes, 'It was only after teaching the Gita for a number of years that it appeared to me, with each re-reading, to be a far more unitary work than most modern scholars had been prepared to concede' (Zaehner, 1973, p. 2).

I am certainly inclined to follow Zaehner's conclusion, and I have never found any striking contradictions in Krishna's words throughout the eighteen chapters. There is no doubt that different spiritual paths are offered, and one supposes that the Christian mind in particular might find this troubling, schooled as it is in a tradition of insistence on doctrinal orthodoxy. But the Hindu religious thought is not like that particularly where the religion as a whole is taken into account. Individual teachers can of course be highly dogmatic in their assertions, but the tradition as a whole is far more comfortable in the presence of differing perspectives on the absolute truth. Ultimately, it is up to the individual to find his or her own path, and the Gita is offering a number of different options in the pursuit of that ultimate goal. These paths are certainly not identical, but that is not to say that they are therefore contradictory.

Who are the main commentators on the Bhagavad-gita?

According to the teachers of the Vedanta system, there are three scriptural bases for the establishment of the truth about absolute reality. These are the Upanishads, the Brahma Sutra, and the Bhagavad-gita, which are known collectively as the *prasthana-traya*, the three foundations. Hence, the Bhagavad-gita has for centuries been one of the most sacred and authoritative texts for orthodox Hindus and has been commented on by some of the most important *acharyas* in the history of the Hindu tradition. Shankaracharya's Bhagavad-gita-bhashya is probably the most well known of these. Here, the commentator tries to demonstrate that the Gita is teaching the doctrine of Advaita Vedanta in a form that is wholly compatible with the Upanishads, though one might feel that the Gita's emphasis on devotion to a higher Deity makes this problematic. Shankara overcomes this difficulty by contending that Krishna is the *atman*, or soul, within each being, and so 'devotion to Krishna' is to be understood as dedicating oneself to realisation of the *atman*. Moreover, on the level of contingent rather than absolute reality, devotion to a personal God is an essential feature of religious life, and as this is the level of reality that most of us inhabit, Shankara himself approved of such worship.

The two great Vaishnava *acharyas*, Madhvacharya and Ramanujacharya, have also left us detailed commentaries on the text of the Gita. According to Robert Zaehner, 'It is Ramanuja who probably comes nearest to the mind of the author of the Gita'. And on balance, one is tempted to agree with this assessment, as Krishna does seem to emphasise both the identity of the *atman* with himself and also the distinction between the *atman* and God in the process of worship, or *bhakti*. Madhva offers us a very lucid commentary based on his own Vaishnava beliefs, but some have found his emphasis on the absolute distinction between the self and God somewhat difficult to reconcile with the Bhagavad-gita's teachings. Vallabhacharya and Baladeva Vidyabhushana have also provided lesser-known Vaishnava commentaries on the text, as has Abhinavagupta, the great teacher of Kashmiri Shaivism.

In the modern era, a number of new interpretations of the Bhagavad-gita have appeared, perhaps most notably that of Dr Radhakrishnan, which follows Shankara's commentary quite closely. In the push for reform and independence, both Tilak and Gandhi provided Gita commentaries, though with very different interpretations. Furthermore, several of the founders of modern Hindu movements have seen fit to give their followers their own interpretations of the text. Here, we might note the works of Chinmayananda, Swami Sivananda, Maharishi Mahesh Yogi, and A. C. Bhaktivedanta Swami Prabhupada. Swami Prabhupada's translation and commentary have become very widely read both in the Western world and in India, and many people possess a copy of this work. Much of this commentary is aimed at those accustomed to Western lifestyles, but it is interesting to note that the philosophical commentary tends towards Ramanuja's interpretation rather than that of Madhva, despite the fact that the author is formally a member of one of the branches of the *sampradaya* descended from Madhvacharya.

MAIN THEMES OF THE BHAGAVAD-GITA

Despite its relative brevity, the Bhagavad-gita contains a complexity of ideas, which it presents to its readers and hearers either in brief or in some detail. I would suggest the following as the big ideas with which Krishna is most preoccupied.

Karma-yoga

This is the main idea that dominates Chapters 2–5 and is an important means of resolution offered by Krishna for Arjuna's preliminary dilemma. Essentially, the teaching here is that action does not
produce a binding future result if it is performed without selfish
desire. So, *karma-yoga* could be defined as action based on dharmic
duty that is performed without desire for personal gain.

The nature of God and the worship of God

The final verse of the sixth chapter marks an abrupt change of
direction for the Gita as it moves forward in its teachings towards
defining the nature of God, identifying the Deity as Krishna himself, and prescribing acts of devotion to Krishna as the best means
of gaining liberation from rebirth. At the heart of this teaching,
we have the startling revelation of the divine *vishva-rupa* in which
the whole of this existence – past, present, and future – is revealed
as the body of God. This line of discourse continues until the end
of Chapter 12, when we are confronted by another abrupt change
of direction.

Interpretations of samkhya concepts

The final six chapters of the Bhagavad-gita contain a variety of
ideas, and the one more or less consistent theme we can detect
here is the use of concepts derived from the Samkhya philosophical
system. The emphasis here is firstly on analysing the component
elements of matter of which the world is comprised, including
the three *gunas*, or fundamental qualities, and then rigidly differentiating the inner self from matter in any form. Throughout the
final six chapters, or at least up until the summary of contents in

Chapter 18, we find these ideas being used creatively by Krishna in order to present a range of teachings.

Whilst these three could be regarded as the main themes of the Bhagavad-gita's discourse, there is a multiplicity of ideas that are touched on during the course of its progression. And of these, some would seem to be sufficiently significant to warrant a mention even at this preliminary stage.

Dhyana-yoga: The path of meditation

This is what is often referred to as *jñana-yoga*, the path of knowledge, when the teachings of the Bhagavad-gita are analysed, and, in fact, it could be included as a fourth major theme. At the end of Chapter 5, we suddenly encounter a couple of verses that refer to the process of yoga meditation based on regulation of the mind and senses. This idea is taken up again in Chapter 6, where it becomes the principal line of discussion. Here, Krishna gives an outline of the basic principles and ultimate goal of the yoga system in a manner that is broadly equivalent to Patañjali's exposition in the *Yoga Sutras*. The topic is touched on again in Chapter 8 and finally in Chapter 18, where the contents are summarised.

Atman: The transcendent soul

One of Krishna's first responses to Arjuna's lament is to remind him that the true self is a spiritual entity that cannot be touched by any wound inflicted on the body. Drawing on the Katha Upanishad, the Bhagavad-gita insists that the *atman* is a spiritual entity entirely distinct from its present embodiment, which transmigrates to another bodily form at the time of death.

Dharma and social order

Another of Krishna's preliminary arguments, prior to his exposition on *karma-yoga*, is based on the notion of *varna-dharma*. Arjuna's duty is to fight because of his birth in a particular social stratum, the *kshatriya* class, whose dharmic duty is to administer, rule, and fight. At different points throughout the Gita, Krishna insists that Arjuna must adhere to his social *dharma*, but in the eighteenth chapter the point is explored again in more detail. Here, we have definitions of the duties of the four *varnas* (social classes), and then an explanation that each person is preconditioned by their inherent nature to act in the manner designated by their birth identity.

GITARTHA SAMGRAHA

The initial division of the Bhagavad-gita into three broad strands is not an original idea and is derived from Yamunacharya, who explains it more fully in his Gitartha Samgraha, dividing the text into three equal portions of six chapters each (1–6, 7–12, and 13–18). Yamunacharya was one of the early teachers of the Sri Vaishnava sect and was a senior contemporary of Ramanujacharya. We conclude this introduction with the Gitartha Samgraha before proceeding to the text of the Gita itself.

THE GITARTHA SAMGRAHA OF SRI YAMUNACHARYA

In the Bhagavad-gita, Narayana is declared to be the Supreme Brahman. He can be attained only through *bhakti*, which is performed by the acceptance of one's own *dharma*, through acquisition of knowledge and through renunciation of attachment.

1. In the first six chapters, the performance of desireless karma and the acquisition of true knowledge through yoga practice is enjoined, so that one can realise the *atman*.
2. In the middle six chapters, *bhakti*, which is brought about through karma and *jñana*, is discussed. *Bhakti* brings realisation of the truth concerning Bhagavan.
3. The final six chapters cast further elucidation on what has gone before. Here, matter (*pradhana*) and the soul

(*purusha*) are explained as well as *Ishvara*. In addition, the disciplines related to work, knowledge, and devotion are further discussed by way of supplementing what has gone before.

4. This treatise was spoken for Arjuna's sake when he was overwhelmed by misplaced love and compassion and when he was perplexed about *dharma* and *adharma* and took shelter of Sri Krishna.

5. In the second chapter, Samkhya and Yoga are described. Samkhya describes the transcendent self, whilst Yoga refers to desireless action. These lead to unwavering knowledge and are taught to remove Arjuna's delusion.

6. In the third chapter, the need to perform karma without any desire except for the pleasure of the Lord and the protection of the world is taught. The agency for action is to be seen as the three *gunas* and the Supreme Lord.

7. The following subjects are covered in the fourth chapter: an incidental explanation of Krishna's nature, that *karma-yoga* is also connected to true knowledge; the varieties of *karma-yoga* and the significance of knowledge within *karma-yoga* are also emphasised.

8. The ease and instant effect of *karma-yoga* are explained in the fifth chapter, as well as some of its component stages and how *brahman* is known as the self.

9. In the sixth chapter, concentration and meditation are presented as forms of yoga and the four types of successful yogin, the means of success in yoga and the highest status of the yoga that has Krishna as its object.

10. In the seventh chapter, Krishna teaches knowledge of himself, his concealment within *prakriti*, surrender to him as a means of release, the practices of different types of devotees, and the highest status of the devotee who possesses knowledge.

11. The eighth chapter reveals the distinctions of what is understood and what is acquired by each of the three classes of devotees: those who seek prosperity, those who seek the true nature of the self, and those who are devoted to the Lord.

12. In the ninth chapter, the Lord speaks of his own supremacy as the divine even when he comes to earth as *avatars* and of the excellence of the *mahatmas* who seek God alone and of the discipline of *bhakti*.

13. In the tenth chapter, He describes in detail the infinite auspicious attributes of the Lord and his absolute control over all things so as to generate a mood of *bhakti* in the minds of aspirants.

14. In the eleventh chapter, it is stated that the divine vision which gives immediate vision of God was given to Arjuna and that *bhakti* is the only means for knowing and attaining him in this way.

15. In the twelfth chapter, the superiority of *bhakti* is taught, as well as the means to practise *bhakti*, directions for meditating on the self, details of the desired qualities, the modes of *sadhana* (religious practice) to be adopted, and the vast love of the Lord for his devotees.

16. In the thirteenth chapter, the nature of the body, the means of realising the self, the nature of the self, the cause of bondage, and discrimination between the self and the body are described.

17. In the fourteenth chapter, the bondage of the *gunas*, their agency in the performance of action, and how to eliminate their influence are described. It also describes how the three ends of heaven, abiding in the self, and existence within the Lord may be attained.

18. In the fifteenth chapter, the Supreme Lord is declared to be different from the self both in its state of union with

matter and in its liberated state, because He pervades, sustains, and rules over the individual souls and the world.

19. The sixteenth chapter first describes the differences between the devic and the asuric natures in order to establish the truth and proper conduct, which can be pursued only by submission to the *shastras*.

20. In the seventeenth chapter, the following topics are dealt with: rejection of paths not recommended by the *shastras*, the injunctions of the *shastras* in accordance with the *gunas,* and the characteristics of the three words 'om', 'tat', and 'sat'.

21. The final chapter describes the mental state necessary for allowing that the Lord is the real controller, the necessity of developing the sattvic nature, the spiritual end gained by fulfilling one's duties, and *bhakti-yoga,* which is the essence of the Gita Shastra.

22. *Karma-yoga* means 'to practise austerity, pilgrimage, charity, *yajña*, and other such acts'. *Jñana-yoga* means 'to control the mind and then to abide within the purified self'.

23. *Bhakti-yoga* means 'to practise meditation and other forms of worship with undeviating love for the Supreme Being'. These three yogas are interconnected.

24. Obligatory and occasional duties are connected to all three yogas, as they are means of worshipping the Supreme Lord. All three grant vision of the self, but *bhakti* can be practised before such vision by means of *japa, bhajan*, pilgrimage, etc., even with only superficial love of God.

25. When ignorance is removed and one perceives the self as subservient to God, one attains supreme devotion and thereby reaches his domain. There is *vaidhi* (regulated) *bhakti, para* (higher) *bhakti,* and finally *parama* (supreme) *bhakti.*

26. *Bhakti-yoga* can grant prosperity and sovereignty if one desires them. If one desires to attain the self, all three yogas are effective in the attainment of *kaivalya* (separation from matter).

27. The understanding that Bhagavan (God) is the highest end is common to all three types of yogin, but if one overlooks the other two and aspires only for the Lord, one will attain him completely.

28. The *jñanin* is one who is devoted exclusively to the Lord and whose whole existence depends upon him. Contact with God is his only joy, separation his only grief. His thoughts are focussed only on God.

29. When one finds pleasure only in thinking, meditating, speaking, worshipping, and praising the Lord, then the senses, intellect, mind, and vital forces all become concentrated upon him.

30. Regarding all disciplines just as means of pleasing the Lord, without any other motive, one should give up dependence on anything but him and abandon any fear that this means one will be incomplete.

31. Such a person finds pleasure only in undeviating service to God. He then attains his domain. This Gita Shastra is meant mainly for such a devotee. This is a summary of its meaning.

Oh Lord of the Earth, kindly position my chariot
in the space between the two armies. —1.21

CHAPTER 1

The main function of this opening chapter is to introduce the conversation that ensues and to provide a setting for Krishna's instructions. In fact, verses 2–19 are taken almost verbatim from a later chapter of the *Mahabharata* (Chapter 47 of the *Bhishma-parvan*), in which the preparations for the second day of the battle are described.

Hence, the setting for the Gita discourse really begins from verse 20, and it is from this point on that we need to be more precisely aware of what is taking place. Arjuna asks Krishna, his friend and charioteer, to take up a position between the two armies so that he can look across at those he must fight. The sight of all his friends and relatives gathered there ready for battle fills Arjuna with dismay, and he decides that he will in effect withdraw from the conflict. In understanding the Bhagavad-gita, it is important to note the arguments that Arjuna then gives to support his decision to give up the fight, as these provide at least the preliminary stimulus for Krishna's response.

THE FIELD OF DHARMA

1. Dhritarashtra said: On the field of dharma at Kurukshetra, what did my sons and the sons of Pandu do when they assembled there seeking battle, O Samjaya?

2. Samjaya said: On seeing the battle array of the Pandava host, King Duryodhana approached the acharya and spoke these words.

3. Behold this mighty army of the sons of Pandu, acharya, arranged in battle array by the son of Drupada, your intelligent disciple.

4. There are heroes and great bowmen in that host, the equals in battle of Bhima and Arjuna: Yuyudhana, Virata, and Drupada, that great chariot warrior.

5. Then there are Dhrishtaketu, Chekitana, and the heroic King of Kashi; Purujit, Kuntibhoja, and Shaibya, who is a hero amongst men;

6. The mighty Yudhamanyu, the heroic Uttamaujas, the son of Subhadra, and the sons of Draupadi; all of them are great chariot warriors.

7. Now learn about those who are most prominent on our side, O best of brahmins. For your understanding, I will inform you about the captains leading my army.

8. There is yourself, and then Bhishma, Karna, the all-conquering Kripa, Ashvatthaman, Vikarna, and the son of Somadatta as well.

9. And many other heroes are willing to lay down their lives for my sake. They carry many different types of weapon, and all of them are skilled in the arts of warfare.

10. Guarded by Bhishma, our strength is unlimited, but their strength, guarded by Bhima, is limited indeed.

11. Situated in each of your allotted stations, all of you must give protection to Bhishma.

12. The senior member of the Kuru house, Duryodhana's mighty grandfather, then roared as loudly as a lion and blew on his conch shell. This sound brought joy to Duryodhana.

13. Conch shells, kettledrums, panava drums, anaka drums, and horns then immediately resounded, all together making a tumultuous sound.

14. Mounted on a mighty chariot yoked to white horses, Madhava and the Pandava then blew their celestial conch shells.

15. Hrishikesha sounded the Panchajanya and Dhanamjaya blew on the Devadatta. Vrikodara, the performer of formidable deeds (bhima-karma), blew the great conch shell known as Paundra.

16. King Yudhishthira, the son of Kunti, blew the Anantavijaya, Nakula blew the Sughosha, and Sahadeva sounded the Manipushpaka.

17. That mighty bowman the King of Kashi, Shikandin the great chariot warrior, Dhrishtadyumna, Virata, the unconquerable Satyaki,

18. Drupada and all the sons of Draupadi, O lord of the earth, as well as the mighty son of Subadhra then blew their respective conch shells.

19. That sound shattered the hearts of the sons of Dhritarashtra, for the tumult resonated across both the sky and the earth.

20. Seeing the sons of Dhritarashtra gathered there and the weapons starting to fly, the Pandava with a monkey on his banner took up his bow.

21. He then spoke the following words to Hrishikesha, O lord of the earth. Kindly position my chariot in the space between the two armies, Acyuta,

22. So that I can look upon all those who have assembled here seeking battle. Let me see those with whom I will have to fight in this warlike endeavour.

23. I see them assembled here intent on battle, seeking to please the ignorant son of Dhritarashtra by fighting on his behalf.

24. Addressed in this way by Gudakesha, O Bharata, Hrishikesha positioned that wonderful chariot in the space between the two armies.

THE BHAGAVAD GITA

25. In the presence of Bhishma and Drona and all the kings of world, he said, Behold, Partha, the Kurus gathered here together.

26. Partha could see fathers and grandfathers standing there, as well as the teachers, maternal uncles, brothers, sons, grandsons, allies,

27. Fathers-in-law, and friends who were present in the two armies. On seeing all his family members standing nearby, the Kaunteya

28. Was overwhelmed with profound compassion and spoke these words in a mood of dejection, On seeing these relatives here, Krishna, standing ready and seeking battle,

29. My limbs are failing me, my mouth is drying up, there are tremors all over my body, and its hairs are standing erect.

30. The bow named Gandiva slips from my hand and my skin is burning. I can no longer stand up, for my mind has become dizzy.

31. I see unfavourable omens, Keshava; I cannot see how anything good can come from killing my own kinsmen in this battle.

32. I have no desire for victory, Krishna, nor for a kingdom or for worldly pleasure. What is the point of our gaining a kingdom, Govinda, or objects of enjoyment or even maintaining our lives,

33. When all those for whom we might desire a kingdom, objects of enjoyment, and the pleasures of life are taking part in this war, giving up their lives and their wealth?

34. By that I mean our teachers, fathers, sons, grandfathers, maternal uncles, fathers-in-law, grandsons, brothers-in-law, and other relatives.

35. Though they may kill me I have no wish to kill these men, Madhusudana, not even if we could gain dominion over the three worlds thereby, how much less then for acquiring this earth?

36. After killing the sons of Dhritarashtra, what pleasure would there be for us, Janardana? Sin alone would come to us by killing these men who seek to kill us.

37. We have no right to kill the sons of Dhritarashtra, for they are our own relatives. How could we ever be happy again after destroying our family, Madhava?

38. Even if their consciences have been obliterated by greed and they cannot see the evil inherent in causing the destruction of their family or the sin involved in betraying a friend,

39. How can we fail to have wisdom enough to turn away from such a sin, for we can certainly see what a crime it is to bring about the destruction of the family, Janardana.

40. When a family is devastated in this way, the ancient traditions of dharma relating to the family also perish. And when such dharma perishes, adharma predominates over the entire family.

41. And as a result of the predominance of adharma, Krishna, the women of the family become degraded; and when the women are thus degraded, a mingling of the varnas arises.

42. Such a mingling leads both the destroyer of the family and the family itself to hell. Deprived of the ritual offerings of *pinda* and water, the ancestors of such families fall from their position.

43. As a result of the wicked acts of those who harm the family, acts which lead to a mingling of the varnas, the eternal forms of dharma rooted in caste (jati) and family are destroyed.

44. And we have heard, Janardana, that there is undoubtedly an abode in hell for those men who are destroyers of family dharma.

45. Alas! Alas! We are bent on performing a most sinful deed by slaying our family members in battle due to our greed for the pleasure of sovereignty.

46. If the sons of Dhritarashtra, weapons in hand, were to slay me in battle, unresisting and unarmed, that would be better for me.

47. After speaking in this way on the field of battle, Arjuna sat down on the seat of the chariot and cast aside his bow and his arrows, his mind agitated by sorrow.

CONCLUSION:
A SUMMARY OF CHAPTER 1

There are a number of points we could make here in summarising Arjuna's response to the situation he finds himself in. In verse 28, we read that he was overwhelmed by a deep sense of compassion, and it is this that initially gives rise to his misgivings about the course of action he is set on. The Sanskrit word used here is *kripa*, which is usually regarded as a very positive quality, reflecting a person's concern for others who are in distress.

The first point made by Arjuna himself is a very logical one – victory in this war will not make them happy. Deprived of their rightful share of the kingdom, the Pandavas have been living a wretched life as exiles. Now they are seeking to regain the position that is rightfully theirs so that they can find satisfaction once more. Arjuna's point here is that in order to recover their kingdom, they will have to kill many of their own family members, a course of action that will mean that any resulting gains will not bring them the happiness and satisfaction they seek.

From verse 38 onwards, Arjuna begins to reflect on the matter in relation to *dharma*, the proper execution of religious duty. The Pandavas are *kshatriyas*, and hence, for them, waging war is not in conflict with *varna-dharma*. Arjuna argues, however, that a war of this type does contravene dharmic duty because it will lead to the destruction of their family and a concomitant collapse of family *dharma*. In verse 43, he refers to *kula-dharma* and *jati-dharma*, *dharma* relating to the family and *dharma* relating to his caste or community.

Although waging war is action in accordance with his *varna-dharma* as a *kshatriya*, an internal family war is in breach of these other forms of *dharma* and will lead only to the degradation of the family. It is interesting to note here the extent to which Arjuna is set against any mingling of the *varnas*, which he sees as a cause of immorality amongst the women of the family. It is sometimes said that this is an idea espoused by the Bhagavad-gita, but as we shall see, Arjuna's words here are not accepted by Krishna.

A further point made by Arjuna is that the killing of family members is a sinful action because it leads to a decline in *dharma*. In verse 45, he describes the course of action they are proposing to follow as *mahat papam*, a great sin, which will lead to terrible misfortune in the future as the law of karma shapes their unfolding destiny. Here, Arjuna expresses the view that a sin as great as this will condemn the Pandavas to existence in hell, for they will be acting as the destroyers of *dharma*. Moreover, their motives in waging war are not represented as being particularly noble ones. In verse 45, he describes the impetus for war as *rajya-sukha-lobha*, greed for the joy of sovereignty. So, inspired by selfish desire, the Pandavas are about to follow a course of action that will destroy the *dharma* of their family and their community. How can this be righteous?

Although Arjuna is described initially as being overwhelmed by compassion, his objection to warfare is not based on any advocacy of non-violence or even a moral perspective. One suspects that his fundamental response to the situation is an emotional one and that he is then constructing a line of rational argument to justify his emotional impulses, and this view is confirmed by Krishna's initial response at the start of Chapter 2. The argument he constructs rests on the idea that the right course of action must be one that either brings benefit to the performer or else is in accordance with *dharma*. According to Arjuna, his waging war at Kurukshetra will meet neither of these two criteria. Now, let us go on to see how Krishna responds to this argument.

There was never a time when I did not exist,
nor you, nor these lords of men;
nor shall any of us cease to exist in the future. —2.12

CHAPTER 2

In looking at the opening phase of the Bhagavad-gita's exposition, we will take Chapters 2 and 3 in order, breaking them down into discrete passages and trying to identify the points Krishna makes and the reasons why he makes them. Underlying this approach is the view that the Gita is an ordered discourse that proceeds step by step to set out a specific form of religious teaching. Let us now move on and consider the second chapter.

KRISHNA'S REBUKE

1. Samjaya said: Madhusudana then spoke the following words to Arjuna, who was filled with compassion, whose eyes were agitated and full of tears, and who was lamenting.
2. The Lord said: Whence could such faintheartedness have come upon you at this time of trial? This is not proper for a civilised man, it does not lead to heaven, and it will bring dishonour.
3. Do not give up your manhood in this way, Partha! Such a mood ill becomes you. Giving up this pathetic weakness of heart, arise, O destroyer of the foe.

It is interesting to note here that Krishna's initial response to the points made by Arjuna in Chapter 1 is to dismiss the whole case as being nothing more than an emotional outpouring that is not worthy of a reasoned reply. Arjuna may have presented some viable arguments, but here, Krishna seems to regard the whole thing as a form of mental weakness. Hence, his first reply is also on the emotional level; he does not seek to answer any of Arjuna's arguments, but turns immediately to the emotional trauma that is at the heart of them. In other words, he is saying that Arjuna's speech is not worthy of a reasoned response because it is the product of emotional turmoil rather than logical analysis.

ARJUNA AGAIN REFUSES TO FIGHT

4. Arjuna said: O Madhusudana, how can I employ my arrows in fighting with Bhishma and with Drona on the field of battle? They are worthy of my worship, O slayer of the foe.

5. It would be far better to refrain from killing such noble-minded teachers and to live in this world by begging for our food. Our teachers are desirous of wealth, but if we kill them, the rewards we would enjoy would be tainted with blood.

6. Nor do we know which would be better for us, defeating them or being defeated by them, for after killing the sons of Dhritarashtra, now positioned before us, we would have no wish to live.

7. My very existence is afflicted by problems caused by weakness and my mind is confused about dharma. So now I am asking you which is the best course to adopt. Answer me clearly, for I am now your student. Instruct me, for I have surrendered to your guidance.

8. I cannot see anything that will dispel the grief that is drying up my senses, not even attaining a prosperous kingdom on earth without any rival, nor even gaining lordship over the gods.

9. Samjaya said: After speaking in this way to Hrishikesha, Gudakesha said to Govinda, 'I will not fight'. He then fell silent, O destroyer of the foe.

Despite Krishna's rebuke and the implication that he is a coward, still Arjuna cannot be roused to battle. His words may be based on emotion rather than reason, but it is going to take more than an emotional response to change his mind. In verses 4–6, he repeats the point he has made earlier that a victory achieved by slaying the sons of Dhritarashtra and the elders of the family will not bring them any sort of happiness. They are fighting the war to win back their rightful inheritance so that they can live happily in a state of prosperity, but a victory gained in this way will not achieve that goal.

In verse 7, he turns again to the question of *dharma*, which he has also covered in Chapter 1, but here, he admits that he does not really understand what his dharmic duty is; moreover, he admits that the rationality of his thoughts has been undermined by the intensity of his emotions. So now he turns to Krishna for a proper explanation of his dilemma in relation to *dharma*, although he cannot see any way that he can be persuaded that he should fight.

THE ATMAN, THE INNER SELF

10. With a slight smile, Hrishikesha then spoke these words to the lamenting Arjuna whilst they were situated in the space between the two armies.
11. The Lord said: Whilst grieving for those who should not be lamented over, you speak words that appear wise. But learned men grieve for neither the living nor the dead.
12. There was never a time when I did not exist, nor you, nor these lords of men; nor shall any of us cease to exist in the future.
13. Even as the embodied soul present in this body goes through childhood, youth, and then old age, in the same way it then acquires a different body. One who is wise is not confused about this.
14. It is contact of the senses with their objects, Kaunteya, which leads to sensations of heat and cold, pleasure and

pain. Being impermanent, such sensations come and go, and so you must learn to endure them, Bharata.

15. If these sensations do not distract a person, O best of men, and if he can remain equal in sorrow and happiness, then such a wise person gains the state of immortality.

16. That which is unreal never comes into being, and that which is real never ceases to be. Those who perceive the truth can recognise this conclusion concerning these two.

17. You must understand this to be the indestructible principle that pervades this whole world. No one can bring about the destruction of this unchanging principle.

18. This eternal embodied soul is indestructible and beyond comprehension. The bodies it inhabits, however, are said to be finite. Therefore, fight, O Bharata.

19. Neither the person who thinks this self is the killer nor he who thinks it is killed properly understands it, for it does not kill and it cannot be killed.

20. It is never born and it never dies. It is existing now and it will never cease to exist. It is unborn, eternal, everlasting, and most ancient. It is not killed when the body is killed.

21. How can a person who properly understands this as indestructible, eternal, unborn, and without decay cause the death of anyone or kill anyone? What will he cause the death of? What will he kill?

22. Just as a person casts aside old clothes and puts on other ones that are new, so the embodied soul casts aside old bodies and accepts other new ones.

23. Weapons cannot cut it, fire cannot burn it, water cannot make it wet, and wind cannot dry it.

24. This cannot be cut, it cannot be burned, and it cannot be moistened or dried. It is eternal, all-pervasive, fixed, immovable, and everlasting.

25. It is said that it is imperceptible and inconceivable and it is not subject to transformation. Understanding it in this way, you should lament no more.

26. And even if you think that it is born repeatedly and repeatedly dies, still you should not lament over it, O mighty one.

27. For one who has been born death is certain, and for one who has died birth is certain. Therefore, you should not lament over something that cannot be averted.

28. The beginning of living beings is unknown, their interim stage is visible, and their end is again unknown. So why should there be any lamentation over this?

29. One person sees it as wonderful, another person may speak of it as wonderful, and yet another person may come to hear about it as wonderful; but even after hearing about it no one truly understands it.

30. This embodied soul present within the bodies of all beings is eternal and can never be killed. Therefore, you should not lament for any living being.

Here, then, we encounter the first of Krishna's teachings in response to Arjuna's plight. It is, moreover, the first teaching that the Bhagavad-gita presents to its readers, although this is not a theme that Krishna pursues in any great detail after this initial exposition.

Discussion: The essence of Krishna's argument

Krishna's first argument to Arjuna rests on the traditional Hindu understanding of the soul as being distinct from the body, and it is no surprise to find quotations from the Katha Upanishad included here, as the transcendent nature of the *atman*, the inner self, is the main topic of that Upanishad's discourse. Verses 19 and 20 are both taken from the Katha Upanishad (although the wording is changed slightly) and are used to demonstrate that the death of the body does not entail the death of the true self. (As an aside, it is interesting to note that 2.19 of the Bhagavad-gita is virtually a quotation of 2.19 of the Katha Upanishad; this may be a coincidence, but I like to think it is done deliberately).

So, Krishna's argument here is a relatively simple one. Arjuna is lamenting because he cannot bear the thought of the death of his relatives and teachers, but one who possesses the higher knowledge taught by the Upanishads will know that the true self will not die. Therefore, Arjuna should give up his sorrow over the death of family members, realising that for the true self there is no death. When the body is destroyed, the soul within moves on and enters another bodily form, just as we discard our old worn-out clothes and put on new ones. However much the body may be afflicted by physical circumstances, the eternal principle that is the true self remains untouched. Therefore, Arjuna should understand that the deaths he will cause on the battlefield do not pertain to the true self and he should give up his grief.

This, then, is the main thrust of Krishna's argument at this point as he begins to reason with Arjuna. Within this passage, however, there are specific verses that different Hindu *acharyas* have used to support their own religious teachings. In commenting on verse 12, Ramanujacharya argues that because Krishna says that the self will never cease to be, the position of Advaita cannot be sustained. The Advaita philosophy insists that liberation from rebirth occurs when one realises one's own identity with Brahman and when individual existence ends as a result of that realisation. Here, however, Krishna seems to be suggesting that the individual existence of the soul will never end. As might be expected, Shankaracharya does not accept this reading and suggests that the verse should not be overinterpreted or used as the basis for philosophical discussion. Krishna is speaking conventionally here, beginning his discourse to Arjuna, and the only point he is trying to make concerns the eternality of the soul.

Verse 16, on the other hand, might be used to support the Advaitic argument that the world is unreal. Krishna is differentiating here between the eternal spiritual principle and the material embodiment, but in doing so he uses the word *sat* to designate the soul, and *asat* to refer to the body. *Sat* and *asat* are often used in the sense of real and unreal, and so the verse could be taken as supporting Shankara's position that the variegated world we inhabit is an illusion created by ignorance, for everything is Brahman. However, Ramanuja and others contend that here, *sat* and *asat* should be understood as meaning 'temporary' and 'eternal'. These are rather subtle arguments, and for our purposes we can note that the main point here is to understand the existence within the body of a higher self, a spiritual entity that survives the death of the body and then transmigrates into another bodily form. Krishna is here explaining the conventional doctrine of reincarnation, which is a major feature of Hindu, Buddhist, and Jain religious teaching. Because death pertains only to the body and not to the true self, Arjuna can engage in battle without worrying about the consequences.

We might like to pause for a moment at this point and reflect on whether the argument Krishna presents here is morally acceptable. At this stage, one might feel a bit uneasy about the Gita's position, but of course this is just the first point that is made, and it has to be taken within the wider context of the text as a whole. Moving quickly on, Krishna now offers Arjuna a second argument to convince him that he should fight.

THE DHARMA OF A KSHATRIYA

31. Considering the nature of your personal dharma, you should not hesitate. For a kshatriya, there is nothing superior to fighting in accordance with dharma.

32. Kshatriyas who encounter a war of this type become joy-ful, Partha; it comes unsought and yet opens the door to heaven.

33. And if you do not engage in this dharmic battle, then you will destroy both your personal dharma and your honour, and you will accumulate sin.

34. Then people will always speak of your dishonour; and for a person who has achieved renown, dishonour is worse than death.

35. The great chariot warriors will think that you have left the battle due to fear. Those who had previously thought highly of you will now hold you in contempt.

36. Your enemies will speak many insulting words about you, condemning your prowess. What could be more painful than that?

37. Either you will die and reach heaven, or else you will con-quer and rule the earth. Therefore, arise, Kaunteya, with your resolve set on battle.

38. Become equal-minded towards happiness and distress, gain and loss, victory and defeat, and then engage your-self in battle. You will not acquire sin by acting in this way.

Discussion:
Krishna's second argument

We will recall that in Chapter 1, when Arjuna lost his resolve, he expressed a fear of sin and its consequences in terms of his future rebirth. He suggested that by killing the elders of the family, the *dharma* of the family would be destroyed and, as a result of this sinful act, he would be condemned to hell. Here, Krishna responds to that argument by insisting that waging war is indeed Arjuna's *dharma*. Arjuna is a *kshatriya*, a member of the social class whose religious duty is to govern society and to wage war against invaders and wrongdoers. Hence, for Arjuna, waging war is a religious duty, his *dharma*. In verses 32 and 37, Krishna responds to Arjuna's fear of sin by insisting that because waging war is *kshatriya-dharma*, he will, in fact, gain great merit by engaging in this type of action, and this merit will elevate him to the heaven of the gods after death. This view is confirmed elsewhere in the *Mahabharata,* where we are shown Duryodhana, Shakuni, and Duhshasana elevated to heaven after death, not because of their virtue but because they fought and died in battle in accordance with the *dharma* of their social class.

This, then, is Krishna's second argument. Arjuna must fight because his social *dharma*, his *varna-dharma*, obliges him to do so. He will not be guilty of any sin by executing his *dharma*; rather, he will gain rewards both in this world and in the world to come. Krishna also warns Arjuna that if he leaves the field of battle, no one will applaud him for his virtue. His enemies will despise him as a weak-minded coward who did not have the courage to fight. And for a *kshatriya*, dishonour of that type is unbearable. This short passage is confirmed at the end of the Gita, in Chapter 18, where Krishna lists the duties of the four *varnas,* or social classes. The list of *kshatriya* duties (18.43) includes *yuddhe apalayanam*, never fleeing from battle, and so Arjuna is obliged to stand and fight because it is his *dharma* as a *kshatriya* to do so.

As with the insistence on the eternality of the soul, the emphasis on social *dharma* is not one of the Bhagavad-gita's main ideas and should not be taken in isolation from its other teachings. Here, Krishna is providing us with an introduction to the main idea of these opening chapters, the concept of *karma-yoga*. This entails the performance of action without any desire for personal gain. Here, Krishna is briefly explaining to Arjuna what his duty is; now he will go on to explain the consciousness of detachment with which that action should be performed. So, rather than taking this passage out of context as an insistence on *varna-dharma*, we should probably see it as an introduction to the main teaching on *karma-yoga*.

It is this big idea that Krishna turns to now, though he has some more introductory words to speak before giving the full explanation.

AN INTRODUCTION
TO KARMA-YOGA

39. I have spoken so far on the basis of Samkhya, but now listen to this concerning Buddhi Yoga, the yoga of the intellect. When you engage in action on the basis of this understanding (*buddhya*), you will free yourself from the bondage of action.
40. There is nothing to lose in this attempt and neither can there be any failure, for even a slight engagement in this dharma frees one from great danger.
41. Here, the resolute intelligence becomes fixed on one point, O child of the Kurus, but the understandings of those who are irresolute have many branches and diversify without limit.

In these three verses, Krishna is introducing the next topic and explaining the effectiveness of the type of yoga he will now explain to Arjuna. There are, however, a few points that we should note here:

In verse 39, Krishna says that the teachings he has given up until this point are in relation to Samkhya. Samkhya is one of the main branches of Hindu religious philosophy; it seeks to analyse the elements of matter and then to demonstrate that the soul is different from matter. So here, we should probably understand that Krishna is referring to the teachings on the soul he gave earlier in the chapter rather than those on *kshatriya-dharma* he has just presented.

He then gives the title 'Buddhi-yoga' to the teachings he is now going to impart. The word *buddhi* means 'intellect' or 'understanding', but the teachings that follow from this point are related to *karma-yoga*, the yoga consisting of desireless action. Hence, we must conclude that *buddhi-yoga* and *karma-yoga* are one and the same. Perhaps *karma-yoga* is here designated as *buddhi-yoga* because the focus is on the intellect detaching itself from selfish desire, thereby transforming the consciousness that motivates us to act.

Here, we might also note Krishna's insistence that there can be no failure in the spiritual endeavour, only degrees of success. No spiritual achievement is ever lost or wasted. This point is further explained at the end of Chapter 6, where Krishna tells us that even if one engaged in yoga practice does not achieve complete success, he can carry on from the same point of achievement in a future life.

CRITICISM OF THE VEDIC RELIGION

42. Persons lacking in insight who are attached to the religion of the Vedas speak in flowery language. 'There is nothing more than this', they say.

43. Filled with desires and seeking the heavenly worlds, they advocate many different types of rituals, which lead to a higher birth as the result of that action. Pleasure and power are the goals they seek.

44. The resolute form of intelligence existing in the state of *samadhi* can never arise for such persons who remain attached to pleasure and power and whose minds are carried away by such desires.

45. The Vedas are concerned with the three *gunas*, but you must become free from the three *gunas*, Arjuna. One who is self-possessed transcends duality, always adheres to the quality of *sattva*, and has no interest in gain or protection of what has been gained.

46. As with the purpose served by a reservoir of water when the whole area is flooded with water, so it is with the purpose of the Vedas for a brahmin who is enlightened by knowledge.

This is a very interesting passage from the Bhagavad-gita, as it contains a fairly strident criticism of the Vedic religion and the Vedic ritual practices. Two questions arise here: Why does Krishna take this attitude towards Vedic ritual? And why does he include this instruction at this point in the Gita? Let us take these in turn.

We must be aware that the Bhagavad-gita is not 'anti-Vedic'. The criticism made here is not of Vedic ritual per se but of ritual that is performed on the basis of selfish desire and is hence a materialistic endeavour. When the religion of the Veda is pursued in this manner, it is related to the three qualities of matter (*gunas*): *sattva*, *rajas*, and *tamas*. It is not dedicated to spiritual goals. Krishna is especially critical of those who perform such materially motivated rituals and claim that this is all there is to religious life. In other words, they themselves condemn other forms of religion based on spiritual goals by stating *na anyad asti*, there is nothing other than this. The Gita may be critiquing the Mimamsa philosophy here, which does indeed contend that the Vedic religion is based on ritual alone and that the ritual is performed in order to gain defined goals. Here, we also find a clear resonance of Shankaracharya's great debate with the *acharya* of the Mimamsaka school named Mandana Mishra. The Veda consists of a *karma-kanda* portion, which emphasises ritual leading to prosperity in this world, and a *jñana-kanda*, consisting of the Upanishads that teach spiritual wisdom leading to liberation from rebirth. Here, Krishna is not denying the Veda, as the Buddhists do, but is criticising those who emphasise only the *karma-kanda* portion and deny the value of the *jñana-kanda* with the words *na anyad asti*. It is very interesting to note that this is exactly the position taken by Mandana Mishra in the debate with Shankaracharya.

Why, then, does Krishna include this passage at this point in his discourse, where he is about to introduce the *buddhi-* or *karma-yoga?* I think the answer to this question is that he wishes to draw a clear distinction between karma and *karma-yoga.* Karma means 'any type of action', but specifically 'ritual action performed in order to gain a desirable result'. The Vedic ritual falls into this category, and it is hence a material action. *Karma-yoga* may externally appear to be identical to karma in terms of the action performed. The key difference is in the *buddhi,* or consciousness, that is the basis for that action. In the case of karma, it is selfish desire, but in the case of *karma-yoga,* the same action is performed without selfish desire. Duryodhana and Arjuna both perform the same action on the battlefield, but Duryodhana is involved in karma, whilst Arjuna, acting without desire, is urged to perform *karma-yoga.* So here, in his criticism of ritual, Krishna is stating from the outset that the *karma-yoga* he is about to reveal is entirely different from the karma he here condemns, though they may appear to be identical in terms of the physical actions undertaken.

Now, with the preliminaries complete, we can at last enter into the discussion of *karma-yoga,* which is the main teaching offered by the Bhagavad-gita in its earlier chapters.

AN OUTLINE
OF KARMA-YOGA

47. You only have a right to the action itself and never to the fruits of that action. Do not make the rewards of action your motive, and do not develop any attachment for avoiding action.

48. Situated in yoga, perform your duties whilst giving up all attachments, Dhanamjaya. Remain equal in success and failure, for such equanimity is what is meant by yoga.

49. Action alone (karma) is greatly inferior to Buddhi Yoga, Dhanamjaya. Seek shelter in the intellect (*buddhau*); those motivated by the fruits of action are petty-minded.

50. By focusing the intellect in this way (*buddhi-yukto*), one sets aside both righteous and unrighteous deeds. Therefore, engage yourself in this yoga, for yoga is the true art of performing action.

51. Wise men who engage in the yoga of the intellect abandon the fruits that are born of action. Free from the bondage of rebirth, they attain a position that has no blemish.

52. When your intellect breaks free of the dense thicket of illusion, you will reach a state of indifference for what should be heard and what has been heard in the past (*shruta*).

53. Your intellect becomes perplexed by the Shruti, but when it remains steady and fixed in the state of *Samadhi*, without any wavering, you will then have achieved success in yoga.

This is quite a short passage, but it does set out the essential principles of the Bhagavad-gita's doctrine of *karma-yoga*, here again referred to as *buddhi-yoga*.

Buddhi-yoga as described in verses 47–53

The practice of *buddhi-yoga* consists of the performance of proper action in a mood of complete detachment, without any desire for personal gain and being unmoved by the success or failure of the action undertaken. It is interesting to note how verse 49 makes a direct comparison between karma and *karma-*(*buddhi-*)*yoga*, thus continuing the theme of the previous passage that condemned karma in the form of ritual actions.

What does 'prescribed action'
in verse 47 mean?

One must presume that 'prescribed action' means 'action in accordance with one's personal *dharma*'. Here, we seem to have a reference to the discussion of *kshatriya-dharma* contained in verses 31–37, but now this is placed into the context of *buddhi-yoga*. Arjuna should perform his *kshatriya-dharma* by fighting, but he must divorce himself from the selfish form of consciousness with which *kshatriya-dharma* is performed by Duryodhana and others.

What is the goal attained
by the practice of buddhi-yoga?

In verses 50 and 51, we are told that those who follow the path of *buddhi-yoga* become free of both virtue and sin (*sukrita* and *dushkrita*). In other words, they break free from the control of the law of karma that keeps us bound to this world. This is referred to in verse 51. Having freed ourselves from the domain of karma and rebirth through this practice, we then attain a *padam anamayam*, a position that is free from any blemish or contamination. Of course, the precise meaning of this phrase can be interpreted in different ways, but it is clear that the practice of *buddhi-yoga* is designed to lead a person to *moksha*, liberation from rebirth. So again we see a fundamental difference between karma in the form of Vedic ritual and *karma-(buddhi-)yoga*, which is a form of religious practice aimed at achieving release from rebirth. It is hence a type of *moksha-dharma*.

Attitudes towards the Veda
as expressed in the Bhagavad-gita

In line with the attitude of the previous passage, verses 52 and 53 suggest that the practice of *buddhi-yoga* takes the practitioner beyond the teachings of the *shruti* or Veda. Here, one must presume that Krishna is referring to the *karma-kanda*, or ritual portion, and is showing that *buddhi-yoga* belongs to the *jñana-kanda* revealed by the Upanishads. And, in fact, the opening verses of the Isha Upanishad do seem to refer to the same idea of desireless action the Gita is advocating here.

Now Krishna expands on the initial idea of the *buddhi-yoga*, responding to a question from Arjuna by explaining the type of consciousness that should be assumed in order to practise it effectively. It is noteworthy that Gandhi once wrote that these verses were 'inscribed on the tablet of my heart', claiming that all his activities in the area of politics and social reform were, for him, a part of his practice of *karma-yoga*.

THE CHARACTERISTICS OF ONE WHO PERFORMS BUDDHI-YOGA

54. Arjuna said: What is the defining feature of a person whose realisation is steady and who remains firm in this state of *samadhi*, Keshava? How does such a steady-minded person speak? How does he sit? How does he move?

55. The Lord said: When a person sets aside all the desires running through his mind, Partha, and satisfies himself in the self alone, he is then described as one whose wisdom is steady.

56. When the mind does not grieve over life's sorrows, when a person remains untouched by the joys of life and free from passion, fear, and anger, he is described as a sage whose understanding is steady.

57. When a person has no affection for any object at all and feels neither joy nor loathing when he gains desirable and unwanted results, then his wisdom is firmly established.

58. When a person withdraws all his senses from their objects, like a tortoise withdrawing its limbs, then his wisdom is firmly established.

59. The objects of pleasure cannot touch the embodied soul when it abstains from them. Although one can restrict one's inclination in this way, the attraction still remains, but after perceiving the Supreme, one completely renounces such attraction.

60. The agitating senses can forcibly carry away the mind of even a perceptive person who makes the proper endeavours, Kaunteya.

61. Restraining all these senses, one engaged in this practice should remain dedicated to me. When he has his senses under control, then his wisdom is firmly established.

62. When a person thinks about the objects of the senses, attachment for them inevitably arises. Due to that attachment, desire appears, and from desire, anger comes into being.

63. From anger comes delusion, and as a result of that delusion, one's thinking is degraded. When thinking is degraded, one's intelligence is destroyed, and when intelligence is destroyed, a person is lost.

64. But one who possesses self-control can move amongst the sense objects using senses that are free of desire and loathing and are directed by his will alone. Such a person attains a state of absolute tranquillity.

65. In that state of tranquillity, all his sufferings disappear. And when one's mind is thus at peace, the realisation (*buddhi*) then becomes steady.

66. But there can be no realisation for one who does not engage in this practice and indeed no proper engagement of the mind. Without engaging the mind properly, there is no peace, and how can there be happiness for one who is not at peace?

67. Whichever of the roaming senses the mind becomes attached to will carry away a person's understanding, just as the wind carries away a boat on the waters.

68. Therefore, O mighty one, only if a person completely draws back his senses from their objects is his wisdom firmly established.

69. One who practices this restraint is awake when it is night for all living beings. And that period in which living beings are awake is night for the perceptive sage.

70. Just as rivers flow into the sea, which is always full and remains steady and immovable, so all these desires flow into such a person. It is he who attains peace, not one who seeks to fulfil those desires.

71. Giving up all desires, such a person moves through life without attachment. He has no sense of 'mine' or 'I'; it is he who attains peace.

72. This is the transcendental state, Partha, and on reaching such a position, one is no longer deluded. If one can remain situated in this state of consciousness even at the time of death, then one attains *brahma nirvana*.

The characteristics of a person
engaging in buddhi-yoga

The main point that Krishna emphasises throughout the passage is that the *yogin* should renounce his desires for material pleasure. This is the vital difference between karma and *karma-yoga*; the action is the same, but the *karma-yogin* acts without selfish desire. Verses 56 and 57 further explain that such a person remains undisturbed by the vicissitudes of fortune; he is not elated when things go well and not downcast over the misfortunes that inevitably befall us in life. He remains always aloof from the fluctuations of fortune, hence free from passion, from fear, and from anger. His senses are still active, and so desires still arise in his heart, but he has the intellectual strength to resist those desires and act on the basis of a higher consciousness. He is the master of his own being and not the servant of the uncontrolled senses; here, again, we might note the teachings of the Katha Upanishad, which gives the example of the chariot with the intellect as the driver and the horses as the senses that must be brought under control.

The significance of verses 59 and 61

Verse 59 indicates that control of the senses and selfish desires is made possible by the perception of something higher than this world. This can be interpreted as some form of spiritual realisation or experience, or could just be the recognition of a higher goal in life. The Gita just says *param drishtva*, which means 'seeing something higher'. However, the word *rasa*, meaning 'taste', is also used here, and this does indicate that restraint of the senses becomes possible when one starts to experience the joy of spiritual realisation. In verse 61, Krishna uses the phrase *mat-parah*, meaning 'dedicated to me', to describe the way in which the practitioner should perform *buddhi-yoga*. The reference that Krishna makes here to himself is something new and is a forerunner of the ideas on *bhakti*, devotion to God, that appear in later chapters. Later on, we will see how *karma-yoga*, or desireless action is brought into the realm of *bhakti* and represented as being action, performed as devotion to Krishna. At this point, however, this idea is only hinted at in this verse. Shankaracharya consistently regards Krishna as identical to the *atman*, the inner self; hence, he interprets this verse as meaning that the *karma-yogin* is dedicated to gaining knowledge of the *atman* and its identity with Brahman, the ultimate reality.

The difference between karma and karma-yoga

Verse 69 again reminds us of the contrast between Arjuna and Duryodhana. To an observer of the battle, they may appear to be acting in an identical manner, but the difference between karma and *karma-yoga* is as dramatic as that between night and day. One type of person moves through the world of desire, sensual pleasure, and material gain. For the *karma-yogin*, this is night, for he does not operate in this sphere. He explores the domain of the spirit, seeking to achieve spiritual realisation by renouncing materialistic aspirations. For one whose life is dedicated to material acquisition, this domain of spiritual pursuits is like night, for he is not active there.

What goal does the karma-yogin gain?

The goal achieved by this type of spiritual endeavour is described in verse 71 as *shanti*, or absolute tranquillity, absolute peace of mind – *sa shantim adhigacchati*. Those active in the material domain of gain and loss suffer constant anxieties, but a person who seeks the spiritual domain attains transcendence and tranquillity. The final verse of the chapter, verse 72, concludes with the words *brahma-nirvanam ricchati*, or 'he reaches the *brahma-nirvana*'. Now, the precise meaning of *brahma-nirvana* is rather difficult to determine; we might note the connection here with the Buddhist notion of *nirvana* as the final goal, though we cannot say whether there is any direct influence. However, the phrase is clearly a reference to the cessation of worldly existence and entry into the spiritual domain that is Brahman. So again, it is made clear to us that the teachings here are about *moksha*, how to gain complete liberation from the cycle of suffering and rebirth.

CONCLUSION:
A SUMMARY OF CHAPTER 2

A lot of ground has been covered in this second chapter, and we might summarise the contents, point by point, as follows:

- Though rebuked by Krishna for a lack of manliness, Arjuna continues to assert his unwillingness to fight in the battle.
- Krishna then speaks of the eternality of the true self in all beings. Even though the warriors will die in battle, it is only the body that is ended, not the embodied soul.
- Krishna reminds Arjuna that as a *kshatriya*, he is bound by his *dharma* to fight in battle and never withdraw.
- Vedic ritual performed purely for material gain is criticised. This is karma.
- However, ritual action should not be given up, and for Arjuna, ritual action is the action ordained by the rules of *dharma*. Hence, he must fight in battle. However, he must do so without any desire for personal gain. This desireless action is designated as *buddhi-yoga*.
- One who engages in *buddhi-yoga* must be detached from material desires and remain aloof from emotional attachment to success or failure in the action he performs. When action is performed in this detached manner, one is free of the law of karma and attains the spiritual goal of liberation from rebirth.
- Now, we can proceed to the third chapter, in which Krishna expands on the ideas he has introduced here.

*A person does not gain freedom from action
simply by ceasing to act, and he cannot reach the
ultimate state of perfection by renunciation alone.* —3.4

CHAPTER 3

In Chapter 3, Krishna expands upon the idea of *karma-yoga* he introduced in the second half of Chapter 2. This further explanation is called for because it is clear from Arjuna's opening remarks that he has not yet fully grasped how detachment from the world can be reconciled with engaging in acts of violence. Is it possible to reach this state of detachment whilst remaining engaged in the worldly actions dictated by one's social *dharma*?

ARJUNA'S INQUIRY

1. Arjuna said: If you regard realisation as being superior to action, then why are you urging me to engage in a form of action (karma) that is so dreadful?
2. It seems that you are confusing my understanding by this equivocal instruction. Please tell me conclusively of the one course by which I can obtain the greatest benefit.

Here, Arjuna admits frankly that Krishna's teachings in Chapter 2 have left him confused. If Krishna regards *buddhi* (the intellect) as superior to karma (action), then why does he urge him to engage in action of the most extreme kind? It seems that Arjuna regards worldly action as standing in opposition to spiritual realisation, designated by the word *buddhi*. Krishna has tried to explain how they can be reconciled in his discourse on *buddhi-yoga*, but Arjuna has not quite understood the point. The debate that will now take place is a significant one. The religious ideas of Buddhists and

Jains insist that full spiritual realisation can be gained only if a person renounces the worldly life for the life of a renunciant. For this reason, Buddhist monks still live in large monastic communities, where they can remain aloof from worldly concerns and concentrate on their personal spiritual progress. The Bhagavad-gita is not content with this view, not least because it believes that a person should maintain a concern for the affairs of the world, and so it argues that renunciation is a state of mind and does not depend on living in a state of isolation from human society. This is clearly another feature of the doctrine of *buddhi-* or *karma-yoga*, and it is one that Krishna will now consider in more detail as a response to Arjuna's question.

WHAT IS RENUNCIATION?

3. The Lord said: O sinless one, I have already alluded to a twofold system that exists in this world. For Samkhyas, it is by the yoga of knowledge (*jñana-yoga*), and for yogins, it is by the yoga of action (*karma-yoga*).

4. A person does not gain freedom from action simply by ceasing to act, and he cannot reach the ultimate state of perfection by renunciation alone.

5. No one can remain still without performing any action, not even for a moment. Everyone is helplessly engaged in some form of action by the *gunas* that are born out of *prakriti* (matter).

6. One who restricts his organs of action but continually dwells on the objects of the senses within his mind is a deluded soul. Such a person is referred to as a hypocrite.

7. But one who continues to act whilst controlling the senses with the mind, Arjuna, using his organs of action to perform *karma-yoga* without any attachment, is certainly superior.

8. You should continue to perform your prescribed duties, for performing action is superior to refraining from action. You cannot even sustain your bodily functions without acting.

I would say that this passage is directed against those who say that renunciation of material desires is possible only if one withdraws from the world to become either a wandering *sadhu* or a monk living in a monastic community. Wherever one lives, action must be performed, for one cannot live without acting. And one may restrain and regulate one's activities by refraining from worldly action, but if one's mind still dwells on the objects of desire, then there is no real renunciation, for it is the state of one's consciousness that is more important than physical action. Verse 6 seems to refer to one who renounces the world physically but remains dominated by material desires. As well as the more obvious forms of desire for sensual pleasure, these can be of a more subtle nature, such as desire for the fame and prestige that often come to religious leaders.

Verse 7 refers to one who remains active within the world but does not seek to enjoy the objects of the senses. Here, Krishna refers to this type of practice as *karma-yoga* rather than *buddhi-yoga*, though there is no suggestion of any difference in terms of the way it is undertaken, as both consist of performing one's duties in the world without desire for personal gain. Krishna clearly considers that the *karma-yogin* who lives in the world is in a superior position spiritually to the monk who has renounced the world but still nurtures material desires. So the message here seems to be that it is better not to physically renounce the world, but to cultivate a mood of inner renunciation whilst remaining active in the world. This view certainly marks a distinction between Hindu and Buddhist teaching on how to gain liberation from rebirth.

The Vedic Ritual
and Karma-yoga

9. Except where action is performed in the execution of *yajña*, this world remains in the bondage of action. Remaining free of attachment, Kaunteya, you should therefore perform action for that purpose alone.

10. In the beginning, after creating living beings along with *yajña*, Prajapati said to them: You will flourish by means of this ritual; this will be the cow that grants all your desires.

11. You should sustain the gods in this way, and the gods will then sustain you. Sustaining each other in this way, you will achieve the highest benefit.

12. Sustained by *yajña*, the gods will bestow upon you all the food you may desire. One who consumes the foods given by the gods without making offerings to them is certainly a thief.

13. Righteous people who consume food left after a *yajña* are freed from all blemishes. But wicked people who cook just for themselves consume only sin.

14. Living beings exist on food, and food is produced due to rain. The rain comes as a result of *yajña*, and *yajña* is performed by ritual action.

15. You should understand that ritual action is derived from the Veda (Brahma) and the Veda appears from the *akshara* (undecaying). Hence, the all-pervasive Brahman is always present within the *yajña*.

16. In this world, a malicious person who delights only in the senses, and does not perpetuate the turning of the wheel thus set in motion, certainly lives a worthless life.

This passage makes an interesting contrast with the apparent criticism of Vedic ritual we encountered in Chapter 2 (verses 42–45). Here, Krishna insists that the Vedic *yajña*, the ritual offering into the sacred fire, must be performed, for the welfare of the world is dependent on the ritual. The gods are nourished by the offerings made into the sacred fire, and when the gods are pleased in this way, they in turn supply all the necessities of life to human beings on earth. In understanding the difference of perspective between this passage and 2.42–45, we must note again the distinction between karma and *karma-yoga*. The ritual actions condemned previously were karma in the sense that they were performed by selfish-minded individuals desirous of personal gain. Here, *yajña* is to be performed not on the basis of selfish motivations but for the welfare of the entire world. And this is an important feature of *karma-yoga*. Almost by definition, *moksha-dharma* involves indifference to the world, for the practitioner is interested only in breaking free of the world. The Bhagavad-gita, however, will not accept that this world is of no importance as one seeks the higher goal of liberation. Rather, it offers us a *karma-yoga* that reconciles the quest for *moksha* with a concern for life, well-being, and prosperity in this sphere of existence. This reconciliation of two apparently contradictory goals is certainly one of the major contributions to Hindu religious thought made by the Bhagavad-gita. Here, we can see how the performance of the Vedic ritual is transformed into a form of yoga that aims at liberation from rebirth; the *yajña* is to be performed without any attachment or desire for personal gain, but only as a duty that will bring about prosperity, happiness, and well-being for the people of the world.

WHY SHOULD A YOGIN PERFORM RITUALS?

17. But for a person who seeks pleasure in the self alone, finds contentment through the self, and is fulfilled by the self, there is no prescribed duty to perform.

18. There is nothing for him to gain by either performing or renouncing such duties. Nor is there any reason for him to be dependent on another living being.

19. Remaining always unattached, you should therefore perform your prescribed duty. A person who performs such duty without attachment attains the highest goal.

20. It was solely through the performance of action that Janaka and others attained a state of complete perfection. Just by considering the welfare of the world, you should be inspired to act.

21. Whatever course of action a superior man pursues, lesser persons will follow, and the world will accept the standard he sets.

22. There is no action that I am bound to perform anywhere in the three worlds, nor anything I might need that I have not already attained, and yet still I am engaged in action.

23. For if ever I was to cease from the actions I tirelessly perform, all people would follow my path, Partha.

24. If I did not perform these duties, then these worlds would fall into ruin. I would then be the creator of chaos and thereby cause harm to living beings.

25. People devoid of knowledge perform actions on the basis of worldly attachment, Bharata. The wise should act in the same way but without attachment, seeking the well-being of the world.

26. The wise man should not cause any breach in the understanding of ignorant people attached to performing action.

By acting whilst engaged in his yoga discipline, he should
encourage them to perform all their duties.

I have given a question as the heading for this passage: 'Why should
a yogin perform rituals?' Here, again, we may recall a verse from
the second chapter (v. 46) in which Krishna states that just as a
lake fulfils all the functions of a small pond, so a spiritually realised brahmin has achieved all that the Vedic ritual can offer. The
point made there was that any person who has achieved the highest
level of spiritual awakening has no further need of any ritual that
might help those who are less advanced. But here, we seem to have
a different view set forward, as Krishna suggests that enlightened
persons should continue with their ritual actions.

If we consider the reasons given as to why a person who has
achieved this state of enlightenment should continue to perform
duties related to this world, we might note the following points:
In verses 17 and 18, Krishna states quite clearly that a person who
has realised the *atman* within his own being has no further need to
engage in ritual acts such as the Vedic *yajña* discussed in the previous verses. Such a person is described *atma-rati* (finding pleasure in
the self), *atma-tripta* (completely satisfied by the self) and *atmany...*
samtushta (fully content within his own being). For the self-realised
person, *karyam na vidyate* (v. 17), there is no religious duty that he
is required to perform. So here, in fact, we get confirmation of the
point made earlier in Chapter 2 (v. 46); the realised soul has no need
of any ritual act, for he has already achieved the highest religious
goal. So why, then, should he continue to perform such rituals?

The first point Krishna makes in response to this question is
that the enlightened person has nothing to lose by performing
ritual acts (v. 18). He is already on the level of awakened knowledge, and he is not going to fall from that position by continuing
to act. Because he has achieved the state of self-realisation, there is
nothing that can disturb him; performing or not performing ritual
action is entirely the same.

Verse 19 seems slightly anomalous, because here, Krishna, pauses in his discussion of whether the realised person should perform action and returns instead to Arjuna's position. Arjuna should certainly engage in the ritual action of his *kshatriya-dharma*, but without selfish desire, for this is the *karma-yoga* that will take him to that higher state of consciousness.

It is in verses 20 and 21 that we find the real heart of the issue. It is all to do with the well-being of the world. The realised saint may have transcended the world through spiritual enlightenment, but that does not mean that he should be indifferent to the situation of the world. Verse 20 cites the example of King Janaka (presumably the father of Sita from the Ramayana), who was an enlightened sage but who continued his *kshatriya* duty by ruling the kingdom. Why did he not live as a renunciant? The answer given here is *loka-samgraham – sampashyan*, it was because he was concerned over the welfare of the world, the *loka-samgraha*.

Not only did Janaka's enlightened rule bring benefit to his citizens, but his conduct in remaining dedicated to his social duty also served as an example to others. So here is another reason. Not only does the performance of religious duty bring benefit to the world, but its performance also serves as an example to others. The mass of the population should not seek to take up the renounced lifestyle of the *sadhu*, for this will not help them spiritually, and one who is truly enlightened sets the example for others by continuing to perform his or her duty even though he has no personal need to do so.

This passage marks an important addition to our understanding of the *karma-yoga*. The performance of social duty as desireless action is not just a means by which an individual can make personal spiritual progress. It is also a means by which individual spirituality can be reconciled with ensuring order and prosperity in the world; it draws social *dharma* and *moksha-dharma* together in a unique manner. Kings and other leaders are not to abandon their positions and ignore the effect this will have on the world. The welfare of the world does matter, and so *karma-yoga* is recommended as the means by which one can pursue personal spirituality without causing harm to the world by abandoning social responsibilities.

In verses 22 to 24, Krishna refers to himself as an example of the principle of *karma-yoga*. Whether we regard Krishna as the Supreme Deity or as an enlightened teacher, there is no reason why he should concern himself with a world he is not a part of. But still, he is engaged in action. Why? Because he is concerned for the well-being of those who live in the world, and if he did not act, this well-being would be damaged.

In verses 25 and 26, the teaching of the passage is concluded with a further reference to the importance of *loka-samgraha*, the well-being of the world, and a succinct explanation of the *karma-yoga*. The external actions performed by the *karma-yogin* are identical to those performed by a person who is absorbed in this world; the difference lies in the consciousness and the motive. One acts for selfish reasons; this is karma. The other performs the same action out of duty alone, without attachment or desire; this is *karma-yoga*.

KARMA-YOGA AND SPIRITUAL KNOWLEDGE

27. All actions are ultimately performed by the *gunas* inherent in *prakriti* (matter), but a person whose mind is deluded by the sense of 'I' thinks, 'I am the doer'.

28. But one who understands the truth about the distinction between *guna* and action, O mighty one, understands that it is just one set of *gunas* acting on other *gunas*. By understanding action in this way, he remains unattached.

29. Those who are confused about the *gunas* inherent in *prakriti* have attachment for the action generated by the *gunas*. But one who understands all this should not disturb such ignorant persons who have only limited knowledge.

30. Casting off all your deeds onto me by fixing your mind on the true self, remaining free of desire and free of any sense of 'mine', you should now fight with the emotions banished.

31. Persons who are faithful and devoid of envy and who always adhere to the teaching I have just revealed are released from the effects of action.

32. But those who despise this teaching of mine and do not adhere to it are deluded in all their wisdom. You should know that they are lost souls who are completely dull-witted.

33. Even one who possesses knowledge conducts himself in accordance with his nature. Living beings must conform to their inherent nature; what can repression of one's nature achieve?

34. Desire and aversion are the conditions of the senses in relation to objects they perceive. A person must not fall under the control of either of these tendencies, for both are obstacles to him.

35. Even though it may have faults, one's own dharma is still superior to accepting the dharma of another, even if it be perfectly observed. Death in the performance of one's own dharma is better, for another's dharma is a source of danger.

Here, again, we are presented with further discussion around the subject of *karma-yoga*, but in this passage, we see the emphasis being shifted slightly away from a simple discourse on desireless action towards the spiritual knowledge that is associated with that *karma-yoga*. The passage is rather complex and involves several different ideas, and hence, it might be useful to summarise what is being said here point by point, looking at how it refines the previous discourse on *karma-yoga*.

Verses 27 and 28 discuss exactly what is happening when action is performed and show how a person can be detached from the results of action – as is essential in the practice of *karma-yoga* – by understanding the truth of action. The conventional view is that when action is performed, we consider ourselves the doer and the controller of the outcome. Here, however, Krishna suggests an alternative view by means of which we can detach ourselves from the actions we perform. The Samkhya teachings used by the Bhaga-vad-gita reveal that matter, or *prakriti,* is pervaded by three inherent qualities, the *gunas* designated as *sattva, rajas,* and *tamas.* From the perspective of *karma-yoga,* a person sees that he is not the doer of the action he performs, for in fact action is just an interaction of these *gunas.* Action is a process that takes place within the realm of matter. Rather than seeing himself as involved in the process of action and thereby feeling attachment for the outcome, the *kar-ma-yogin* takes up the position of a neutral observer of the action he performs and thereby becomes detached from the outcome. The instruction here is really about how to engage in *karma-yoga* by becoming a detached observer of oneself performing action, rather than identifying oneself as the performer of action.

In verse 30, we have a further hint of the relationship between *karma-yoga* and *bhakti,* devotion to God, a theme that is developed more fully later in the Bhagavad-gita. Here, again, there is further advice on the techniques of *karma-yoga.* In performing action, one becomes detached emotionally by observing it as an interaction of material forces. Now in this verse, one understands that all outcomes are determined by the will of God, and this understanding further assists the process of becoming detached from action.

Verses 31 and 32 simply describe the differing characteristics of those who do and those who do not accept Krishna's teachings on *karma-yoga.* They also describe the different results these two types of person will achieve. Perhaps here, we should connect the Gita to its context within the *Mahabharata* and recognise a reference to the Pandavas on one side and the Kauravas on the other.

In verses 33 to 35, we see another dimension of the doctrines of *karma-yoga* and a reference to the Bhagavad-gita's ideas on the social divisions of *varna*, which are often interpreted in terms of the caste system. The point that Krishna is making here is again intimately linked to the doctrine of *karma-yoga*. It is suggested that every person is born with a predetermined inherent nature, known as *sva-bhava*. How is this predetermined? By the actions performed in previous lives that have shaped the inner nature with which the soul transmigrates. Hence, for the Gita, it is not true to say that all human beings are born equal with their inner nature like a blank sheet. Each of us is born with a specific personal disposition, and it is this inner disposition that is reflected in the division of society into four *varnas*, or social classes: brahmins, *kshatriyas*, *vaishyas*, and *shudras*. The *dharma* ordained for each of these social classes reflects the inner nature of those born into them, and therefore, it is regarded as wrong for people to change their *varna* or to abandon their social *dharma*. This of course applies to Arjuna in his present situation; he is born as a *kshatriya* and hence, he has the *sva-bhava*, or inherent nature, of a *kshatriya*. Therefore, his desire to abandon the battle and renounce his duty is perverse and wholly impractical. Verse 35 is repeated almost verbatim in the eighteenth chapter (v. 47), and at this point, the topic is explained in greater detail. Here, Arjuna is instructed that he cannot give up his *kshatriya-dharma*, because *kshatriya-dharma* is a reflection of *kshatriya* nature and a person cannot change his inherent nature. Therefore, one should continue to perform one's own social *dharma*, but do so without desire or attachment, thereby transforming karma into *karma-yoga*.

THE ROOT CAUSE
OF WICKED ACTION

36. Arjuna said: What is it that impels a person to act sinfully even though he has no desire to do so, Varshneya, compelling him to act in that way as if by force?

37. The Lord said: It is desire, it is anger; this arises from the *guna* known as *rajas*. You should know this as a mighty devouring force, a great source of sin; it is the enemy in this world.

38. As fire is covered by smoke, as a mirror is covered by dirt, and as an embryo is covered by its membrane, so is this world covered by desire.

39. Knowledge is covered by this desire, which is therefore the great enemy of one who possesses knowledge. This enemy in the form of desire, Kaunteya, blazes like an insatiable fire.

40. The senses, the mind, and the intellect are said to be its abode. Covering the true knowledge of the embodied being, it thus places it in a state of delusion.

41. Therefore, you must first regulate the senses, O best of the Bharatas, and then conquer this source of sin, which destroys both spiritual and practical knowledge.

42. They say that the senses are in a superior position and that the mind is superior to the senses. The intellect stands above the mind, but this is superior even to the intellect.

43. Thus, understanding that which is superior to the intellect and making yourself steady by your own self, you must defeat this enemy in the form of desire, O mighty one, though it is difficult to overcome.

This final passage of Chapter 3 is inaugurated by a further question posed by Arjuna relating to the causes of wicked action. It is not entirely clear what prompts Arjuna to pose this question at this particular point. Perhaps it is Krishna's reference to the faulty performance of dharmic duty, or perhaps it is the idea of a person abandoning his own *dharma*, which could also be regarded as wicked action. Anyway, the question is an intriguing one and is related to the idea of *karma-yoga*, for Krishna has already informed us that in practising *karma-yoga*, one must strive to become free of selfish desire.

Arjuna's question about the root cause of wicked action

The wording of Arjuna's question is interesting, for it indicates that people often act wickedly whilst seeking to be virtuous. So, what is the force which compels people to deviate from the virtue they aspire after? Krishna initially gives two answers: *kama esha kro-dha esha*, it is desire and it is anger, but the subsequent discussion focuses on desire alone. It is the burning desire for sensual pleasure that gives rise to selfish actions such as lying, cheating, deceiving, stealing, or harming others, and if this desire cannot be resisted, then a person is compelled to engage in acts he knows in his heart to be wicked.

What is the consequence of giving in to desire for one who is seeking spiritual perfection?

In verses 39 and 40, Krishna points out that true knowledge is obscured when selfish desire prevails. *Knowledge* here refers to the higher understanding of our spiritual identity, which is the key to liberation from rebirth. This knowledge, or *jñana*, can only exist when the covering power of desire is removed.

Overcoming the power of desire

In verse 41, Krishna says that the senses must be brought under control, for desire is stimulated by sensual perception, as we learned in Chapter 2 (v. 62). In the final two verses, however, it is suggested that the enemy known as desire can be defeated by knowledge of the true self, which stands above and beyond even the intellect or personality. When our spiritual identity is realised, then the desire to enjoy the world through the material identity naturally declines.

*What is the connection between this final passage
of Chapter 3 and karma-yoga?*

From the beginning of the discussion on this subject, the Bhagavad-gita has indicated that *karma-yoga* means 'the performance of dharmic duty without any selfish desire'. Hence, it is clear that the presence of *kama*, desire, within the heart and mind of the practitioner will be a major obstacle to the practice. In this passage, the point is pursued in more detail by showing how the presence of desire firstly causes a person to deviate from *dharma* and virtue, and secondly inhibits the knowledge and detachment the *karma-yogin* is striving to achieve.

CONCLUSION:
A SUMMARY OF CHAPTER 3

The Gita's third chapter begins with a question from Arjuna that seeks clarification of the ideas Krishna set out in Chapter 2. Krishna explains again that action performed without desire is superior to the physical renunciation of the world, for no one in any condition of life can completely refrain from action. The Gita then explains why the Vedic *yajña* is to be performed; it is not for personal gain but for the welfare of the world, for *yajña* ensures that the rains will fall and provide food for all. One who has achieved spiritual realisation has nothing to gain from action, but still he will continue to act, not for selfish reasons, but because he seeks the well-being of everyone. Even Krishna himself acts for this reason, embodying the spirit of *karma-yoga*. Hence, even an enlightened *sadhu* will continue to perform his dharmic duty and will not adopt the duties of any other *varna*. The chapter concludes with a further question from Arjuna, this time about the impulse that leads people to act sinfully. Krishna responds by emphasising his insistence that selfish desire should be abandoned. It is desire alone that leads to sinful action; hence, a person should strive to overcome this powerful foe in his quest for spiritual perfection.

The third chapter of the Bhagavad-gita builds on the notion of a *karma-yoga* that Krishna initially established in verses 47 to 54 of the Chapter 2, but here, the practice is explained in more detail. It now becomes clear that a part of the reason for the advocacy of *karma-yoga* is a concern that the welfare of the world should not suffer because its leaders decide to abandon their duties in order to pursue higher spiritual goals. When *karma-yoga* is properly understood, this is not necessary, and the stability of the world is a vitally important factor that cannot be ignored. Moreover, we see here clear indications of the ideas that will become increasingly significant as the Gita continues its discourse, notably *jnana* and *bhakti*, knowledge and devotion. Chapters 4 and 5 continue to explain in more detail various aspects of the practice of *karma-yoga*, but in the sixth chapter, the emphasis on knowledge of the true self comes wholly to the fore. Furthermore, in the chapters that follow, it is the nature of God and devotion to God that emerge as the central themes of the Bhagavad-gita's instruction.

In this world, there is nothing as
purifying as knowledge. —4.38

CHAPTER 4

In the fourth chapter of the Bhagavad-gita, we find further instruction on the practice of the *karma-yoga*, which has already been considered in detail. Towards the end of the chapter, the emphasis of the teachings changes as Krishna begins to shift his focus away from the performance of desireless action towards the higher knowledge that should support this practice. We see this change of emphasis occurring in verse 33, in which *jñana* (realised knowledge) is emphasised as the highest *yajña* (religious practice). The remaining verses reveal the importance of realised knowledge in reaching the ultimate goal. Before taking us through this transition from *karma-yoga* to spiritual knowledge, however, the chapter begins with significant revelations about Krishna's divine identity and his descent to earth. The nature of God is a subject explored in detail in later chapters, but here, we have a taste of what is to come in response to a question from Arjuna.

THE DOCTRINE OF AVATAR

1. The Lord said: I instructed this ever-existing yoga to Vivasvan. Vivasvan instructed it to Manu and Manu taught it to Ikshvaku.
2. It was in this way that the Raja-Rishis (royal saints) understood this yoga, receiving it one from the other in succession, but after a long time had passed, knowledge of this yoga was lost in this world, Paramtapa.

3. This same ancient yoga has today been instructed by me to you because you are my devotee (*bhakta*) and my friend. It is indeed the most profound mystery.

4. Arjuna said: Your birth was later than the birth of Vivasvan, which was earlier. So, how can I understand that you taught this to him in the beginning?

5. The Lord said: There are many births of mine that have passed, and of yours also, Arjuna. I know about them all, but you do not know of them, Paramtapa.

6. Although I am unborn and my identity is unchanging, and although I am the controller (*ishvara*) of all beings, still I resort to my own *prakriti* energy and appear by means of my own power.

7. Whenever there is a decline in *dharma*, O Bharata, and whenever there is an increase in *adharma*, it is then that I manifest myself.

8. For the protection of the righteous (*sadhus*), for the destruction of the wrongdoers, and for the purpose of establishing *dharma*, I appear age after age.

9. He who fully understands the truth about my divine birth and activity does not take birth again after giving up his body. He comes to Me, Arjuna.

10. Free of desire, fear, and anger, wholly dedicated to me and dependent upon me, many persons purified by knowledge and austerity have attained my state of existence.

11. According to the manner in which they dedicate themselves to me, so I devote myself to them. In all circumstances, people follow the path I set for them, Partha.

This is one of the best known of all the passages in the Bhagavad-gita, as it sets out one of the most important elements of Hindu teachings about God, particularly for those Hindus whose religion tends towards Vaishnavism. The idea of *avatar* is a significant feature of Vaishnava theology, and it is here in the Bhagavad-gita that we get the original pronouncement of this teaching. There are a number of points we might note from the passage, some of which will be taken up in more detail later on.

It is the first three verses of the chapter that prompt Arjuna's question. Here, Krishna is demonstrating that the *karma-yoga* he has revealed is not a new idea he has just come up with but has been practised since ancient times. It is interesting to note that the line of descent he refers to in the transmission of this form of religious practice is through *kshatriyas* rather than brahmins. This suggests that *karma-yoga* is primarily for people who have worldly responsibilities; it is a means of pursuing the highest spiritual goals whilst still discharging one's social duties.

It is apparent from the question in verse 4 that at this point Arjuna is still not certain about Krishna's divinity or his identity as an *avatar* of Narayana (Vishnu). Vivasvan is the sun god, one of the twelve Vedic Adityas, but of course the Supreme Deity is the creator of all the gods. So Arjuna's question here suggests that he has not yet accepted Krishna's divine identity.

The use of the word *prakriti* in verse 6 suggests that when Vishnu assumes an *avatar* form, it is in a body composed of matter (*prakriti*). Most Vaishnava commentators do not accept this and interpret *prakriti* here as meaning 'my own (divine) nature'. On balance, the use of *prakriti* might seem to suggest that the Deity takes on a material body in order to play the role of a human being (as in Christian beliefs about Jesus), but it is not conclusive.

Verses 7 and 8 are perhaps the best known of any passage from the Bhagavad-gita, and it is here that the classical doctrine of *avatar* is established with the reasons for a descent being given as the decline in *dharma*, the increase of *adharma*, the need to protect righteous persons, and the need to vanquish the wicked who have destroyed the equilibrium of the world. The Vaishnava *Puranas* provide many *avatar* stories which reflect the definition provided here in the Gita.

Verse 9 is very important in understanding Hindu devotional practice, as it refers to learning about the stories contained in the *Puranas*, which tell of Krishna's birth and activities (*janma* and *karma*). Today all over India, there are story-tellers, bhajan singers, dances, dramas, and recitations based on the lives of Krishna, Rama, and occasionally other *avatars* as well. In the modern era, this form of religious practice has been translated into new media such as comic books, film, television, and the internet. This long and thriving tradition can be derived from the idea given here that learning about the birth and activities of the Deity is one path to *moksha*.

Verse 11 is also one that is well known to many Hindus, and it does seem to confirm the idea of Swami Vivekananda and others that all forms of religion are a part of the path established by the Supreme Deity. Here, then, we find support for the traditional Hindu attitude of religious tolerance, for Krishna does not say 'This is my religion and those who do not follow it are all evil and will be punished'. Rather, he says *mama vartmanuvartante manushyah partha sarvashah*, which suggests that every religious path is a part of Krishna's way – *mama vartma* – and different types of religion are established depending on the extent to which a person is able to surrender to Krishna.

Having deviated somewhat from its main topic, the Bhagavad-gita now returns to its discourse on *karma-yoga*, the performance of ritual action as duty rather than for worldly gain. In this passage, however, we see Krishna once more bringing himself into the equation, as he did in Chapter 3 on a similar topic (vv. 22–3). And here, ritual action does not just mean the performance of the Vedic *yajña* or *murti-puja* (image worship) in a temple, but is the duty one is bound to perform based on one's *varna* or social position.

Krishna and Karma-yoga

12. Seeking success through ritual action, some people worship the gods. In the human sphere, success is quickly attained through ritual acts.

13. I created the system of four *varnas* based on the *gunas* and types of action. And you should understand that although I am the creator of this system, I am still the one who does not act, the one who does not decay.

14. Actions cannot leave a mark on me, and I am unaffected by the fruits of action. He who understands this truth about me is not bound by the actions he performs.

15. In the past this truth was well known to people who sought liberation from rebirth and also performed action. So, you should also perform your designated actions, just as people in the past fulfilled their duties.

16. What is action? What is non-action? Even the wise are confused about this. I will now explain to you what action is; when you understand this you will be freed from evil.

17. One must understand about action, and one must understand about forbidden action. One must also understand what non-action is; the course of action is indeed hard to comprehend.

What does verse 13 tell us about varna and possibly caste as well?

There is an argument to suggest that this verse is saying that *varna* (and hence caste by implication) is not based on birth but on a person's qualities (*gunas*) and the way in which he acts. So it could be used by reformers who want to see the rigidity of the caste system eroded. The point, however, is not conclusive. It could well be that Krishna is merely saying that the *varnas* are defined by the *gunas* that predominate in each of them and by the type of work that is designated for the members of each social class. In their commentaries, Shankaracharya, Ramanujacharya, and Madhvacharya all take the verse in this latter sense.

Why does Krishna bring himself into the discussion of ritual action?

In the second half of verse 13 and in verse 14, Krishna refers to himself as being a person who engages in action and yet is not affected by the law of karma. As he has just revealed himself to be the *ishvara* (v. 6), or Supreme Deity, this statement could be a further reflection on his own divinity, but this is not emphasised here. The real point would seem to be that the performance of action does not necessarily lead to the bondage of rebirth under the control of the law of karma. This idea is raised again in the following verses, especially v. 16, where the question is asked as to what action really is. Here, we are again in touch with the doctrine of *karma-yoga*. Action will only produce future rebirth if it is performed with a selfish motivation. Action performed without desire does not produce any future result, and this means that the actor can attain freedom from karma in a state of *moksha*. Whether or not he is regarded as the Deity, Krishna himself is an example of a person who acts but is not affected by the results of action, for it is not the physical action that produces karma but the state of mind that motivates the action. This is one of the most important teachings of the Bhagavad-gita and is closely related to the teachings of the Yoga system, such as those encountered in Patañjali's *Yoga-sutra*.

Following on from verse 14, verse 15 is again all about *karma-yoga*. Firstly, Krishna is emphasising that it is not just a recent innovation, but that it is part of the traditional religion of the followers of the Vedas, and secondly, he is asserting again that one who performs his worldly duties can simultaneously pursue the spiritual goal of *moksha*. Hence, renunciation of the world by living as a monk or *sadhu* is not a necessary requirement for one who seeks liberation from rebirth.

Non-action

We can now see why Krishna poses the questions he does in verses 16 and 17. What is karma and what is *akarma*? Even the wise men, the *kavis*, find this a confusing subject. Why? It seems very simple to define what action is. But Krishna's point is that desireless action really falls under the heading of non-action because it produces no future result. And then again, refraining from action, *akarma*, can be defined as karma if one refrains from action due to selfish or malicious motivation. For example, if I see someone in distress but selfishly decide not to help, I have performed no action, but still, karma will accrue, because in all cases it is the state of consciousness underlying the action (or inaction) rather than the physical deed itself that is significant.

THE QUESTION ANSWERED – KARMA-YOGA

18. One who perceives inaction in action and action in inaction is intelligent amongst men. He is properly engaged, and he performs all his designated actions.
19. When all a person's endeavours are devoid of any inclination towards desire, his action is burned by the fire of knowledge. The wise ones describe such a person as a learned *pandit*.
20. When a person gives up attachment for the fruits of action, is always satisfied, and is not dependent on any other, then even though he is engaged in action, he performs no action at all.
21. Having no expectation of result, controlling his thoughts, practising self-control, giving up all desire for acquisitions,

and acting only for the maintenance of the body, a person remains free of contamination.

22. If he is satisfied with whatever befalls him, transcends duality, is free of envy, and is equal in success and failure, then even though he engages in action, he is not bound by it.

23. For a liberated person whose attachments have vanished, whose mind is absorbed in higher knowledge, and who acts only in the form of *yajña*, any action he performs dissolves away completely.

We could take these verses as being almost the last word on *karma-yoga*, in which the main points are again re-emphasised. They also provide the answer to the previous question about action and non-action, defining these in terms of the motivation.

Inaction in action and action in inaction

This goes back to our previous discussion. Essentially, one sees 'inaction in action' (*akarma* in karma) when the action in question is performed without selfish desire. It then effectively becomes inaction (or non-action) because it will not produce a future reaction according to the law of karma. And action is to be understood as non-action when a person gives up performing his duty for selfish reasons. That failure to perform action will produce a future reaction, and so in that sense the non-action is action, the *akarma* is karma.

How is it that a person 'performs no action at all even though he is engaged in action'?

Verse 20 again reinforces our understanding of *karma-yoga*. The key phrase here is at the start of the verse: *tyaktva karma-phala-sangam*, meaning 'giving up (*tyaktva*) attachment (*sanga*) to the fruits of action (*karma-phala*)'. When action is performed with this renounced state of consciousness, there is no future karma generated. Hence, in truth, 'he performs no action at all'.

Acts only in the form of yajna

The word *yajña* means 'the Vedic ritual in which offerings are made to the gods through the sacred fire'. Of course, this ritual is often performed in pursuit of some worldly goal, but here, I think *yajña* refers to action that is performed as a ritualised duty as opposed to action performed for personal gain. If *yajña* is taken in this sense, then the connection with the ongoing discourse on *karma-yoga* becomes clearly apparent.

This point about *yajña* is expanded upon in the following verses, in which the concept of *yajña* is broadened so as to include several different types of religious activity, including the yoga practices discussed later in the Gita. The idea seems to be that all these forms of *yajña* can be included under the heading of *karma-yoga* when they are enacted without selfish desire.

VARIOUS FORMS OF YAJÑA

24. The sacrificial offering is Brahman. The oblation is Brahman; it is offered by Brahman into the fire that is also Brahman. Brahman alone is reached by a person who absorbs his mind completely in the ritual act that is Brahman.

25. Some practitioners make *yajña* offerings dedicated to the gods alone, but others make their offerings into the fire of Brahman, performing *yajña* for its own sake.

26. Then there are some who offer hearing and the other senses into the fires of restraint and others who offer sound and the other objects of the senses into the fires of the senses themselves.

27. Others offer all the actions performed by the senses and the movements of the breath into the fire of yoga practice based on self-control, which is illuminated by means of true knowledge.

28. Some sages, strictly adhering to their vows, perform *yajña* with their possessions, some through religious austerity, some through yoga, and some through recitation and knowledge of sacred texts.

29. Others offer the *prana* breath into the *apana* and the *apana* into the *prana*, dedicating themselves to the practice of *pranayama* by restricting the movement of the *prana* and the *apana*.

30. Others restrict their eating and make offerings of the *prana* breaths into the *prana* breaths themselves. All such persons who have knowledge of *yajña* have their contaminations destroyed by means of *yajña*.

31. Consuming the nectar of immortality in the form of the leftover offerings at the end of a *yajña*, they proceed to the eternal region of Brahman. There is nothing in this world for a person who performs no *yajña*, O best of the Kurus, and this is even more the case for the other world.

32. Thus, many different types of *yajña* are expanded within the mouth of Brahman. You must understand that all of them are based on action, for when you understand this you will be liberated.

This passage is a little difficult and requires some careful consideration, although I think it can be identified as a further definition of *karma-yoga*, leading eventually to the emphasis on higher knowledge with which this chapter ends. Let us take it point by point:

Verse 24 defines the various elements of the traditional Vedic *yajña* as Brahman. It is difficult to say precisely what this means. Shankaracharya explains that this is the vision of the enlightened person when he performs the ritual fire offering. He is not looking for material gain through the ritual, but in his detached state of consciousness identifies the ritual and all its component parts as Brahman. Ramanuja suggests that all these parts of the *yajña* are designated as Brahman because they are derived from Brahman, which is the original source of the world. Here, one suspects that Shankara might be closer to the spirit of the text, for the Gita is here again arguing that when it is performed without desire, religious ritual of any sort is a spiritual practice and hence is Brahman.

Verse 25 seems to be the key to this passage, as it indicates that the *yajña* can become a spiritual practice performed by *yogins* rather than the materially motivated ritual that Krishna refers to so dismissively in 2.42–5. This is another important feature of the teachings revealed by the Bhagavad-gita. In the Veda, there is a clear division between the *karma-kanda* consisting of worldly ritual and the *jñana-kanda*, the knowledge revealed by the Upanishads, which leads to liberation from rebirth. Here, however, Krishna achieves a reconciliation of the *karma-kanda* and the *jñana-kanda* by re-branding the Vedic rituals as a form of *karma-yoga* when they are performed without selfish desire. And of course, as we have learned, *karma-yoga* is a path to *moksha*, the goal of the *jñana-kanda*.

The remaining verses of the passage then show that the word *yajña* does not refer solely to the Vedic ritual. Verse 28 describes *yajña* as being performed with objects (*dravya*, presumably those offered into the sacred fire) through religious austerities and vows, through yoga techniques or through understanding and reciting sacred texts. And in verses 28 and 29, reference is made to the yogic practice of *pranayama*, the regulation of the breath within the body, which is also designated as a type of *yajña*. In verse 31, we are back with the Vedic *yajña* and the eating of the food leftover after the offerings have been made into the fire.

Verse 31 seems to provide the conclusion and explanation of the passage, which is essentially that all these types of *yajña* are based on action, and hence, action as *karma-yoga* can indeed lead the practitioner to the realm of Brahman, which is beyond this world of rebirth.

REALISED KNOWLEDGE AS
THE GOAL OF KARMA-YOGA

33. The *Jñana Yajña*, consisting of knowledge, is superior to the *Dravya Yajña*, consisting of physical objects, O destroyer of the foe. Without any exception, Partha, all action finds its proper conclusion in knowledge.

34. You should gain this knowledge through submission, inquiry, and service. Those who have knowledge and perceive the truth will impart knowledge to you.

35. And when you have acquired this knowledge, you never again fall prey to illusion, Pandava, for you will see that all living beings are within your own self and, moreover, within me.

36. Even if you perform sinful acts more heinous than those of all other sinners, still you can cross beyond all such wickedness by means of the boat of knowledge.

37. Just as a blazing fire turns fuel to ashes, Arjuna, so the fire of knowledge turns all actions to ashes.

38. In this world, there is nothing as purifying as knowledge. In due time, a person who is successful in yoga will find this knowledge within himself through himself alone.

39. One who has faith will acquire this knowledge if he devotes himself to the quest and gains mastery over the senses. And when he has acquired this knowledge, he very soon attains supreme peace.

40. But if a person is devoid of knowledge, has no faith, or is beset by doubts, he will meet with destruction. Neither this world nor the world to come is for the doubting soul, and he can never be happy.

41. When his action is given over to the practice of yoga, when his doubts are destroyed by knowledge, and when he is in full control of his existence, a person's actions cannot bind him, Dhanamjaya.

42. Therefore, using the sword of knowledge, cut through this doubt of yours, which has arisen due to ignorance and is now situated in your heart. Take up this yoga and arise, Bharata.

In verse 33 of Chapter 4, the Bhagavad-gita displays a clear progression in the teachings Krishna is giving to Arjuna, for here, we are told that the *karma-yoga* previously advocated is effective because it leads to higher knowledge, or the *jñana* emphasised by the Upanishads as the real key to liberation from rebirth. This transitional verse introduces us to a new topic that runs through Chapter 5 and into Chapter 6, where the quest for spiritual realisation is combined with teachings on yoga practice, although there is a break in this progression in Chapter 5, where Arjuna asks for a clarification of the point.

The relationship between karma-yoga
and jñana (realised knowledge)

In verse 33, we read that all action (karma) finds it conclusion in knowledge (*jñana*). Of course, this could refer just to ritual action, and then the meaning would be that all action is renounced when a person attains higher knowledge. However, it may well be that the meaning is that action in the form of *karma-yoga* culminates in the higher knowledge that brings *moksha*. This would seem to be logical in light of the previous passage, and it is the view taken by Shankaracharya in his commentary. In verse 38, we find it stated that knowledge is *yoga-samsiddha*, the perfection of yoga practice, and up to this point, yoga for the Gita has meant *karma-yoga*. This, again, would seem to support the conclusion that *karma-yoga* finds its natural conclusion in the realisation of higher knowledge.

How can one acquire this knowledge?

Verse 34 indicates that enlightened persons will reveal this knowledge to those who render service to them and make inquiries in a mood of submission. This implies the guru-disciple relationship as the means by which knowledge is transmitted, though there is no suggestion here of the need for a formal relationship of this type. Verse 39 further indicates that faith is a prerequisite for one who is seeking knowledge, as is dedication to the quest and the power to control the senses. And as we noted above, the suggestion is that true knowledge arises naturally in the heart of one who has been successful in his execution of *karma-yoga*.

What is the nature of this knowledge? What does it reveal?

Perhaps surprisingly, the actual nature of the knowledge being referred to here is touched upon only briefly. This is in verse 35, where the knowledge in question is defined as being the realisation that all beings exist within the *atman* and hence within Krishna, who at this point seems to be identified as the inner self of all beings. This view that the *atman* is identical with the Deity is a common theme in Vaishnava and Shaivite thought and reflects the Upanishadic teaching that the *atman* is identical with Brahman. Hence, the knowledge that is being discussed here as arising due to the practice of *karma-yoga* would seem to be close to the advaitic notion of absolute oneness: all beings are identical to oneself and identical to the supreme absolute reality, present here as Krishna.

The result of acquiring spiritual knowledge

In contrast to the paucity of definition, much of the passage is devoted to discussing the results that are to be gained through the acquisition of *jñana*. A number of points are mentioned. Firstly, in verse 35, it is said that knowledge puts an end to illusion; this is important for Shankaracharya, for he regards *avidya*, ignorance, as the single barrier to *moksha*. Then, in verses 36 and 37, we are informed that the effects of previous sinful acts are dispersed through the acquisition of knowledge. In other words, the *jñanin* will not have to suffer the results of any of the actions he has previously performed, for this knowledge takes one beyond the realm of suffering and rebirth. And thirdly, we are told in verse 39 that one who acquires this knowledge will thereby gain the highest state of peace – *param shantim* – a phrase that is usually equated with liberation from the troubles of this world.

CONCLUSION:
A SUMMARY OF CHAPTER 4

I would suggest that we can divide Chapter 4 into three broad sections. In the opening verses, Arjuna's doubt about Krishna as a teacher of ancient wisdom is addressed by a revelation of the doctrine of *avatar*. Here, Krishna is drawn, perhaps prematurely, into a discussion of his own nature and his position as the Supreme Deity who controls the world. But at this point he chooses not to dwell on the subject and moves back to the idea of desireless action, the *karma-yoga*, which has been the main topic up to this point and is here explained in still more detail. From verse 33 onwards, the emphasis is shifted somewhat away from *karma-yoga* towards the acquisition of realised knowledge. In this final section of the chapter, *jñana* is revealed as the factor that overcomes previous *karma*, dispels illusion, and allows the soul to experience absolute tranquillity in the liberated state.

However, before we can proceed towards a fuller exposition of this topic of spiritual knowledge, the natural flow of the discourse is interrupted somewhat as Arjuna seeks clarification as to why Krishna has moved from emphasising *karma-yoga* towards establishing knowledge as the key to spiritual success. The fifth chapter of the Gita opens with this question, which allows Krishna to explain more fully the relationship between the yoga of action and the development of realised knowledge of the *atman*.

*One whose happiness is within, whose pleasure is within,
and whose light is within is indeed a yogin.* —5.24

CHAPTER 5

As mentioned above, Chapter 5 opens with a question from Arjuna in which he apparently seeks clarification of what has been said before. However, it is rather difficult to see exactly how Arjuna's question relates to what Krishna has been saying and at first glance seems to be a bit of a non sequitur. Has Krishna actually recommended renunciation of action?

SAMKHYA AND YOGA ARE ONE

1. Arjuna said: Krishna, you advocate both the renunciation of action and the yoga of action as well. But which of these is the better course? Tell me this definitively.

2. The Lord said: Renunciation and *karma-yoga* both lead to the highest result. But between the two, *karma-yoga* is superior to the renunciation of action.

3. One who neither loathes nor hankers after anything is to be known as a constant renunciant. Transcending such duality, O mighty one, he easily breaks free of bondage.

4. Foolish people say that Samkhya and yoga are different, but not learned *pandits*. A person who properly adheres to one of these paths gains the fruit of both.

5. The position achieved by the followers of Samkhya is also attained by those who adhere to the path of yoga. One who sees that Samkhya and yoga are one and the same, truly sees.

6. But without engaging in yoga practice, renunciation is very difficult to achieve. The sage who engages in yoga practice quickly attains Brahman.

7. One who engages in yoga and has purified his very being, who has gained self-mastery and control of the senses, whose own self has become the self of all beings, is not besmirched even though he engages in action.

So why does Arjuna ask this question? Has Krishna actually praised *samnyasam karmanam*, the renunciation of action? If we look back to the beginning of the third chapter, it seems that he has done just the opposite. Firstly, I think we must accept that Arjuna has still not fully grasped the solution to the riddle posed by Krishna in 4.18 concerning action in non-action and non-action in action. He still seems to think that the renunciation of action means just that, whereas Krishna has been trying to explain that by giving up desire for the fruits of action, true renunciation can be practised even whilst one continues to act. Hence, Arjuna sees Krishna's praise of knowledge at the end of Chapter 4 as an alternative to the path of *karma-yoga*. After all, in verse 37, Krishna did say that the fire of knowledge will turn action into ashes. So it is in order to fully understand the relationship between action and knowledge that Arjuna asks this question, but he is probably mistaken in equating the knowledge Krishna has referred to with the renunciation of action; and Krishna's response to the question suggests very clearly that it is based on a misapprehension.

Let us now move on to look at Krishna's response, from which we can note the following points:

In verse 2, Krishna initially acknowledges the premise of Arjuna's question, accepting that renunciation and *karma-yoga* are two spiritual paths that reach the same goal. *Karma-yoga* is judged to be the better of the two, however, confirming the conclusion given in the first verses of Chapter 3, which formed a response to a rather similar inquiry from Arjuna. In verse 3, we find that renunciation is defined in terms of a state of detached consciousness rather than giving up physical action, which is of course a characteristic of *karma-yoga*.

In verses 4 and 5, it seems that Krishna is rejecting the idea that underpinned Arjuna's question, namely that renunciation and *karma-yoga* are two separate paths, although the words used are different. Here, it is asserted that Samkhya and yoga are in effect the same path, because if a person follows one of them, he derives the result of both. The logical presumption must be that here, Samkhya is equated with the idea of renunciation and yoga is the *karma-yoga* initially offered as an alternative. The point is further complicated by the fact that Samkhya and yoga are two of the traditional systems of Indian philosophy. These are discussed at some length in other passages of the *Mahabharata*, and there also, we find the declaration that the two are virtually the same system. Hence, I think we can take these two verses in two ways simultaneously. Firstly, we have confirmation of the conclusion reached elsewhere in the *Mahabharata* that Samkhya and yoga are essentially one system of thought. Secondly, this conclusion is applied to Arjuna's question about renunciation and *karma-yoga*, in effect saying that the two are really a part of the same spiritual process and that the distinction Arjuna is seeking to draw is an artificial one.

This point is confirmed in verses 6 and 7, where it is said that renunciation without yoga practice is very difficult – *duhkham aptum a-yogatah*. And in verse 7, we see that the practice of yoga involves the renunciation of the fruits of action, a point that is confirmed in verse 2 of Chapter 6. Hence, both are to be taken as a part of the same path of spiritual progress.

In a very real sense, Arjuna's question has helped to move the discussion on in an appropriate manner. In Chapter 4, we had a restatement of the main ideas of *karma-yoga* and a new emphasis on spiritual knowledge. So how do these two ideas fit together? This is the discussion that is taken up in Chapter 5, and, as we shall see, higher realisation of the true self is integrated with the yoga of action.

KARMA-YOGA AND
REALISED KNOWLEDGE

8. One who is engaged in yoga practice and sees the truth thinks, 'I never perform any action'. He thinks in this way even whilst seeing, hearing, touching, smelling, eating, moving, sleeping, breathing,

9. Speaking, evacuating, seizing, opening his eyes, or closing them. He considers, 'It is just the senses engaging with their objects'.

10. One who deposits his actions on Brahman and abandons attachment is not smeared by sin when he acts, as a lotus leaf is not touched by water.

11. Abandoning attachment, *yogins* then act with body, mind, speech, and with the senses in order to purify themselves.

12. Abandoning the fruits of action, the practitioner of yoga attains enduring peace. But one who does not engage in yoga and is motivated by desire remains in bondage, attached to the fruits of action.

13. Giving up all actions mentally, the embodied being easily remains in full control within the city of nine gates, neither acting nor causing action to be performed.

14. The Lord generates neither the means by which action is performed nor the actions themselves as performed by the people of the world. Nor does he create the conjunction between action and its result; it is a person's inherent nature that does this.

15. The mighty Lord does not assume anyone's sin or indeed their virtue. But knowledge is covered over by ignorance, and so living beings become deluded.

Why does the yogin think, 'I never perform any action' (v. 8)?

The obvious answer is given in verse 9: 'It is just the senses engaging with their objects'. There is, however, a little more to it than this. Implicit in this statement is the realisation that my real identity lies beyond the senses as the *atman*, the soul within the body. So I never perform any action, because action is performed by the bodily senses, and my own true identity is the *atman*, which is not the body. Here, then, we begin to see how the philosophy of action is linked to the philosophy of the soul and body: yoga and Samkhya are indeed one and the same.

Who is the lord and the mighty lord
(prabhu and vibhu) referred to in verses 14 and 15?

Some Vaishnava commentators suggest that these verses may refer to the idea of an *antaryamin*, an expansion of the Supreme Deity who exists within each body alongside the *atman*, guiding it through the path of rebirth. This idea gains some confirmation later in the Gita in verses such as 16.18 and 18.61, but here, I think the words *prabhu* and *vibhu* both refer to the *atman*, the individual soul that is the master and controller of the body and senses.

How does karma-yoga combine with higher knowledge?

Here, again, we have a connection between knowledge of the inner self and *karma-yoga*. The yoga demands that we perform our actions without attachment to the result, and this becomes possible when we realise that our true identity lies beyond the body. We are spirit and not matter, and because action is performed by the material body and senses, we can become detached from the results of action by the realisation that we are not the doer and that the result has no effect on our higher spiritual nature.

After explaining how *karma-yoga* is intimately related to spiritual knowledge, how yoga and Samkhya are one, Krishna now returns to the topic he was pursuing prior to Arjuna's interjection, providing us with deeper insight into the path of knowledge, the *jñana-marga*.

KNOWLEDGE, DETACHMENT, AND SPIRITUAL REALISATION

16. But for some people, the ignorance shrouding the inner self (*atman*) is destroyed by knowledge. For such persons, knowledge acts like the sun and illuminates the higher reality.

17. Their intelligence, their life and their conviction are devoted to that goal, for they are fully dedicated to it. Purged of contamination by means of knowledge, they go to the place from which there is no return.

18. The learned *pandit* perceives the same reality within a brahmin endowed with wisdom and good conduct, a cow, an elephant, a dog, and one who eats dogs.

19. Even whilst they are still in this world, persons whose minds are fixed in this state of equanimity conquer the process of creation. It is Brahman that is free of blemish and always the same, and so they are situated in Brahman.

20. Such a person does not rejoice when he gains what is dear to him, nor is he disturbed when he experiences something undesirable. His intellect is steady, he is free of delusion, he has knowledge of Brahman, and he is situated in Brahman.

21. Remaining wholly unattached to external sensations, such a person finds joy in the self within. Absorbing himself in Brahman through yoga practice, he experiences joy that does not decay.

CHAPTER 5

22. The pleasures that arise from sensory contacts are in fact
sources of misery. They have a beginning and an end,
Kaunteya, and so an enlightened person (*budha*) does not
delight in them.

23. Any person in this world who is able to resist the force of
desire and anger before being released from the body is
indeed properly engaged in yoga and is a joyful man.

24. One whose happiness is within, whose pleasure is within,
and whose light is within is indeed a *yogin*. Existing as
Brahman, he attains the state of *brahma nirvana*.

25. It is *rishis* who are free of contamination who gain that
state of *brahma nirvana*. For them, duality is dispelled, they
are self-controlled, and they take delight in the welfare of
all beings.

26. This *brahma nirvana* quickly arises for sages detached from
desire and anger, whose minds are controlled, and who
have knowledge of the inner self.

I think the real significance of this passage is that it shows very
clearly how the *karma-yoga* Krishna has earlier advocated leads to
the realised knowledge that for the Upanishads is the key to moksha. We should note the following points here:

This passage is very close to the doctrine of the Upanishads in
its revelation that *jñana* is the destroyer of the ignorance that is the
cause of the bondage keeping the soul tied to this world. It is this
higher knowledge that dispels the darkness of material existence
and thereby leads the soul to a state beyond rebirth. Above all else,
the Bhagavad-gita is a *moksha-shastra*, a treatise on liberation, and
we may note here how many times and in how many ways this ultimate goal is referred to. In verse 17, it is described as attaining the
state from which there is no return – in other words, from which
one is never again reborn. Verses 19 and 20 refer to being 'situated
in Brahman', which is the liberated state of existence. Verse 21
reveals that the liberated person experiences a joy that does not

decay, which can be contrasted with the temporary happiness we experience in this world. And verses 24 to 26 use the phrase *brahma nirvana* to refer to the liberated condition. The emphasis here is very much on *moksha*, which is gained through realised knowledge of one's own spiritual identity.

The phrase *brahma nirvana*, noted above, has a clear resonance with Buddhist teachings on *moksha*. We cannot say, however, whether this is due to Buddhist influence on the Gita or the Gita's influence on Buddhism, or whether this was a common form of language used in ancient times to refer to *moksha* that was made use of by Krishna here and by Buddhists referring to the same concept.

Verse 18 is an interesting one for a number of reasons. Firstly, it gives some insight into the nature of the knowledge presented here as the means of purging all contamination. The learned *pandit*, presumably one who possesses the knowledge, sees different types of living beings as equal despite their physical distinctiveness – *panditah sama-darshinah*. Why? Again, it is not stated overtly, but the answer would seem to be that it is because he perceives the *atman* rather than the body as the true identity of a living being. It is also interesting to note that Swami Vivekananda repeatedly stressed that a Vedantist who has this view of the oneness of all beings must manifest this knowledge in his attitude towards others; hence, any discrimination against women or against persons of a different caste was incompatible with the realised knowledge of Vedanta, as represented in this verse.

Verses 20–26 emphasise the point that the development of this higher knowledge must be accompanied, and is indeed effected, by a sense of detachment from the world and its pleasures, which are enjoyed through the senses. It is here that we see again the connection between *karma-yoga* and the realised knowledge that is the current topic for consideration. The *karma-yogin* continues to be active in the world, but crucially, he renounces desire for gain and attachment to the result, precisely the qualities that are mentioned here in relation to the development of realised knowledge.

And finally, we might note that the definition of the *yogin* given in verse 24 is somewhat different from that given for the *karma-yogin*, where the emphasis is always on renouncing selfish desire and being detached from the results of action. Here, the *yogin* is defined as one who experiences the joy of self-realisation and has knowledge of his own inner identity. This really leads on to the final verses of the chapter and indeed the discourse on *dhyana-yoga*, the yoga of meditation, which dominates the sixth chapter.

The Bhagavad-gita has now moved definitively on from its advocacy of *karma-yoga*, and the emphasis is very clearly on gaining liberation from rebirth by realised knowledge of the inner self. *Karma-yoga* is never wholly absent from the Gita's thought, however, and throughout its course, we get hints and reminders of this first great discourse. However, the teachings have now moved on, and in the last verses of Chapter 5, we are introduced to the next major idea to be covered – realisation or knowledge of the inner self that is gained through the techniques of yoga meditation.

A Different Kind of Yoga

27. Setting aside external perceptions, fixing his vision between the eyebrows, bringing the *prana* and *apana* breaths into a state of equilibrium as they move within the nostrils,

28. And controlling the senses, mind, and intellect, the sage who constantly dedicates himself to liberation from rebirth and who has given up desire, fear, and anger, is indeed a liberated person.

29. Understanding me to be the true object of *yajña* and acts of austerity, the supreme lord of the all the worlds and the friend of all beings, he attains a state of absolute tranquillity.

Even within these three verses, there are clear differences of emphasis. Verses 27 and 28 introduce us to the yoga techniques that will be discussed in greater detail in Chapter 6, involving concentration of the mind on a single point and the regulation of the breath within the body, a technique referred to as *pranayama*. This discourse follows on logically from what we have been taught earlier in the chapter about the necessity of higher knowledge, for the techniques mentioned here are designed to bring the practitioner to a state of direct perception of the inner self or, in other words, to a state of realised knowledge. But the final verse here seems anomalous, as it suddenly introduces the idea of a personal Deity, a concept that has not figured at all in Chapter 5's discussion of knowledge and *karma-yoga,* and which does not return again until the end of Chapter 6, when the Gita does indeed move on to discuss the nature of God. Robert Zaehner remarks:

> *This very abrupt introduction of the personal God as the only true recipient and experiencer of the sacrifice and religious practices in general is surprising, as it does not seem to fit in with the rest of the chapter which is otherwise quite coherent (Zaehner, 1973, p. 217).*

So what are we to make of it? Some scholars might suggest that the verse is an interpolation, or addition, made by a later Vaishnava editor, anxious to see that the ideas of *bhakti* and devotion appear in all parts of the Bhagavad-gita. This could be true, but as there is no evidence to support such a claim, it must be regarded as an inadequate solution. For Shankaracharya, there is no real problem here. In his Gita commentary, he consistently equates Krishna with the *atman* within all beings, and as this section is about knowledge of the *atman,* reference to Krishna as the Supreme Deity is perfectly logical. But perhaps we must also look at the structure of the teachings of the Gita. It does not move in a purely linear manner of reasoning; it gives us prior hints before dealing with a topic in full and it frequently includes later reminders of previous ideas. So we should probably not be too surprised to find Krishna giving us a small suggestion of what is to come, even though it does not fit precisely into a sequential progression of ideas.

CONCLUSION: A SUMMARY OF CHAPTER 5

Chapter 5 of the Bhagavad-gita begins with a question from Arjuna that sets the agenda for its content as a whole. He asks Krishna to make a definitive decision as to whether *karma-yoga*, or renunciation of action, is the superior path to follow. Krishna responds by reasserting the view given earlier in Chapter 3 that *karma-yoga* is better than renunciation, but he refines his answer by explaining that the higher knowledge he has discussed at the end of Chapter 4 (designated here as Samkhya) is inseparable from *karma-yoga* and hence should not be equated with the renunciation of action. He goes on to explain that *karma-yoga* allows the practitioner to acquire realised knowledge of the *atman* because it entails the withdrawal of attachment from the external world. Only when one's preoccupation with external perception and enjoyment of the results of action is restrained can knowledge of the spiritual reality within one's own being begin to arise. Hence, the process of *karma-yoga* and the attainment of realised knowledge are inseparable and should not be regarded as two distinct paths – *ekam samkhyam cha yogam cha*. This is the fundamental message of the fifth chapter, and now that this link has been established, we can move on to explore how the yoga of meditation allows the adept to gain perception and hence knowledge of the spiritual domain within one's own being.

*For one who sees me everywhere and who sees
everything as existing within me,
I am never lost nor is he ever lost to me.* —6.30

CHAPTER 6

The sixth chapter of the Bhagavad-gita presents us with a wholly new topic, that of *dhyana-yoga*, the techniques of meditation by which one's perception is withdrawn from the external world and turned inwards towards the *atman* that is the true self. The yoga philosophy is one of the six orthodox systems of Hindu thought, and the main text for this system is the *Yoga Sutras* composed by the sage Patañjali. In the Bhagavad-gita, however (and in other passages of the *Mahabharata*), we find the earliest complete exposition of the *yoga-darshan*. Moreover, it is interesting to note the clear similarities between the Gita's teachings here and Patañjali's later treatise. Patañjali offers an *ashtanga-yoga*, a yoga of eight limbs, which is composed of the following parts:

- *yama* – restraint from pernicious practices
- *niyama* – the observance of righteous and religious duties
- *asana* – practising sitting postures
- *pranayama* – regulation of the breathing process
- *pratyahara* – withdrawing the senses from their external perception
- *dharana* – concentration of the mind on a single point
- *dhyana* – deep meditation on that one single object
- *samadhi* – final realisation and absorption in the object of meditation

As we read through the Bhagavad-gita's discussion of yoga practice, we may note the way in which it covers these eight limbs that are presented by Patañjali in a systematic fashion. But we should note as well how Krishna draws his yoga teachings into the wider discourse of the Bhagavad-gita, revealing that above all else, yoga is a practical means of gaining the knowledge of the self he has emphasised firstly in Chapter 4 and then again in Chapter 5. Before that, however, he seeks to demonstrate the line of progression from *karma-yoga* and to show that the renounced state of consciousness inherent in *karma-yoga* is an essential prerequisite for the practice of this yoga of meditation.

RENUNCIATION AS THE BASIS FOR YOGA

1. The Lord said: A person who performs the action he is duty-bound to perform whilst remaining detached from the fruit of action is a true renunciant (*samnyasin*) and a *yogin*, not one who never lights the sacrificial fire and does not perform the ritual.

2. You should know that that which they call *samnyasa* is in fact yoga, Pandava. One who has not given up the inclination for pleasure can never become a *yogin*.

3. For the sage who is a beginner in yoga, action is said to be the means, but for one who is advanced in yoga, tranquillity is said to be the means.

4. When he has no attachment for the objects of the senses or for performing action and when he gives up all material inclinations, he is said to be advanced in yoga.

5. One should elevate oneself by means of the self, and one should never degrade oneself. One is indeed one's own friend and one's own enemy as well.

6. The self is the friend to one who gains self-control by means of the self. But when one has lost his self, then this very self acts like an enemy.

7. When a person has self-control and possesses inner tranquillity, the supreme self is realised, whether there be heat or cold, happiness or distress, honour or dishonour.

8. Satisfied by his knowledge and realisation alone, situated in a higher position and mastering his senses, one who engages in this way is said to be a *yogin*. He regards a lump of earth, a stone, and gold equally.

9. When considering friends, allies, enemies, those who are indifferent, neutrals, those who hate, relatives, righteous persons, and the wicked, one who is equal-minded is in a superior position.

Elaborating upon karma-yoga

Verse 1 seems to be a fairly straightforward reassertion of the doctrine of *karma-yoga*. Its presence here is surely intended to show us that the teachings that will now be given are an expansion on what has gone before rather than an alternative interpretation of yoga.

Verse 2 harks back to Arjuna's question at the beginning of Chapter 5 and makes the same point Krishna previously stressed, namely that yoga and renunciation are not two alternative possibilities, but that renunciation is an inherent feature of yoga practice. In other words, one cannot practise yoga without first withdrawing one's consciousness from worldly ambitions. And of course, this is the main goal of *karma-yoga*.

It is not entirely clear, but there does seem to be an indication in verse 3 of a process of progression from *karma-yoga* towards *shama*, inner tranquillity, which is the desired state of mind for *dhyana-yoga*. Hence, we might conclude that we are being presented with a step-by-step path beginning with *karma-yoga* and then, when its goals have been achieved, moving on to the next stage, which is the meditation that will now be described. Shankaracharya certainly interprets the verse in this way, as he is always keen to demonstrate that knowledge is the only path to *moksha* and action is only a preliminary stage of purification.

How do verses 1–9 define the ideal state
of consciousness for one who practises yoga?

The qualities referred to here include self-control and inner tranquillity (*jita atma* and *prashanta atma*), indifference to the fluctuating fortunes experienced in the world, caring nothing for praise and blame, inner satisfaction, control of the senses, and regarding the world with equal vision. An important point is being made here, particularly in an age in which popular forms of yoga abound. The yoga that is taught here is not a form of fitness regime or stress relief but is in fact the highest expression of personal spirituality. As such, it can only be properly undertaken by a person who has mentally withdrawn from the world in the manner achieved by the successful practice of *karma-yoga*. The goals that will be offered here are the ultimate goals of life, and they are not to be attained without intense prior preparation.

THE PRACTICE OF YOGA

10. Staying in a secluded place, the *yogin* should engage himself constantly. He should remain alone, controlling his mind and self, without any aspiration and without any sense of ownership.
11. He should prepare a firm seat for himself in a clean place, not too high and not too low, covered with cloth, animal hide, and *kusha* grass.
12. Sitting there on his seat, fixing his mind on a single point, controlling the movements of his mind and senses, he should engage in yoga practice in order to purify himself.

13. Holding his body, head, and neck in a straight line, steady and without moving, he should concentrate on the point of his nose whilst not looking in any direction.

14. With his whole being in a state of tranquillity, free of fear, steady in his vow of celibacy, controlling his mind, with his thoughts concentrated on me, the practitioner should sit there, dedicating himself to me.

15. By constantly engaging himself in this way, the *yogin* who controls his mind attains the state of tranquillity, which culminates in *nirvana* and which rests upon me.

16. Yoga cannot be practised if one eats excessively or does not eat at all, nor if one sleeps too much or remains constantly awake.

17. The yoga that destroys suffering can be practised if one displays moderation in eating, leisure pursuits, performance of action, sleeping, and wakefulness.

In these verses, Krishna reveals the techniques to be followed by one who seeks higher realisation through the yoga of meditation. Similar teachings are found in the Shvetashvatara Upanishad (Chapter 2, vv. 8–14), but here, a more detailed account is provided. We may note the following points:

Unlike *karma-yoga*, this *dhyana-yoga* is not to be practised within the context of human society but in a deserted place away from such contact. This might suggest that we have now moved on to consider the way of life followed by one who has renounced the world to live as a *sadhu* or a monk. This view is confirmed in verse 14, which refers to the *brahmachari vrata*, the vow of celibacy, the *yogin* must undertake as a part of this practice.

Verses 11–13 describe the ideal sitting posture for the *yogin* as he begins to engage in this meditation, and it would seem to be very similar to the famous *padma asana*, or lotus position. Here, it is the holding of the head and body in a straight line that is emphasised. In *hatha* and other forms of yoga, bodily exercises are advocated as a means of awakening the dormant Kundalini energy and raising it through the different *chakras* of the subtle body. Patañjali does not refer to techniques of this type, and despite the reference here to *asana*, it seems that the Bhagavad-gita remains similarly focussed on the control of the mind and turning the external perception inwards.

In verse 14, Krishna refers to himself as the object of perception to be sought by one who adopts this process. This could be understood as a theistic interpretation of yoga, with the Supreme Deity becoming the object of yoga practice. In this way, the *dhyana-yoga* is integrated with the ideas of *bhakti*, devotion to God, that dominate later chapters of the Gita. The teachings of the passage as a whole would, however, tend to suggest that in this case, Shankaracharya is quite right to emphasise the identity of Krishna the Deity with the *atman* within each being. Hence, we should probably take the idea of thoughts being concentrated on Krishna as meaning that one's meditation should be fixed on the *atman* at the core of one's own being.

Verse 15 gives us the first idea of the goal that will be attained through this yoga practice. Three words or phrases are used to describe this result: *shanti*, *nirvana-paramam*, and *mat-samstham*. *Shanti* means 'peace or inner tranquillity', *nirvana-paramam* means 'the highest state of *nirvana*', which is really a general term for liberation from rebirth, and *mat-samstham* means 'the state in which Krishna exists'. None of these terms is precise, but they do indicate that this yoga practice is a form of *moksha-dharma* that can grant the practitioner liberation from rebirth, and indeed, this is exactly the goal that Patañjali offers to those who attempt to follow the teachings of his *Yoga Sutras*. Moreover, that condition of freedom from rebirth is one of utter tranquillity in which the afflictions of the world can no longer touch the liberated soul. This is the state in which Krishna himself is always situated, and here, we can regard Krishna either as a manifestation of Vishnu, the Supreme Deity, or the *atman* within every being, or indeed as both of these.

Verses 16 and 17 refer to the lifestyle that must be followed by one who is attempting to practice this form of yoga. Again, there is an emphasis on following a renounced lifestyle that does not allow for excessive indulgence in sensual pleasure, but at the same time, there is a rejection of the extreme mortification of the body through harsh austerity. Here, again, we might note a link between the Gita and the teachings of the Buddha, who similarly recommended a 'middle way' between austerity and indulgence.

THE OBJECT AND THE GOAL OF MEDITATION

18. When a person controls the mind (*citta*) and fixes it on the *atman* alone, untouched by any desires, he is then said to be properly engaged in yoga.

19. *Yogins* who have controlled the mind and who practise yoga in relation to the *atman* have been compared to a lamp in a windless place that never flickers.

20. When the restrained mind ceases from its activities due to the practice of yoga and when the *atman* is perceived by means of one's own faculties, so that a person finds satisfaction within the *atman*;

21. When one experiences that limitless joy, which is grasped by the intellect (*buddhi*) but is beyond the range of the senses, and remains fixed on it never wavering from that focus;

22. Then, after attaining this position, one realises that there is nothing superior to what has been achieved; when situated in this state of being, one cannot be disturbed even by terrible suffering.

23. One should understand that what is known as yoga amounts to the breaking of the connection with suffering. Yoga must be performed with firm resolve and with a state of mind free from despondency.

24. This should be done whilst giving up all the desires that arise from material inclinations and restraining the entire group of senses by means of the mind alone.

25. One should undertake this withdrawal little by little, using the resolutely focussed intellect. Fixing the mind in conjunction with the *atman*, one should not think of any other object.

26. One must withdraw the wavering, unsteady mind from wherever it wanders and bring it back under control, fixed on the *atman* alone.

27. The highest joy comes to that *yogin* whose mind is tranquil, whose passions are quieted, who exists as Brahman, and who has no blemish.

28. Engaging himself constantly in this pursuit, the *yogin* who is free of blemish easily makes contact with Brahman and acquires endless joy.

29. One who engages in yoga practice sees the *atman* within all beings and all beings within the *atman*, maintaining this equal vision everywhere.

30. For one who sees me everywhere and who sees everything as existing within me, I am never lost, nor is he ever lost to me.

31. Regardless of the way he lives, one who adheres to this sense of oneness and worships me as the one situated within all beings is a *yogin* who exists in me.

32. One who thus sees everyone's pleasure and suffering as the same as his own, Arjuna, is considered to be the highest *yogin*.

Here, the Bhagavad-gita describes the higher stages of *dhyana-yoga*, when the mind has been brought under control and can be used as an effective tool of inner exploration. In this passage, we can see very clearly that yoga is indeed a part of the Hindu religious quest and is wholly spiritual in its orientation, at least in terms of the meditation techniques Krishna reveals here.

What is the ultimate object on which the mind should concentrate?

This passage makes it very clear that the whole of the yoga process – beginning from regulation of one's lifestyle, restraint of the senses, and control of the mind – culminates in the realisation of the *atman* within one's own being. We are currently unaware of the spiritual nature that is our true identity because our senses, mind, and intellect are all directed outwards to the external world. But when we gain control over these faculties, they can be restrained and turned inwards, and the end result of this process is that we gain direct perception of the *atman* within. We may now recall how at the end of Chapter 4, the Gita moved its emphasis away from *karma-yoga* towards realised knowledge, and how this topic was pursued further in Chapter 5. The yoga techniques taught here in Chapter 6 are directly related to this discourse on *jñana* because they provide a means through which knowledge of the self can be gained by direct perception of the inner reality. This point is emphasised in verses 18, 19, 20, 25, and 26, all of which reveal that the object of this yoga process is direct knowledge of the *atman* that is the core of our being.

The result of yoga practice

The immediate result of this realisation is a sense of joy and the ending of the suffering that is our usual lot in this world. Here, again, the Gita seems to share the Buddhist perspective in teaching that this world is a place of suffering (*dukka*, or misery, is the first of the Buddha's four noble truths), though it differs markedly from Buddhism in revealing the presence of the eternal *atman*. This sense of unbreakable joy is closely related to the notion of *moksha*, a word that literally means 'release'. We are at present in the domain of suffering, but knowledge of the *atman* brings us release from this distress; we experience *sukham atyantikam* ('limitless joy', v. 21) because the nature of the *atman* is *sac-cid-ananda* – existence, consciousness, and pure bliss.

Verses 25 and 26 suggest that we should not expect this realisation of the *atman* to come immediately. This is not an easy process, as Arjuna's response in verses 33–34 confirms, and success will come only gradually as a result of constant and diligent practice. The mind is naturally unsteady, and the ability to fix it in concentration on a single point is rarely achieved. Verse 25 indicates that there will be many setbacks in the endeavour, but a practitioner must continue with the attempt until mastery of the mind is finally achieved. Anyone who has tried to practice yoga by fixing the concentration on a *mantra* or a single object of vision will confirm how difficult it is to restrain the mind from wandering away into its usual pattern of thoughts.

What significance can we see in Krishna's references to himself in this passage?

Verses 29 and 30 are significant here, as they make virtually the same statements. However, verse 29 is in relation to the *atman* and verse 30 is in relation to Krishna, the speaker. The obvious implication is that of identity between the *atman* and the Deity, an idea that Shankaracharya consistently emphasises. Verse 31, however, uses the word *bhajati*, meaning 'worship', in relation to Krishna, who is situated in all beings. This choice of words is rather unusual in the present context but does provide the beginnings of a link with the discourse on devotion to God that begins from Chapter 7. Hence, we might suggest that for the Bhagavad-gita, there is a Supreme Deity who creates and controls the world and who is to be worshipped with devotion, but this Deity is identical with our own inner self. And finally, as something of an aside, we might note that verse 29 makes a similar equation between the *atman* and *brahman* when it suggests that the *yogin* makes contact with *brahman, brahma-samsparsha*, thereby confirming the Upanishadic view that the *atman* is *brahman – ayam atma brahma*.

ARJUNA'S MISGIVINGS ABOUT YOGA

33. Arjuna said: I see no firm status for this yoga you have explained as being based on equal-mindedness, Madhusudana, because of this unsteadiness.
34. The mind is unsteady, Krishna, it is dominating, powerful, and very firm. I think controlling the mind is harder to achieve than controlling the wind!
35. The Lord said: Without doubt, O mighty one, the mind is flickering and difficult to restrain. But through constant endeavour and renunciation it can be restrained, Kaunteya.
36. In my opinion it is difficult for a person who lacks self-control to follow the path of yoga. But one who makes this endeavour after achieving self-mastery is able to do so by employing the proper means.

This passage is quite straightforward, though it is important to note both Arjuna's objection here and also Krishna's response to it. Arjuna's point is that the yoga system Krishna has just outlined is too difficult; the mind is so powerful that it cannot be brought under volitional control simply by an effort of the will. Again, one might see here something of an introduction to the teachings on *bhakti*, devotion to God, for there, we find that the Deity himself intervenes in the process and delivers his devotee so that one does not have to rely solely on one's own mental prowess.

Here, however, Krishna does not accept Arjuna's objection. This *dhyana-yoga* is certainly a difficult path to follow, but if one can achieve self-mastery, then it is not at all impossible, as Arjuna is suggesting. The key to success is given in verse 35 – *abhyasena tu kaunteya vairagyena cha grihyate*. The mind can be controlled through *abhyasa*, constant regulated practice, and through *vairagya*, proper renunciation of worldly aspirations. In other words, Krishna is saying that this is not a cheap or easy process of spiritual endeavour, but if one is serious and dedicated, it is possible to gain the highest goals by the means he has revealed in this chapter.

THE FATE OF THE
YOGIN WHO FALLS SHORT

37. Arjuna said: A person who does not endeavour enough but is endowed with faith may be distracted from yoga by the fluctuations of the mind and so fail to gain the goal of yoga. What result does he achieve, Krishna?

38. With both his aims unachieved, is he not lost like a divided cloud without any real position, O mighty one, deluded from the path to Brahman?

39. You should completely dispel this doubt of mine, Krishna. Except for yourself, there is no one who can dispel it.

40. The Lord said: Neither here nor in the next world, Partha, is such a person ever lost. No one who does good will ever attain a bad result thereby.

41. After reaching the worlds enjoyed by the righteous and residing there for innumerable years, the failed *yogin* takes birth in the house of pure-hearted, prosperous people.

42. Or he may be born into a family of *yogins*, possessed of wisdom. A birth in this world of that type is very rarely attained.

43. There, he regains the state of consciousness he achieved in his previous body and once more endeavours for perfection, O child of the Kurus.

44. He is drawn in that direction even against his will due to the regulated practice he previously undertook. Even a

person who merely attempts to gain an understanding of yoga transcends the teachings of the Veda.

45. Through his continuous endeavour, the *yogin*, engaged in his practice and purified of faults, will gain perfection after several births and then proceed to the highest destination.

46. The *yogin* is superior to one who undertakes austerity. He is also regarded as being superior to one who possesses knowledge and to one who performs ritual action. Therefore, Arjuna, become a *yogin*.

47. And of all *yogins*, he who has faith and who worships me with his inner self absorbed in me is the most advanced in yoga. That is my opinion.

Here, again, we have an inquiry from Arjuna, which really follows on from his previous expression of doubt about the viability of the *dhyana-yoga* process. His point is that because this spiritual path is so fraught with difficulty, there will be some practitioners who fall short in their endeavours and fail to achieve the ultimate goal. What is the fate of such persons? They have given up their worldly aspirations to seek spiritual rewards, and so if they fail in their yogic endeavours, they are doubly the losers and end up with nothing at all.

Responding to this question, Krishna makes a very significant point not just for our understanding of yoga practice but also for Hindu religious thought as a whole. Because Indian religion generally includes a belief in reincarnation, complete spiritual success in the present lifetime is not absolutely essential, as it is for most followers of Western religions. If we fail to achieve absolute perfection in this life, the progress we have made is not lost, and in our next birth we can take up the path once more and build on the progress previously made. And if we look ahead to the next chapter (verse 3), we will see that in fact, it is only a very small number of aspirants who do achieve *moksha* in the present life. So

Hindu spirituality is a gradual, progressive process extending over a number of lifetimes as we move towards the final goal. And I would suggest that this is one of the reasons that Hindus are more tolerant of diversity than is sometimes the case in world religions. Hinduism can readily accept that different persons are at different stages of spiritual progression and so require different forms of religion to take them forward. Here, this point is very clearly made in a manner that fully answers Arjuna's misgivings and at the same makes a significant point about Hindu spirituality as a whole. There are a number of further points that we might also note here:

The worlds of the righteous, the *punya-kritam lokan*, mentioned in verse 41 are almost certainly the worlds of the Vedic gods. These 'heavens' are frequently mentioned in the *Mahabharata* and the *Puranas* as the destination achieved by those who live righteously and adhere to *dharma*. This is not *moksha*, however, as those who gain elevation to these worlds must ultimately return to earth and resume the cycle of rebirth. It seems that the failed practitioner of yoga is first rewarded by existence in these worlds and is then able to resume his spiritual progress after taking birth again in this world.

Verse 44 suggests that a person is attracted towards spiritual matters at least partially as a result of endeavours made in a previous life. We see that some people have an almost instinctive attraction for spiritual pursuits, while others remain entirely indifferent to the religious way of life. The indication here is that these varying dispositions are a result of one's previous existence, which shapes the nature of the subtle body in which the soul transmigrates.

Verse 45 indicates that even if a person commits himself to the path of *dhyana-yoga*, it may take several births before perfection is achieved. This is indeed a slow and arduous path to follow.

In verse 46, the statement that the *yogin* is superior to the *jñanin*, the one who possesses knowledge, might strike us as rather unusual. After all, the practice of the yoga of meditation has been shown to be a means of gaining knowledge. Shankaracharya explains that here, the word *jñanin* refers to one who has theoretical knowledge derived from scripture but not the realised knowledge of the self that leads to *moksha*. Ramanuja agrees with Shankara on this point and suggests that the knowledge referred to here means 'knowledge of different subjects'. In other words, the *jñanin* mentioned here is a learned scholar rather than an enlightened person.

In the last verse of the chapter, we again find that the discourse moves on to discuss the worship of God, just as it did in the last verse of Chapter 5. The statement here is interesting for our understanding of the Gita as a whole, for we are now informed that one who worships Krishna is the best of all *yogins*. From this, we must presume that the devotee is in a better position even than one who undertakes the *dhyana-yoga* revealed in this chapter. So, just as we had indications that the acquisition of realised knowledge is the next stage after *karma-yoga*, here, the suggestion is that *bhakti*, devotion to God, is the next stage beyond the acquisition of higher knowledge. Many Hindus believe that *jñana* is the goal attained through *bhakti*, but the Bhagavad-gita does not appear to share this view, as it consistently refers to *bhakti* as the highest form of spirituality. Again one might suggest that this verse is a later addition, as it seems to be in contrast to the previous teachings of the chapter. Here, however, it marks a fundamental transition in the progression of the Gita's discourse, setting the tone for the chapters we will next encounter.

Linking the Bhagavad-gita to the Yoga Sutras

At the beginning of Chapter 6, I referred to the eight limbs of yoga delineated by Patañjali in his *Yoga Sutras*. Below, I have compiled a list that shows how the Gita's yoga teachings in Chapter 6 appear to refer to each of the eight limbs. This is not necessarily the 'right' answer, as the link between the Bhagavad-gita and the *Yoga Sutras* is not exact, but I hope it shows how the Gita is closely related to the classical *yoga-darshan* of Patañjali.

YAMA AND NIYAMA

In his *Yoga Sutras*, Patañjali gives lists of five *yamas* and five *niyamas*, which are restraints from sensual indulgence and the practise of designated virtues. The topic is not dealt with in the same systematic manner in the Bhagavad-gita, but in the opening ten verses we do see a similar insistence on the necessity of regulating one's personal conduct as a prerequisite for the practice of yoga. Later on, verse 14 refers to the vow of celibacy, which is one of Patañjali's five *yamas*, and in verses 16 and 17, we find further reference to the necessity of a controlled, regulated lifestyle.

ASANA

Verses 11–13 describe how the seat should be established and then the ideal posture to be adopted by one who is practising *dhyana-yoga*.

PRANAYAMA

The sixth chapter of the Gita does not include any reference to *pranayama* in its discourse, though elsewhere this element of yoga is noted, as in 4.29–30, 5.27, and 8.10–12. It is hard to say why *pranayama* is overlooked in Chapter 6, though we must be aware that Krishna is here providing only a summary of the techniques rather than an exhaustive treatise.

PRATYAHARA

The withdrawal of the senses from the process of external perception is an essential prerequisite for turning one's concentration inwards. This is referred to in verse 24, where the phrase *indriya-gramam viniyamya* is used, meaning 'restraining the collection of senses'. Krishna also refers to controlling the mind and drawing it back under control – as in verse 26 – and this includes restraint of the senses from external perception.

Dharana

Before internal meditation can be successfully performed, the mind must be regulated so that it remains fixed on a single point without any deviation. This is probably what is indicated in verses 12 and 13, where Krishna says that the *yogin* must concentrate on the point of the nose and become unaware of all directions. The idea here is that the mind is focussed so rigidly on a single point that its perception of everything else is suspended. The process referred to in verse 26 also seems to be one of *dharana*, whereby the practitioner repeatedly draws back the wandering mind and by an effort of will forces it to remain concentrated on a single object.

Dhyana

When the mind is brought under strict control by the practice of *dharana*, it can then be used as a tool for the realisation of the *atman* within one's own being. The Bhagavad-gita places a lot of its emphasis on this higher realisation as the goal of yoga practice. Verses 20–26 refer several times to the fixing of the mind on the *atman*, and it is this higher perception that is meant by the term *dhyana* (which, incidentally, is used in Tibetan Buddhism, where it becomes 'zen' rather than *dhyana*).

Samadhi

When the yoga practice reaches a successful conclusion, the state known as *samadhi* is attained. This is the position of spiritual enlightenment in which the adept leaves behind the illusion of worldly existence and perceives the reality of his own spiritual identity. In Chapter 6 of the Bhagavad-gita, this is referred to as a state of unlimited joy and realised knowledge. We could say that verses 27–32 all refer to the condition of *samadhi* in which a different perception of existence is attained and the world as we now know it is transcended.

CONCLUSION:
A SUMMARY OF CHAPTER 6

Chapter 6 of the Bhagavad-gita is dominated by the discussion of *dhyana-yoga*, the yoga of meditation, which Krishna presents here as the next stage in the consideration of spiritual knowledge that has been a major topic in Chapters 4 and 5. The opening verses refer again to the progression from *karma-yoga* to *jñana* and the internal renunciation of worldly desires as a prerequisite for the practice of *dhyana-yoga*. We are then given a brief outline of the practice, which consists of sitting in the correct posture, withdrawing the mind and senses from the external world, and then fixing the perception unwaveringly on a single point. Through this practice, the mind is brought under the control of the intellect and can then be used as a tool for meditation. When the mind is turned inwards, it eventually comes to perceive the soul that is our true identity and becomes wholly absorbed in this realisation, experiencing the limitless joy that is an inherent quality of the spirit. At this point, the knowledge Krishna has been referring to earlier is no longer theoretical but is based on direct perception and enlightened realisation. In the final verses of the chapter, Arjuna expresses doubts as to whether this process of controlling the mind is actually possible, and asks about the fate of one who endeavours on this path but fails to achieve its ultimate goal. Krishna responds by asserting that this process may be difficult, but it is not impossible if one is dedicated to following it. And even if one fails to achieve success in the present life, any gain or progress that has been made will provide a basis for further endeavours in the next life.

As jewels are strung on their thread, so
this whole world is strung upon me. —7.7

CHAPTER 7

At the end of the sixth chapter, we saw how Krishna suddenly ended his discourse on *dhyana-yoga* and seemed to indicate that there is a form of spirituality that is even higher than the *karma-yoga* and realised knowledge he has previously taught. In the last verse of Chapter 6, he asserted that the one who is best situated in yoga (*yuktattama*) is one who worships Krishna himself with faith – *shraddhavan bhajate yo mam*. This sudden change of emphasis sets the tone for the very different teachings we will now encounter, which focus on the position of the Supreme Deity as the creator and controller of the world and on the spiritual path based on loving devotion to that Deity. This is the way of *bhakti*, and here, again, we see why the Bhagavad-gita is such an important work in establishing Hindu religious doctrine.

In traditional and contemporary Hinduism, the idea of worship, devotion, and love dedicated to the Supreme Deity is one that predominates in the minds of most believers. The Upanishads speak of the higher knowledge of the self that is identical with Brahman, the ultimate reality, but they have little or nothing to say about worship, love of God, or devotion. Indeed, in some passages the Upanishads appear to reject any such notion. But in the Bhagavad-gita, this form of spirituality is brought to the fore in a most dramatic manner as Krishna's role is transformed from that of teacher of religion to the Supreme Lord of all creation. Up until this point, the focus of the Gita's teaching has been on self-transformation. Arjuna has been urged to renounce his selfish desires so as to break free from the bondage of future karma and then to seek out knowledge of his own spiritual identity. Here, however, we find the introduction of a very different idea, that of an external Deity who will respond to our prayers and worship, and who will bless and guide us in this world even to the ultimate stage of *moksha*, which is now revealed not so much as a goal we strive to achieve ourselves but as a gift of God, granted to those he loves as an act of divine grace. So much of what is referred to as Hinduism is based on this idea of divine love, and its original philosophical basis is to be found here in the Bhagavad-gita.

KRISHNA AS THE SOURCE OF THE WORLD

1. The Lord said: Now hear, O Partha, how you can have full knowledge of me without any doubts by attaching your mind to me and practising yoga dedicated to me.
2. I shall explain to you in full both the *jñana* and the *vijñana*. When this is understood, there is nothing else remaining that should be known.
3. Amongst thousands of men, only one will endeavour for perfection, and amongst those who do endeavour and achieve that goal, only one will come to know me in truth.
4. Earth, water, fire, air, space, mind, intellect, and the sense of ego comprise the eight component parts of my energy known as *prakriti*.
5. This is the inferior *prakriti*, but you should also know about my higher *prakriti*, which is distinct from it. This is the element of life, O mighty one, the *jiva-bhuta*, by means of which this world is held in place.
6. You should understand that these two are the origin, the womb of all living beings. I am the source of the entire world and its passing away as well.

7. There is no other thing superior to me, Dhanamjaya. As jewels are strung on their thread, so this whole world is strung upon me.

The difference between jñana and vijñana

These are very difficult terms to define at this preliminary stage. As we have noted earlier, *jñana* means 'realised knowledge of spiritual truth', and here, one must presume it refers to knowledge about Krishna, as this is what is indicated by the first verse. Krishna is no longer talking about the *atman,* as he did in Chapter 6, but has turned the discussion towards knowledge of his own identity. The term *vijñana* here is slightly problematic. It is a word that is still used in modern Indian languages to mean technical or practical knowledge – computer science or car mechanics, for example. So, in that sense, *jñana* and *vijñana* could be theoretical and practical knowledge. For Madhvacharya, *jñana* means 'basic knowledge' and *vijñana* is a more detailed exposition; for Ramanuja, *vijñana* means 'the specific knowledge by which God can be distinguished from the world'; and for Shankara, *jñana* is theoretical knowledge and *vijñana* is realised knowledge. All of these are possible, but I would suggest that *jñana* refers to philosophical understanding of the nature of God, whilst *vijñana* indicates the practice one should undertake in light of that knowledge; this explanation recommends itself primarily because this is what the Gita's next set of teachings consists of – understanding God's supremacy, and religious action based on this knowledge of the Deity. We will refer again to these two types of teachings.

Verse 3 is noteworthy in that it explains that the spiritual path is one that is only rarely trodden and, secondly, that knowledge of Krishna is the ultimate goal of this path. One could take this to mean that knowledge of the *atman* (and perhaps its identity as Brahman) is the highest goal, but there also seems to be a suggestion here that *bhakti* stands above even knowledge of the *atman.*

Defining the term 'prakriti'

In verses 4–6, Krishna refers to two types of *prakriti*. The word *prakriti* is usually used to indicate matter as opposed to spirit, but here, the *apara*, or lower, *prakriti* refers to matter, whilst the *para*, or higher *prakriti*, is the *jiva-bhuta*, which is a term used for the *atman* whilst it exists within the body. The material energy is shown here to be eightfold: the five great elements of earth, water, fire, air, and space, and then the three components of our mentality, mind, intellect, and *ahamkara*, the sense of ego. We must presume that the higher *prakriti* here refers to the *atman* existing within its material embodiment; this is the *jiva-bhuta*, and all living beings exist as a combination of these two *prakritis*. Above and beyond them both, however, is the Deity identified here as Krishna himself. They are both his energies, and he is the creator and the destroyer of the world. So here, we encounter an idea stressed in the Shvetashvatara Upanishad, which indicates three eternal principles: matter, the individual soul, and the Supreme Deity who presides over them. This is *jñana* in relation to God; the *vijñana* is to come.

The metaphor of the jewels and the thread

I think verse 7 is a very important one for all people to reflect upon. In this world, we see that there is an order that prevents the onset of chaos. The world moves forward in accordance with designated rules, and yet we cannot perceive the principle of existence which directly sustains that order. Similarly, a necklace of jewels is held in place by the invisible thread that is its sustaining principle; if the thread is broken, chaos immediately ensues. Here, Krishna proclaims himself to be the invisible thread that sustains the order of the world. He is invisible to us, but he is present here within the world, and without that presence, the world could not continue. This notion of the transcendent Deity being immanent yet invisible within the world is one that dominates the Gita's theology and is ultimately revealed to Arjuna when the *vishva-rupa* is displayed in Chapter 11. This verse is also very significant in demonstrating that Hindu teachings can be monotheistic. Here, Krishna says very clearly, *mattah parataram na anyat kimcid asti*, which means, 'There is nothing else that is superior to myself', thereby establishing one of the fundamental principles of a monotheistic theology.

KRISHNA'S PRESENCE
WITHIN THE WORLD

8. I am flavour in water, Kaunteya. I am the effulgence in the moon and the sun. I am Pranava (Om) in all the Vedas; I am sound in space and manliness in men.

9. And I am the primal aroma in earth; I am the heat in fire. I am life in all living beings; I am the austerity of those who undertake such austerities.

10. You should know me as the eternal seed of all beings, Partha. I am the intelligence of those who are intelligent; I am the energy of all energetic sources.

11. And I am the power of the powerful when it is devoid of desire and passion. I am desire in living beings, O best of the Bharatas, when it does not transgress dharma.

12. You should understand that the states of existence based on *sattva, rajas,* and *tamas* come into being from me. But I am not in them; they are in Me.

13. Being deluded by these three states of being, in which the three *gunas* are inherent, the whole world cannot understand me, for I am beyond all three states and I am undecaying (*avyaya*).

14. This divine *maya* of mine consisting of the *gunas* is difficult to go beyond, but those who surrender to me alone cross beyond this *maya*.

15. The wrongdoers, the foolish, the lowest of men, persons whose knowledge is taken away by illusion (*maya*) and

> those who take to the asuric form of existence do not
> surrender to Me.

This passage can be divided into three phases:

Verses 8–11 are included as an illustration of the point made by Krishna in verse 7. He pervades the world, and it is his presence that makes the world what it is. He is the essential nature of the various aspects of the world around us. This, again, is an important point and one that distinguishes Hindu monotheism from that of Christianity, Islam, and Judaism. In those faiths, the one God exists on high in a domain that is wholly distinct from this world. But here, we see that God is not only the creator of the world but he is also present within the world as its invisible sustaining principle. He is both transcendent and immanent. Perhaps we should not be too preoccupied with looking for a literal meaning here; the verses are probably better understood as a poetic form of expression that illustrates and illuminates the theological truth revealed in verse 7.

Verse 12 provides a succinct summary of the main point that is being made here. All the states of existence we can observe in the world, which are shaped by the three qualities of *sattva*, *rajas*, and *tamas*, arise ultimately from out of the Deity himself. Here, the word *mattah* means 'from me'. The last line here refines the understanding still further; God is not present in these manifestations (*na tv aham teshu*), but they are present within him (*te mayi*). Shankara, Madhva, and Ramanuja all explain this in terms of dependence. Krishna may be present as the world, but he is not dependent on the existence of the world for his existence. However, the world is entirely dependent upon him. Another interpretation could be that although the world exists as a part of his existence and is within him, his existence expands far beyond the range of the world, and hence, his full presence is not here. Thus, there is identity between the world and God, but it is not a symmetrical identity; the world is nothing but a manifestation of God, but he himself is the world and more than the world. The word *maya* is often understood in the sense of magic or delusion, but it is also used to refer to *prakriti*, the material energy, and it is probably used here in this latter sense.

In verses 13–15, we get the first hint of the implications of gaining (and not gaining) this understanding of the nature of God. Perhaps here, we see the beginning of a move from *jñana* to *vijñana*, from theoretical knowledge about God towards the practical implications of this knowledge in terms of the way we live. Those who do not understand the presence of Krishna in the world are deluded by the three *gunas* – *sattva*, *rajas*, and *tamas* – mentioned in verse 12. Krishna himself is beyond these qualities, and here, again, we see the meaning of what has been said before; the material world exists entirely within the existence of Krishna, and yet he transcends the world as well. The different groups of people who are thus deluded are defined in verse 15 as being of four types. They are the lowest of men, the rough, ill-mannered, violent, and materialistic people. As the Katha Upanishad states, such people cannot acquire spiritual enlightenment, and conversely, when one has the higher knowledge, it is immediately reflected in personal conduct. Here, also, we get the first hint of how a person will respond when he gains this knowledge of God, and this is contained within the word *prapadyante* used in verses 14 and 15. *Prapadyante* means 'to surrender, to take shelter of and to become dependent upon', and this notion forms one of the main strands of Ramanuja's religious teachings, for he consistently stresses *prapanna*, absolute surrender, as a spiritual goal. He teaches that if one becomes wholly dependent upon the grace of God, then God will certainly bestow his mercy on such a devotee and deliver him from all the difficulties we face. This point is graphically confirmed at the end of the Gita (18.66) in a verse that is highly revered by the Shri Vaishnavas, who follow Ramanuja. And here, also, in verse 14, there is a suggestion of divine grace. This world is very difficult to cross over, as Arjuna asserted at the end of Chapter 6, but one who surrenders to Krishna can indeed cross over it. How can this be? It is explained later in 12.7 and 18.66 that surrender invokes the grace of God and that grace has the power to easily deliver the devotee from the ocean of birth and death – *mrityu-samsara-sagarat* (12.7).

THE FOUR TYPES
OF DEVOTEE

16. There are four types of righteous person who worship Me, Arjuna: one who is in distress, one who wishes to understand, one who seeks prosperity, and the *jñanin* who possesses knowledge, O best of the Bharatas.

17. Amongst these four, the *jñanin* who is always properly engaged and has one-pointed devotion is the best. I am very dear to such a *jñanin,* and he is dear to me.

18. They are all noble persons, but I regard the *jñanin* as my very self (*atma*). He is unwavering in dedicating himself to me alone as his ultimate goal.

19. At the end of many births, one who possesses knowledge finally resorts to me, realising, 'Vasudeva is all things'. Such a *mahatma* is very rarely found.

Four types of sukritins, righteous persons

It is recognised that people may engage in acts of worship, or *puja*, for a variety of different reasons, sometimes for material gain and sometimes for motives that are entirely spiritual. This applies today just as much as it did at the time the Bhagavad-gita was spoken. The point made here is that even if the worship is performed in pursuit of material gain, the performer is still to be regarded as a righteous person. He is a *sukritin*, in contrast to the *dushkritins* mentioned in the previous verse, who never worship the Deity.

'I am very dear to such a jñanin, and he is dear to me'.

Here, we see an expansion of the concept of *bhakti* that has been introduced so far. Up until this point, we have been told that one who understands the presence of God within the world will surrender to him – *mam prapadyante*. Here, however, the word *priya* is introduced, which suggests a relationship between the Deity and the devotee based on mutual love – *priyo hi jñanino 'tyartham aham*, I am an object of love for the *jñanin* – and by way of reciprocation, *sa cha me priyah*, he is loved by me. This idea of a loving relationship with God is one that flowers in later expressions of devotional Hinduism, epitomised in the poetry of Mirabai or the Tamil Alvars, but here, again, we find the origins of another form Hindu spirituality contained within the Gita.

How might one interpret the meaning of verse 18?

One might take a literal reading here and suggest that *jñani tv atmaiva me*, the *jñanin* is my very self, confirms the Upanishadic view of the individual *atman* achieving a state of absolute unity with Brahman. This is Shankaracharya's reading of it, and he summarises the *jñanin*'s realisation as being, 'I myself am the Lord Vasudeva, I am none else'. The Vaishnava commentators, however, do not share this view. For Ramanuja, the verse means that the devotee and the Lord are united in love because they cannot bear to be apart from one another, whilst Madhva explains that it means 'being most beloved of him'. This is a slightly less literal interpretation, but given the context, it is no less valid.

What is the significance of the ideas expressed in verse 19?

Firstly, verse 19 reveals again the immanence of God as being present within the world as was first indicated in verse 7 and will later be revealed directly in the manifestation of the *vishva-rupa* (Chapter 11). There is also a suggestion here that *bhakti*, or devotion, is the next stage on from realised knowledge in terms of spiritual progression. We have seen that *karma-yoga* provides the requisite mood of renunciation for the pursuit of realised knowledge, but here, we are told that one who possesses such knowledge moves to the position of *prapanna* only after many births when he comes to realise that Vasudeva (a name for Vishnu or Narayana) is all things – *vasudeva sarvam*. Shankara naturally takes this as meaning that Vasudeva or Krishna is the *atman*. And as the *atman* is non-different from Brahman, then there is no problem in reconciling this verse with his Advaitic philosophy.

WORSHIPPING OTHER GODS

20. But those bereft of knowledge due to their pursuit of this or that desire surrender to other gods, accepting the appropriate discipline for worship as dictated by their own inner nature.

21. Whatever the form the devotee wishes to faithfully worship, I bestow upon him the firm faith that enables him to do so.

22. When endowed with such faith, he then engages in the worship of that god and as a result attains what he desires. These desired objects are, however, granted by me alone.

23. The results of the worship performed by such unintelligent persons are all temporary. The worshippers of the gods go to the gods; my devotees come to me.

I stated above that this chapter of the Bhagavad-gita reveals a mono-theistic understanding of the nature of God, but this is a peculiarly Indian form of monotheism, which is completely compatible with polytheism. Although there is only one Supreme Deity, there are also lesser gods, the *devas*, who have power over our existence and yet are still mortal beings who exist subject to the laws of nature. These have already been referred to in Chapters 2 and 3, and are the objects of praise and worship for the hymns of the Veda. So, what about the person who chooses to worship these Vedic gods rather than Krishna himself, as has been instructed so far in this chapter? Here, the answer is given.

Worship of other gods is not condemned outright, but those who perform such worship are referred to as *hrita-jñana*, devoid of proper knowledge, and *alpa-medhas*, having little intelligence. Hence, there is no prohibition, but the practice is hardly approved of here.

The tendency to worship a particular god or goddess is derived from a person's nature, which dictates the mode of conduct one is drawn towards. In verse 20, it is indicated that worship of the gods is based on material desire, or *kama*, whilst the words *prakritya niyata svaya* indicate that one is almost compelled to act in this way as a result of the nature one is born with.

Although he does not particularly approve of this worship, it is Krishna who facilitates it from within. He is in the heart of every being, and he guides a person in the direction that most suits his or her inherent nature, and that includes religious life as well. More-over, although the rewards gained from religious practice appear to be granted by the gods, as indicated earlier in Chapter 3 (vv. 11–13), it is actually Krishna himself who grants them, as he is the ultimate controller of the world and of the gods.

It is sometimes said that one can worship any deity one is drawn to and the result will be the same, as all gods are symbolic manifestations of the same ultimate reality. The Bhagavad-gita does not appear to share that view, and in verse 23 it is stated that those who worship Krishna and those who worship the Vedic gods achieve a very different result. I think the point here is that as he did in Chapter 2 (vv. 42–45), Krishna is anxious to distinguish the spiritual path he is advocating from the Vedic rituals of the *karma-kanda*. One might confuse the way of *bhakti* Krishna is teaching here with worship of the Vedic gods, and the Gita is anxious to show that they are not part of the same process.

PERCEPTION OF KRISHNA

24. Those who lack intelligence think of me as a non-manifest entity taking a manifest form. They do not know my higher nature, which is unfading and unsurpassed.

25. I am not manifest to all, because I am concealed by *yoga-maya*. So, this deluded world does not comprehend me, the one who is unborn and unfading.

26. I know the living beings of the past, the present, and the future, Arjuna, but there is no one who knows me.

27. Through the illusion of duality, Bharata, arising from desire and loathing, all living beings in this created world pass into a state of ignorance, Paramtapa.

28. But persons whose wickedness has reached an end and who are engaged in virtuous acts become free from the illusion of duality. They worship me and remain firm in their vows.

29. Those who resort to me and thereby endeavour for liberation (*moksha*) from old age and death fully understand Brahman and have complete knowledge of *adhyatma* and of action (*karma*).

30. Those who also know me in relation to the *adhibhuta*, the *adhidaiva*, and the *adhiyajña* can, with their consciousness fixed, know me even at the time of death.

These verses take us back to the imperceptible presence of Krishna, the invisible thread that sustains the order of the world.

Interpreting the meaning of verse 24

The 'non-manifest entity taking a manifest form' probably refers to the imperceptible soul assuming a bodily identity, which is the condition of living beings in this world. This is Shankaracharya's interpretation. If we accept this view, then the meaning of the verse becomes clear. Foolish people (*a-buddhi*) regard Krishna as an ordinary mortal being and fail to realise that he has a higher identity (*param bhavam*). Here, it seems that it is the *avatar* form that is being discussed, and one might even suggest that the verse is making an oblique reference to the *Mahabharata* narrative in which the Pandavas accept Krishna's divinity, whilst Duryodhana and his faction refuse to accept that he is anything more than an ordinary person.

What is the reason given as to why people
in this world are unaware of Krishna?

The reason given is that living beings in this world have their higher knowledge covered over by ignorance. This is referred to in verse 25 as *yoga-maya* and in verse 27 as *dvamdva-moha*. *Yoga-maya* is a rather tricky phrase to interpret. The word *maya* can be used as a synonym for *prakriti*, meaning 'matter or nature', and if this interpretation is accepted, *yoga-maya-samavrittah* might mean that Krishna is concealed because the people of this world see only the material manifestation and not the higher reality that lies behind it. This view is supported by the phrase *dvamdva-moha*, which means 'the illusion of duality or the materialistic consciousness that perceives the world in terms of happiness and distress, good and bad'. On the other hand, *maya* can also mean 'magic or trickery', and it is just possible that Krishna is saying here that when he appears in a human guise as an *avatar*, he uses his mystical powers to delude the world and cover over his divine identity. This interpretation would again seem to relate primarily to the role played by Krishna in the stories of the *Mahabharata*.

> *What means are recommended here for the*
> *acquisition of knowledge of Krishna?*

It is interesting to note that verse 28 recommends moral conduct and righteous activities as the means one should adopt in order to break free of this illusion. This is referred to as *anta-gatam papam*, sin being at an end, and *punya-karmanam*, engaging in righteous activities. This refers back to the assertion in verse 15 that those who are wicked and low-minded do not surrender to Krishna, and to the statement of the Katha Upanishad (2.24) that wicked persons never realise the *atman*.

I have purposely refrained from discussing the final two verses of the chapter because they contain difficult terminology and are hence hard to comprehend without further elucidation. This is the case for Arjuna as well, and at the beginning of the eighth chapter we find him asking Krishna to explain exactly what he means by his concluding words here. So we will postpone that discussion until we have looked at Krishna's explanation in Chapter 8.

CONCLUSION:
A SUMMARY OF CHAPTER 7

Chapter 7 marks a dramatic change of direction in the teachings of the Bhagavad-gita as Krishna brings himself to the forefront of the discourse and verbally reveals his own identity as the one Supreme Deity. This is a very different form of spirituality from what has gone before. The earlier chapters of the Gita focus on self-transformation and gaining *moksha* by means of renunciation of desire and knowledge of the inner self. Now, however, the focus is on the nature of an external Deity who creates, controls, and pervades the world, and on the worship of that Deity. *Moksha* is still the ultimate goal, but now that goal is attained not by self-transformation and self-knowledge but by the blessing of the Deity. At the beginning of the chapter, three eternal principles are established: matter, the individual soul, and the Deity who controls both of these. That Deity is present within this world and is in fact the fundamental basis that allows it to exist; most people are unaware of his existence because they are under the sway of ignorance and illusion. Those who are righteous, however, worship Krishna, and the wise devotee forms a relationship with him based on mutual love. This worship is not the same as that offered to the Vedic gods, although that worship is dependent upon Krishna and the rewards gained are ultimately bestowed by Krishna as well. So Krishna is present in this world both as an *avatar* and as the all-pervasive supreme principle that sustains the order of the world. The fools will never know of his presence, but those who are righteous may come to know him and ultimately surrender to his grace.

At the time of death, a person should absorb himself
in devotion with an unwavering mind,
using the power of yoga practice. —8.10

CHAPTER 8

The eighth chapter of the Bhagavad-gita follows a direction that is set primarily by questions from Arjuna, which in turn are prompted by the rather obscure instructions with which Krishna concluded Chapter 7. Brief definitions are given for some of the terminology employed there, but the crucial issue that is raised relates to the statement made in verse 30 of Chapter 7 to the effect that even at the time of death – *prayana-kale* – persons whose minds are properly engaged can have knowledge of Krishna. In verse 2 of Chapter 8, Arjuna picks up on that point and asks for further explanation. It is this point that then becomes the predominant topic for the chapter as a whole. It is not quite the case that the main subject of the nature of God and worship of God is forgotten here, and yet there is a sense that this chapter is a slight deviation from the main theme of the discourse, which is picked up again in Chapter 9 when Arjuna's question about the time of death has been fully answered.

SOME DEFINITIONS

1. Arjuna said: What is that Brahman? What is *adhyatma*? What is karma, O Purushottama? And what is it that is defined as *adhibhuta*? What is it that is called *adhidaiva*?
2. What is the *adhiyajña*, O Madhusudana, and how is it present within this body? And how are you to be known at the time of death by those who have attained self-mastery?

3. The Lord said: That which decays not (*akshara*) is the Supreme Brahman; it is one's inherent nature (*sva-bhava*) that is referred to as *adhyatma*. The creative force producing the existence of living beings is known as *karma*.

4. *Adhibhuta* is the existence that decays (*kshara-bhava*), and *adhidaiva* is the soul within (*purusha*). I alone am the *adhi-yajña* here in this body, O best of embodied beings.

Arjuna's questions in the first two verses are inspired by the language Krishna used at the end of Chapter 7. There, it was said that persons who pursue the goal of *moksha* come to exist as Brahman and understand the concepts of *adhyatma* and *karma*. They also come to know Krishna in relation to *adhibhuta*, *adhidaiva*, and *adhiyajña*. So now, perhaps not surprisingly, Arjuna wants to know what Krishna means by these terms, and Krishna responds by giving brief definitions. The terms *adhyatma*, *adhibhuta*, *adhidaiva*, and *adhiyajña* are derived from the Upanishads (see, for example, Chapter 4 of the Kena Upanishad), where the affix *adhi* means 'in relation to'. So literally, the four terms given here mean in relation to the self, in relation to the elements or living beings, in relation to the gods, and in relation to the Vedic ritual. We can list the definitions given by Krishna as follows:

Brahman: The word is defined simply by the term *akshara*, which can refer either to the sacred syllable *om* or to 'that which does not decay'. We will encounter the division between *kshara*, that which decays, and *akshara* later on in relation to body and soul. But here, Brahman can be defined either as *om* or as the non-material principle that does not decay.

Adhyatma: This is defined as *svabhava*, the inherent nature with which one is born and which is shaped by previous acts.

Karma: The definition given here is interesting. Karma is the creative force that gives rise to the existence of a living being. In other words, we are now creating our future existence through the actions we are performing. I once heard a Christian ask a Buddhist monk about who created the world if there was no God. To this the Buddhist replied that we ourselves are our own creators through the past actions we have performed. It seems that here, the Gita is making precisely the same point.

Adhibhuta: This is defined as the *kshara bhava*, the form of existence that decays. This, of course, stands in contrast to the term *akshara* used to define Brahman, and one must presume that it refers to the material embodiment contrasted with the *atman* within, which is Brahman.

Adhidaivata: Here, the *adhidaiva* is defined as the *purusha*, a term used in Samkhya to refer to the soul within the body, a synonym for *atman*. This, again, is in contrast to the *adhibhuta*, which is the temporary identity based on the material body.

Adhiyajña: Somewhat surprisingly, Krishna claims that the *adhiyajña* is himself. This assertion may be connected with the idea presented in the last verse of Chapter 5, in which Krishna stated that he is to be regarded as the true recipient of the offerings made in the Vedic *yajña*.

Up until this point, however, the crucial question that Arjuna raises is yet to be answered. How can Krishna be known at the time of death? This question is answered in far greater detail in the verses that follow.

FIXING THE MIND ON KRISHNA

5. And one who leaves the body at the time of death whilst focusing the mind on me alone attains my existence. There is no doubt about that.

6. Whatever the state of being a man's mind is fixed upon at the time of death as he leaves his body is the state he then attains, Kaunteya, for a person develops into the type of existence he constantly dwells upon.

7. At all times, therefore, you should concentrate upon me and engage in battle. If your mind and intellect are fixed

on me, you will be free from doubt and then you will come to me.

8. It is through the consciousness being absorbed without deviation in the disciplined practice of yoga that a man goes to the Supreme Divine Being, upon whom his thoughts are fixed.

9. One should thus fix the mind upon the one who is the ancient seer, the controller who is smaller than the smallest thing, the ordainer of all that comes to pass, whose form is inconceivable, who is dazzling like the sun, and who is beyond all darkness.

10. At the time of death, a person should absorb himself in devotion (*bhakti*) with an unwavering mind, using the power of yoga practice. Placing the life breath between the eyebrows in the proper way, he thereby attains that original Supreme Person.

11. I shall now briefly explain to you that *akshara* (undecaying) principle, which those who know the Vedas expound upon and which sages who are devoid of passion enter into. It is due to their desire for this position that they take vows of celibacy.

12. Sealing all the entrances of the body, fixing the mind upon the heart, and keeping the life breath (*prana*) within the head, a person should remain steadfast in yoga concentration.

13. One who gives up his body and departs this world whilst reciting 'Om', the single syllable that is Brahman, and fixing his mind on me attains the highest destination.

14. For a person who always sets his mind on me and never allows his concentration to wander, a *yogin* constant in his practice, I am very easy to attain, Partha.

15. Each rebirth is miserable and temporary, but after attaining me, the *mahatmas* never take birth again, having achieved the highest state of perfection.

16. Repeated birth occurs in all the worlds right up to Brahmaloka, Arjuna. But after attaining me, Kaunteya, there is no more rebirth.

This passage provides a clear link between the *dhyana-yoga* teachings of the sixth chapter and the emphasis on *bhakti* we encountered in Chapter 7 and further emphasises the identity the Gita reveals between the inner self and the Supreme Deity. And it is interesting to note how Krishna starts off by referring to himself as the Deity and then speaks of the Supreme Being in the third person; there seems little doubt, however, that they are one and the same.

'How are you to be known at the time of death?'

This is really the main theme of this passage. In verses 5 and 6, Krishna asserts that those who are able to fix their minds on him at the time of death will attain him because the state of consciousness at the time of death dictates the nature of the form of existence into which the departing soul transmigrates. But how is this to be achieved? Essentially, Krishna teaches that one must condition oneself to fix the mind upon him at all times; if one can do that, then the mind will naturally revert to this condition at the time of death. And this fixing of the mind on Krishna is achieved by the yoga process referred to here, which is similar but not identical to the technique revealed in Chapter 6. The practice referred to here consists of fixing the mind on one point in the region of the heart where the *atman* is located, moving the air of life to the top of the head and vibrating the *mantra* 'om' as one leaves the body. So, the answer to Arjuna's question is that one must condition the mind by yoga techniques, and then apply those techniques as one gives up one's life.

Is this passage about yoga practice or
about bhakti–devotion to the Supreme Deity?

The answer to this question is that it is about both, and here, in Chapter 8, we find that *dhyana-yoga* and *bhakti* are integrated into one spiritual path. This is particularly apparent in verse 10, where the word *bhakti* is used in close association with a discussion of yoga techniques – *bhaktya yukto yoga-balena chaiva*, which means 'by means of devotion (*bhakti*) and the power of yoga (*yoga-bala*) as well'. It is also significant to note how the Deity is again identified as the *atman* within, a teaching that is particularly emphasised in the Katha Upanishad. Hence, meditation on the inner self is equivalent to always thinking of Krishna, and so *dhyana-yoga* is in effect a manifestation of *bhakti*.

Yoga techniques at the time of death

Verses 12 and 13 form part of Krishna's answer to Arjuna's question about how one can think of him at the time of death. Here, we have an addition to the yoga teachings of Chapter 6 with more emphasis on bodily exercises and not just mental concentration. We noted that Chapter 6 did not refer to *pranayama*, the regulation of the breath, but here, this is the main focus. The apertures of the body are to be blocked by physical exercises, and the *prana* is then to be raised to the point known as the *brahma-randhra*, which is located at the top of the skull where the three fissures meet. Here, also, we find reference to the use of *mantra* as a part of the yoga techniques and in particular the recitation of the sacred syllable *om*, which in the Upanishads is identified as being non-different from Brahman.

What instruction is given in verses 15 and 16?

Firstly, verse 15 confirms the Vedantic view of the world as primarily a place of suffering from which one should seek liberation or *moksha*. The terms used here are *duhkhalaya* and *a-shashvata*, beset with suffering and temporary by nature. Every living being in this world must undergo the process of rebirth, even the gods above, but if one can reach Krishna, then the process of rebirth is stopped. The phrase used here to define *moksha* is *mam upetya*, reaching me. Now, this could mean attaining Vaikuntha, the heavenly domain of Vishnu, or it could mean the merging of the *atman* with Brahman in line with the ideas presented in the Upanishads. Liberation is the ending of the process of rebirth, but the actual state of being attained is not precisely explained – perhaps because it is beyond the reach of the human mind.

THE MATERIAL
AND THE SPIRITUAL DOMAINS

17. Those persons who understand his day and his night recognise the limit of Brahma's day as one thousand *yugas* (ages), and they understand his night as also lasting for a thousand *yugas*.
18. When the day commences, all beings emerge from the *avyakta* (the non-manifest state of matter) and thereby become manifest. When the night comes, they merge once more into that which is designated as the *avyakta*.
19. Coming into being time and again, this host of living beings is helplessly merged back once more when the night comes. And at the coming of the day, they appear again.
20. Beyond that *avyakta*, however, there is another *avyakta* (non-manifest) existence, which is eternal. When all

living beings are destroyed, that *avyakta* principle is not destroyed.

21. This *avyakta* is referred to as the *akshara*, non-decaying. They say it is the ultimate goal, for on reaching this position, one does not return. It is my supreme abode.

22. That Supreme Being (*purusha*), Partha, is attained by undivided devotion. The living beings are situated within him, and he pervades this entire world.

I mentioned above that Arjuna's questions at the start of the chapter seemed to draw the Bhagavad-gita away from the theme it had been pursuing concerning the nature of God and devotion to God. In particular, the question about how one can fix one's mind on Krishna at the time of death has led to an extensive detour and something of a return to the type of yoga teachings considered in Chapter 6. In this passage, the diversion continues as Krishna expands upon the statements made about *moksha* in verse 16. There, it was asserted that rebirth occurs in every part of this world, but if one can attain Krishna's domain, then rebirth will end. Now, this notion of two distinct realms of existence is explained further. We may note the following points:

Verses 17–19 provide more information about the domain of rebirth, and here, some elements of cosmology are presented, including reference to the duration of the creation. Indian cosmology reveals that the world is constantly manifested and then withdrawn, an eternally repeated process of creation and destruction. Here, each period of manifestation is designated as a day of Brahma, and the period of non-manifestation is Brahma's night. Each creation lasts for a period of one thousand *yugas*. Elsewhere in the *Mahabharata* and in the *Puranas*, this idea is explained in more detail. There, we learn that there are four ages, or *yugas*: *Satya-yuga*, *Treta-yuga*, *Dvapara-yuga*, and the present age, known as *Kali-yuga*. Each of these *yugas* has different qualities, and each lasts for thousands of years. Here, one must presume that when it is stated that each creation lasts for a thousand *yugas*, it means 'a thousand cycles of the four *yugas*'.

At the beginning of a creation, when the daytime of Brahma begins, the living beings transmigrating under the control of past karma emerge from a non-manifest state and resume their activities once more. And when the creation ends after a thousand *yugas* have passed, they return once more into a condition of stasis, or non-manifestation.

The next three verses, 20–22, turn to consider the second of the two domains, that in which rebirth does not take place, referred to by Krishna in verse 16 when he mentioned liberation as reaching himself. Like this world during the night of Brahma, that state of being is also non-manifest because it cannot be perceived from a position in this domain. It is not subject to repeated creation and destruction, as this world is. This domain is *akshara*, it does not decay, and it is the domain of Krishna, his *dhama*, in line with the statement of verse 16.

Verse 22 presents an interesting perspective because here, the higher domain in which there is no rebirth is referred to as the Supreme Person himself. Hence, we must understand that Krishna's abode is not the place where Krishna resides, but is Krishna himself; the Supreme Being and his abode are one and the same.

TIMES FOR
LEAVING THE BODY

23. Now I shall speak of the time of departing in which the *yogins* do not return to this world and the time in which they do return, O best of the Bharatas.

24. Persons who have knowledge of Brahman (or the Vedas) and who depart during the fire, the light, the day, the bright half of the moon, or the six months when the sun is in the northern transit go to Brahman.

25. But a *yogin* who departs during the smoke, the night, the dark fortnight of the moon, or the six months when the sun is in its southern transit come back to this world after entering the light of the moon.

26. Thus, it is understood that there are these two paths from this world, the light and the dark, which exist eternally. By following one, there is no return, but by following the other, one comes back once more.

27. By understanding these two paths, Partha, the *yogin* is never bewildered. So engage yourself in the practice of yoga at all times, Arjuna.

28. A specific reward is ordained as the fruit of the merit (*punya*) acquired through study of the Vedas, sacrifice (*yajña*), religious austerity (*tapa*), or acts of charity, but by fully understanding this wisdom, the *yogin* goes beyond this world and attains the supreme, original position.

Here, the topic raised by Arjuna is pursued still further as Krishna turns to consider an idea that is to be found in the Chandogya Upanishad (5.10.1–6) and the Brihad Aranyaka Upanishad (6.2.15). Two different paths are described for the departure of the soul, one of which leads to the domain in which there is no rebirth, whilst the other leads to a continuation of the cycle. The Gita here summarises these verses and puts a slightly different interpretation on them, suggesting that the time at which one departs from the body is significant in terms of the destination one achieves. The Upanishadic version is not quite the same, as it refers to the path taken rather than the time of death. This is why the words 'departs during the fire' (v. 24) and 'departs during the smoke' (v. 25) seem a little odd here. It is because they are quotations from the Upanishads placed into a rather different context. The interesting point to note is that here, the Gita is providing something of a commentary on the works of the *shruti*, or Veda, as they are relevant to the topic it is presently dealing with. But why does the Gita include this passage? Why does Krishna feel the need to refer to the ideas of the Upanishads?

Clearly, the passage from the Upanishads is regarded as being relevant to the main topic covered in Chapter 8, which is all about the two alternative destinations one can achieve at the time of death: the domain of rebirth and the domain from which one does not come back. This is what Krishna has just considered in verses 17–22, and so it is appropriate that some consideration should be given to Vedic ideas on this topic.

It is interesting to note the times which are regarded as auspicious and inauspicious here. The auspicious times are listed as the daytime, the bright fortnight of the lunar month, and the six months beginning from the festival of Makara Sankranti (Pongal in Tamil Nadu). These months are known as *uttarayana* and are still regarded by Hindus as being more auspicious. The inauspicious times are the nighttime, the dark fortnight of the lunar month, and the six months of the year when the sun travels on its *dakshinayana*, or southern path. But what is the point Krishna is making here?

We might suggest that the key to the passage is to be found in verse 27, which refers to the *yogin*, presumably one who has adhered to the teachings given in verses 8–16. I think what Krishna is saying here is that if one is successful in the yogic endeavour he has outlined, and is able to fix the mind on him at the time of death, then the rules presented in the Veda do not apply. He attains the domain from which there is no return regardless of any other circumstances. I would thus interpret the words 'the *yogin* is never bewildered' (v. 27) as meaning 'the *yogin* is not troubled by these rules about the time for leaving the body' because he has entirely transcended the Vedic strictures by means of his spiritual perfection. This view would seem to be confirmed in verse 28, where it is shown that the *yogin* who adheres to the instructions Krishna has given gains all the rewards obtained through other forms of religion. Hence, the rules of that religion cannot constrain him.

CONCLUSION:
A SUMMARY OF CHAPTER 8

As stated above, the eighth chapter of the Bhagavad-gita appears to be something of a digression from the main theme of this middle section of the text, a digression provoked by the last of Arjuna's questions in verse 2 about how one can think of Krishna at the time of death. Krishna's reply is that at the time of death, the mind will remain fixed on whatever it has been accustomed to dwell on during one's lifetime. Therefore, one should practice a form of yoga that trains the mind to become fixed upon the Supreme Deity who exists within one's own being. One should employ yogic techniques such as *pranayama* and the recitation of the sacred mantra 'om' in order to achieve this goal of concentrating on Krishna at the very moment of death. The Gita then explains that there are two domains of existence that we can dwell in. One is the domain of rebirth, where there is repeated creation and annihilation, and the other is the domain of the Deity, which is the Deity. And if we can reach that sphere of existence, then rebirth is ended and liberation is achieved. Finally, Krishna reflects upon the teachings of the Upanishads on this subject, which appear to suggest that if one departs from the body at different times of the day, the month, and the year, one will achieve one or the other of the two domains. Krishna's point here seems to be that one who achieves success in the yoga practice he has recommended need not be concerned or bewildered by these injunctions, for the *yogin* has achieved the absolute success that transcends all other considerations.

When it is presented in a mood of devotion, I will
accept the devotional offering of a leaf, a flower, a fruit, or water
from one who is pure at heart. —9.26

CHAPTER 9

With the discourse of Chapter 8 completed, Krishna now returns to the theme he was pursuing in the seventh chapter, namely that of the nature of God and spiritual practices based on that knowledge – the way of *bhakti*, the *bhakti-marga*. In many ways, the ninth chapter is the very heart of Krishna's discussion of the nature of God, of his own identity, and of the ways of worshipping God. And here, we will find the ideas first presented in Chapter 7 revisited and expanded upon.

Introduction
to the Chapter

1. But now, O non-envious one, I will reveal to you this greatest of mysteries, including both the *jñana* and the *vijñana*. When this is understood, you will be liberated from evil.

2. This teaching is the king of knowledge, the king of mysteries. This is the purest of all things. It can be realised by direct perception, it is based on dharma, it is very easy to perform, and it is unfading.

3. Persons who have no faith in this dharma do not attain, me, Paramtapa. They return to the path of death and rebirth.

These first three verses form an introduction to the teachings that follow, in which Krishna emphasises the high status of the ideas he will now reveal. He refers to this teaching as *raja-vidya*, the king of knowledge, a phrase which probably means that this is the highest knowledge presented in the Gita. Persons who do not gain an understanding of this *dharma* that is based on *bhakti* will return to the 'path of death and rebirth', the implication being that as well as revealing the nature of God, this teaching is a revelation of the path to *moksha*. And, just as in Chapter 7, we find the teaching defined in terms of *jñana* and *vijñana*, and again I would suggest that this probably refers to theoretical knowledge about the nature of God and then to knowledge of religious practice.

GOD AND THE WORLD

4. This whole world is pervaded by me in my non-manifest form. All beings are situated in me, but I am not present in them.

5. And yet, the living beings are not situated in me; you should see this as my magical opulence. My own self is what causes living beings to exist; it sustains the living beings but is not situated within them.

6. The great wind, constantly moving through all places, is situated in space. You should understand that it is in this sense that all living beings are situated in me.

7. At the end of the period of creation (*kalpa*), Kaunteya, all beings enter into my *prakriti*, and at the beginning of a *kalpa*, I manifest them again.

8. Making use of this *prakriti* of mine, I repeatedly create this entire host of living beings. They are helpless, for they are under the control of *prakriti*.

9. And these actions do not bind me, Dhanamjaya. It is as if I am situated in a position of neutrality, unattached to these actions.

10. It is through me alone that *prakriti* brings the moving and non-moving beings into existence, for I am the Controller. This is the reason why the world proceeds on its course.

This is a rather difficult passage in which the Bhagavad-gita continues to speak about the nature of the Deity it is extolling and in particular the relationship between God and the world he creates. In seeking to understand these verses, we might try to find answers to the following questions.

Is there a contradiction between verses 4 and 5?
Is there a solution for this paradox?

The obvious contradiction here is that in verse 4, Krishna says, 'All beings are situated in me' and then in verse 5, he says, 'The living beings are not situated in me'. The Gita is well aware of the paradox, as Krishna then says, 'This is my magical opulence'. In other words, what would be a contradiction or logical impossibility in the context of the material domain is possible in the higher domain where God resides.

What relationship exists between God and the
living beings, as explained in verses 4–6?

This is a difficult passage, but I think what is being said here is that the created world and the living beings are within the existence of God. As we saw in Chapter 7, he is not a remote purely transcendent Deity, but rather he shares the identity of the Upanishadic Brahman and pervades the whole world by his divine presence. Here, I think we are getting an early hint of the *vishva-rupa* revealed in Chapter 11 through which Krishna shows that this existence is his bodily form. And the contradiction or paradox might be explained, again, by the asymmetrical identity between God and the world. The world and the living beings are nothing but God; they are entirely dependent upon God. Yet, it would be wrong to turn the equation around and say that God is nothing but the totality of the world and the living beings; he is all of that, but this is not the limit of his identity. The metaphor of the wind in space reinforces the point. Wind cannot exist without space to move through; it is wholly dependent on space for its existence. Yet, space can exist with or without wind blowing through it. In the same way, the living beings are wholly dependent on God for their existence, but God is not dependent on the living beings. There is identity between them, but it is not symmetrical or absolute identity.

The relationship between God and prakriti

The word *prakriti* is used in Samkhya philosophy and elsewhere to designate matter in its basic undifferentiated state. Hence, we might translate *prakriti* as 'the material substance', and it is from out of *prakriti,* that the varieties of material manifestation evolve. It is important to note that in Samkhya thought, unlike Advaita Vedanta, the material manifestations are real, though temporary. In verse 4 of Chapter 7, Krishna defined *prakriti* in terms of eight elements and listed those eight. He also claimed that he is the possessor of *prakriti,* and in these verses it is revealed that *prakriti* is a tool owned and used by God in order to create the world inhabited by living beings. He is the ultimate creator of the world, the source from which it emerges, but he makes use of *prakriti* in order to enact this process. Here, we might conclude that the Bhagavad-gita is offering us a form of theistic Samkhya that stands in contrast to the atheistic or non-theistic Samkhya encountered elsewhere.

'I am the controller'

In verse 9, we have a slight return to the ideas on action and reaction that loomed so large in the earlier chapters of the Gita. In 3.22–24 and 4.14, we saw Krishna refer to himself as a *karma-yogin* who performs action but is not under the control of the law of karma. The same point is made here. He is active in the process of creation, but one should not therefore think that he is under the control of the laws of action and reaction that act upon other living beings.

The conclusion given in verse 10 is really quite a simple one. The world of matter with all the varieties of living being is manifested by means of *prakriti*, but we should not think that *prakriti* is the ultimate source of the world, as claimed in the classical Samkhya philosophy. It is the Deity who controls *prakriti* and is the ultimate creator of the world; *prakriti* is just the tool he uses for creation.

WORSHIP OF KRISHNA

11. Fools despise me when I accept this human form. They do not understand my higher nature as the Supreme Lord of the living beings.
12. The hopes, deeds, and understanding of these unintelligent persons are futile. Falling prey to delusion, they adopt the nature of *asuras* and *rakshasas*.
13. But the *mahatmas* inherit the divine nature, Partha. Understanding that I am the unchanging source of all beings, they worship me with undeviating minds.
14. Constantly singing my praises, engaging in resolute vows, and bowing before me with devotion, they are always engaged in acts of worship.
15. There are others who make their offerings through the *jñana-yajña*, the sacrifice of knowledge, and who worship me as that which is one and yet still exists in many different forms, with faces turned in every direction.

I have suggested previously that the *jñana* and the *vijñana* referred to at the start of Chapter 7 and Chapter 9 refer to theoretical and practical knowledge. If that suggestion is accepted, then we might say that verses 4–10 are *jñana* in the sense of providing a theological explanation of the presence of God within the creation, and that now we are moving on to the *vijñana* in the form of worship of the Deity thus defined. Let us note the following points here:

Verses 11 and 12 are about worshipping God, but only in a negative sense, as in verse 15 of Chapter 7. We see the same pattern here. First, the types of person who do not worship Krishna are described, and only then do we learn about the worshippers and the acts of worship.

Here, I would again suggest that we look at the *Mahabharata* context. The fools referred to here do not accept Krishna's status as a divine *avatar*, and they adopt the nature of demonic beings, *asuras* and *rakshasas*. It is well known that Duryodhana and his close associates refused to accept Krishna as a divine being. Even when he displayed an aspect of his *vishva-rupa* before them, they regarded it as a manifestation of magical ability rather than of divinity. And we are informed on several occasions in the *Mahabharata* that the reason for Vishnu's appearance as Krishna was the fact that *asuras* and *rakshasas* had taken birth in the royal families on Earth. Hence, there does seem to be a reference to the *Mahabharata* narrative in these two verses.

The devotees are here referred to by the term *mahatma*, literally 'great soul'. They have acquired the knowledge, the *jñana* revealed by Krishna in the previous verses, and understand that he is the *bhutadi*, the source of the living beings. And because they possess this *jñana*, they therefore adopt the *vijñana*, the religious practices by which the Supreme Deity is worshipped and adored.

Verses 14 and 15 are interesting because they seem to suggest that there are two ways by which an enlightened person may worship the Deity. In verse 14, the usual practices associated with *bhakti* are mentioned. These include *kirtan*, singing the praises of the Deity, accepting regulated vows, and bowing down before the Lord. But in verse 15, it is said that others worship Krishna by means of the *jñana-yajña* that seeks to establish and realise the all-pervasive aspect of God. So, in this sense, the Bhagavad-gita is non-dogmatic; it accepts that there are two ways in which devotion can be expressed, one through overt acts of worship and the other by the acquisition of higher knowledge. We have had suggestions of these two paths earlier on at the beginning of Chapter 3 and again at the start of Chapter 5, and the topic will be revisited later on in Chapter 12, where Arjuna raises a specific question about these two approaches.

THE IMMANENCE OF KRISHNA

16. I am the ritual, I am the sacrifice, I am the offering made to the ancestors, and I am the herbs. I am the *mantra*, I am the ghee, I am the sacred fire, and I am the offering made into the fire.

17. I am the father of this world, the mother, the ordainer and the grandfather. I am the object of knowledge, I am the purifier, I am the syllable *om*, and I am the Rik, the Sama, and the Yajus.

18. I am the goal, the sustainer, the lord, the witness, the abode, the refuge, and the friend. I am creation, destruction, and the foundation, I am the treasury, and I am the imperishable seed.

19. I bring forth warmth, I hold back the rain, and I then release it. I am immortality and I am death. I am both being and non-being, Arjuna.

These four verses seem to be returning to the discussion of verses 4–10, which gave instruction about the connection between the Deity and the world he creates. Here, however, I think we should take these verses as an expansion upon the second form of devotion spoken about in verse 15 relating to the acquisition of realised knowledge. We may note the following points:

In verse 16, Krishna identifies himself as the different aspects of the Vedic *yajña*, and here, we might look back to Chapter 4 (v. 24), where elements of the *yajña* were identified as Brahman. Here, I think we have an expansion on the idea of the *jñana-yajña* mentioned in verse 15. Krishna is represented as being all the various aspects of the metaphorical ritual referred to as the 'sacrifice of knowledge', which aims at the realisation of the presence of God in all things.

Verse 17 proclaims again Krishna's position as the controller and original source of the world, but here, we should note that he also refers to himself as *vedyam*, the subject realised by higher knowledge, and as *omkara*, the sacred syllable identified by the Upanishads as being non-different from Brahman. So, again, it is explained how the realised knowledge that Krishna referred to earlier is in fact a way of worshipping and of realising Krishna himself.

Verses 18 and 19 emphasise the immanence of Krishna within this world in a manner that reminds us of the metaphor of the jewels on a thread given in Chapter 7 (v. 7). It is his presence within the world that allows the order of the cosmos to prevail, and the goal of the *jñana-yajña*, the sacrifice based on knowledge, is to realise that presence, which is usually *avyakta*, or invisible. Here, we might look back to verse 4 of the present chapter, in which Krishna started his discourse by stating that he pervades the entire world in an invisible or non-manifest form, an *avyakta-murti*. He cannot be seen, but his presence in this world is the fundamental principle that sustains the cosmic order, as is emphasised in these two verses. The goal of the *jñana-yajña* is to achieve knowledge of this imperceptible presence, and if we look ahead to the awesome vision of Chapter 11 we might see this as being the *avyakta-murti* becoming *vyakta*, the invisible presence becoming visible, with terrifying consequences for Arjuna.

WORSHIP OF THE GODS AND
WORSHIP OF KRISHNA

20. Drinking Soma, purged of sin (*papa*), those who follow the three Vedas seek the heavenly destination by worshipping me with *yajñas*. By this means, they attain the pure domain presided over by the lord of the gods, and in that heaven, they experience the celestial pleasures enjoyed by the gods.

21. But after enjoying the delights of that extensive heavenly domain, they must re-enter the mortal world when their stock of piety (*punya*) is exhausted. So, by adhering to the dharma of the three Vedas, persons who seek to fulfil their desires merely go there and then again come back.

22. But then there are persons who worship me with undeviating concentration. For those who engage constantly in this way, I bring both prosperity and security.

23. Those who are devoted to other gods and worship them with faith actually worship me alone, Kaunteya, but not in the manner that is properly ordained.

24. It is I alone who am the enjoyer and also the master of all *yajñas*. Such persons do not know me as such and so fall down from the position they attain.

25. Devotees of the gods go to the gods, devotees of the ancestors go to the ancestors, those who worship spirits go to the spirits, but those who worship me go to me.

I mentioned earlier that in this ninth chapter, Krishna seems to return to his main line of discourse that was interrupted somewhat by Arjuna's questions at the start of Chapter 8. And now that he has returned to his principal theme, we find that several of the same topics are being touched upon, including the difference between veneration of the Vedic gods and the devotion to Krishna that is being discussed here.

Are there any differences between this passage and the
parallel passage in Chapter 7 (vv. 20–23)?

In Chapter 7, Krishna revealed that the inspiration that leads people to worship the gods comes from himself within their hearts, as
this manner of worship corresponds with their inner nature. And
Krishna also pointed out there that the reward gained by such worship is in fact bestowed by himself alone rather than the deity who
appears to grant boons. These points are not referred to here. In
this passage, there is a greater emphasis on the fact that the worship of the gods is performed by means of the Vedic *yajña*, and both
chapters emphasise the fact that the rewards gained by this worship are limited and temporary. Both passages also point out that
the worshippers of the gods are elevated to the domain of the gods,
whilst those who worship Krishna attain the domain of Krishna.
And both emphasise the fact that worship of the gods is not the
highest form of spirituality. In Chapter 7, the worshippers were
referred to as being of limited intelligence and devoid of knowledge, whilst here that worship is described as *a-vidhi-purvakam*,
meaning 'not done in the proper manner'. The main point of both
passages is to stress the fact that the worship of the Vedic gods
prescribed in the *karma-kanda* portion of the Veda is different from
the way of *bhakti* Krishna is recommending here, which clearly falls
under the heading of *moksha dharma*.

Externally, it may appear to be that the ritual worship of the
Vedic gods is the same as the worship of Krishna, but the reward
gained by such worship is material and temporary, whilst worship
of Krishna leads to the eternal domain and liberation from rebirth.

Who is actually worshipped through the Vedic yajña?

One of the points Krishna makes here is that he himself is the true
object of worship and the recipient of the offerings made into the

sacred fire. This point was established at the end of Chapter 5, where Krishna referred to himself *bhoktaram yajña-tapasam*, the true object of *yajña* and of acts of austerity. The same point is made here, but it is shown that the worshippers being described do not understand this point and think they are worshipping the gods named in the hymns of the *Rigveda*. This point is made clear in verse 24. Krishna is indeed the true object of worship in Vedic ritual, but because the enactors of the ritual do not understand this, they do not gain the full reward of devotion to Krishna, which will now be discussed.

WORSHIP OF KRISHNA– THE WAY OF BHAKTI

26. When it is presented in a mood of devotion, I will accept the devotional offering of a leaf, a flower, a fruit, or water from one who is pure at heart.

27. Make whatever you do, whatever you eat, whatever you sacrifice, whatever charity you give, and whatever austerities you undertake into an offering to Me, Kaunteya.

28. It is in this way that you will be liberated from both the good and evil results, which are the bonds of action. By engaging yourself in this yoga of renunciation, you will become liberated and you will come to me.

29. I am equal towards all living beings; no one is hated by me and no one is beloved. Those who worship me with devotion, however, are in me and I am in them.

30. Even if a person who thus worships me as his only object performs the most wicked deeds, still he is to be considered a *sadhu*, for his resolution is correct.

31. He quickly becomes a *dharmatma*, committed to dharma, and attains enduring peace. Make it known, Kaunteya, that my devotee does not perish.

32. Having sought shelter with me, Partha, even those of evil births, as well as women, *vaisyas*, and *shudras*, go to the highest destination.

33. How much more so, then, in the case of righteous brahmins, and those religious kings (*raja-rishis*) who show devotion. So, having reached this temporary world that is devoid of happiness, you should engage in worshipping me.

34. Fix your mind on me, become my devotee, worship me, and bow down to me. By engaging yourself in such acts and dedicating yourself to me, you will surely come to me.

It is in this passage and the opening verses of Chapter 10 that Krishna's discourse on devotion to the Supreme Deity reaches its ultimate conclusion, although he has more to say on the subject later on. Here, the teaching is completely focussed on ways of worshipping Krishna and the result gained by this type of religious practice. There is nothing of this kind to be found in any of the major Upanishads, and it is the emphasis placed on the idea of a personal God and loving devotion to that God that marks the Gita out as being such an important text in the development of Hindu religious thought.

Devotional practice

It is not stated overtly, but one might reasonably presume that verse 26 is referring to *murti-puja*, the worship of sacred images as performed within the Hindu *mandir*, or temple. This is implied because it is hard to imagine any other setting in which offerings of the type mentioned here could be made to Krishna. If this is accepted as advocating *murti-puja*, it is significant because it is probably the earliest reference we have in Hindu scripture to this type of religious practice, which does not form any part of the ritual of the Veda.

How is bhakti connected to the earlier teaching on karma-yoga?

This is an interesting point. When Krishna was teaching the doctrines of *karma-yoga* in the earlier chapters of the Gita, he made little reference to himself as the Deity. The idea of *karma-yoga* is simply that one performs one's duty in a mood of renunciation without any desire to enjoy the results of action. In verses 27 and 28, however, we see that desireless action is transformed into action done as an offering to Krishna. As in the earlier teachings, it is asserted that action of this type will not lead to any future karma, and so the process of rebirth can be ended. However, it is interesting to note how the earlier teaching on *karma-yoga* has now become integrated into the prevailing idea of devotion to the Supreme Deity.

Is Krishna equal to all living beings?

Krishna certainly states very clearly that he is equal to all living beings – *samo 'ham sarva-bhuteshu* – but there does seem to be an exception made in this verse (v. 29). Here, the word *tu* plays a very important role, for it means 'but' or 'however' and, in this context, suggests an exception to the rule established in the first line. That rule is that Krishna is equal to all, 'but' this rule does not apply to those who worship him in a mood of devotion. The clear implication is that Krishna is partial to his devotees, and as revealed later on, this partiality is an expression of his love for them.

Continued sinful activities while on the path of bhakti

Verse 30 seems to suggest that the way of *bhakti* enables a person to continue with sinful activities and still attain the highest spiritual goals, but I think we need to look more carefully. In verse 31, the situation becomes a little clearer, because here, it is asserted that the wrongdoer who takes to the worship of Krishna quickly ceases from his previous mode of conduct and instead becomes a *dharmatma*, a person dedicated to *dharma*. The idea seems to be that any person who engages in worship of the Deity will be transformed by this action and will therefore cease to behave in an unrighteous manner. The verses certainly do not give license for immoral behaviour whilst one is engaged in acts of devotion.

The wording of verse 32

Verse 32 is rather controversial, and even the precise translation of the words is open to debate. In fact, the thrust of what Krishna is saying here is liberal in intent, as it opens up the possibility of gaining the highest spiritual goals to any person, regardless of caste or gender. Hence, the teaching here is that a *sadhu* or a saint can be a man or woman from any background; the only criterion is devotion to Krishna. The problem arises, however, over the term *papa-yonayah*, which means 'those of sinful birth'. I have translated the verse here as if *papa-yonis*, women, *vaishyas*, and *shudras* were four items in a single list, but it could be understood that *papa-yonayah*, or sinful births, are being defined as women, *vaishyas*, *shudras*. In either case, it does raise serious questions about the Gita's view of women and members of the lower castes, though, as stated at the beginning, the primary intent behind the verse is probably to elevate rather than to degrade.

The goal achieved through devotion and worship

In verse 28, it is said that one who performs these acts of devotion will be liberated (*mokshyase*) from the bondage of action and will then attain Krishna (*mam upaishyasi*). Verse 32 states that devotees of any background go to the highest destination (*yanti param gatim*), and verse 34 repeats the words of 28 in saying that devotees come to Krishna. The point is that the Bhagavad-gita is above all else a treatise on gaining liberation from rebirth, a *moksha-shastra*, and this emphasis is clearly perpetuated even where the main topic of the discourse is devotion to the Supreme Deity.

CONCLUSION:
A SUMMARY OF CHAPTER 9

We have now almost reached the end of Krishna's main teachings about the nature of God and worship of God, though a dramatic twist to the topic is about to occur in response to further requests from Arjuna. These teachings are more or less concluded by verse 11 of Chapter 10, when Arjuna begins to seek further understanding; however, in Chapter 12, we encounter a further intensification of the idea of divine love and divine grace. In Chapter 9, following the introductory verses, we find a repetition of some of the main ideas introduced in Chapter 7 and an expansion on the main themes of the discussion contained therein. We first encounter a discourse on the relationship between the Deity and the world we inhabit, which is his creation and is entirely under his control. The God of the Bhagavad-gita is certainly an omnipotent, transcendent, monotheistic Deity, but one of the main differences from Western monotheism is to be found in the idea of the immanence of God. Krishna is transcendent, but his invisible (*avyakta*) presence pervades the world, preserving the order and balance of creation. Foolish people do not understand Krishna's divine identity, but there are great souls who do, and on the basis of this realisation, they engage in acts of devotion either by praising and worshipping him or by pursuing realised knowledge of his identity as it pervades and controls the world. This worship is not the same as that which forms a part of the Vedic *yajña*. The Vedic ritual is performed without knowledge of the Supreme Deity and yields only temporary results, whilst worship of Krishna leads to liberation from rebirth. Therefore, Arjuna should worship Krishna with devotional offerings, and he should dedicate all his actions to Krishna. The Deity is by nature equal to all living beings, but he is particularly inclined towards those who become his devotees. Hence, anyone who worships Krishna will attain the highest spiritual goal of liberation, regardless of their birth, lifestyle, or background. The conclusion of the chapter is thus that Arjuna should absorb his mind in Krishna, be his devotee, and worship him.

Among secrets, I am silence, and
I am the wisdom of the wise. —10.38

CHAPTER 10

Chapter 10 begins with a continuation of the ideas we have been exploring in Chapter 9, and verses 8–11 provide a useful summation of the main principles of doctrine relating to God and devotional practice. In verse 12, however, Arjuna begins to redirect the discussion, firstly by proclaiming his absolute acceptance of Krishna's divinity and then by asking how one who exists in this world can conceive of Krishna. The answer to this question dominates the latter half of the chapter as Krishna gives a poetic account of how his presence can be recognised in the opulence and glory of the world. The point is made philosophically in the final verses of the chapter, which serve to explain the significance of what has been said before. The focus here is still on the nature of God and developing a mood of devotion to God, but Arjuna's request leads the line of discussion to take a different form.

KRISHNA AS THE ORIGIN OF THE WORLD

1. The Lord said: Listen again, O mighty one, to the excellent words I will speak to you. You take delight in such matters, and I desire your welfare.
2. The gods cannot comprehend my origin, and neither do the great *rishis*. Indeed, it is I who am the only source of the gods and the great *rishis*.
3. One who knows me as unborn and without beginning, as the great Lord of the worlds, is the one who is not

deluded amongst mortal beings. He is liberated from all sins.

4. Intelligence, knowledge, freedom from illusion, tolerance, truthfulness, self-control, tranquillity, joy, misery, existence, non-existence, fear, fearlessness,

5. Not harming, equanimity, satisfaction, austerity, charity, fame, and infamy are the varied dispositions for living entities, which arise from me alone.

6. In the beginning, the seven great *rishis* and the four Manus were endowed with my nature because they were born from my mind; all these living beings existing in the world are descended from them.

7. One who properly understands this glory and mystical power of mine is properly engaged through unwavering yoga discipline. There is no doubt about this.

Krishna opens this chapter by repeating that he is the source of this world, though here, he does not mention his use of *prakriti* to achieve this. Everything is produced from the Supreme Deity who exists beyond this world; again, we have a clear statement of a monotheistic theology. Here, we might note the following points:

The *rishis* referred to in verse 2 are the seers who perceive the Vedas and then reveal them to the rest of humanity. But even they cannot comprehend Krishna, for it is Krishna who first creates the *rishis*, as we hear again in verse 6. And here, also, we see that Hindu monotheism is quite compatible with polytheism. There are different gods, but these gods are a part of this world. There is only one Supreme Deity who creates and controls these secondary gods, so in this way monotheism and polytheism are reconciled.

The various states of existence experienced by living beings in this world are all created by the Supreme Deity. These are the qualities individual possess as a result of their inherent nature, the *svabhava* derived from previous actions. Buddhists would suggest that this cycle of karma and rebirth is an automatic one and that it is one of the inevitable laws of the universe. Here, however, the Gita indicates that the process continues under the direction of Krishna, who is the creator and controller of the world.

According to accounts contained in the *Mahabharata* and the *Puranas*, the seven great *rishis* and the Manus mentioned in verse 6 were the first living beings created at the beginning of the world. They then give rise to all the different creatures that inhabit this creation. The point here is that the primal cause of the world is Krishna, who is the creator of the creators.

Verses 3 and 7 once again refer to the necessity of understanding Krishna as the controller of the world, an idea we have encountered several times before. This knowledge frees a person from the effects of previous sinful actions and is the basis for religious practice referred to here as *avikampa-yoga*, yoga that is unwavering. The indication of the next verse is that here, the word 'yoga' refers to acts of devotion performed to worship the Deity.

WORSHIP OF KRISHNA

8. I am the origin of all things; everything comes into being from out of me. Understanding this, the enlightened ones worship me, filled with loving attachment.
9. Their minds are absorbed in me and their lives are given over to me; they enlighten one another about me. Talking constantly about me, they find satisfaction and delight.
10. To those who engage constantly in such practices, worshipping in a mood of love, I give that yoga of the intellect by means of which they come to me.
11. I am situated within their very being, and out of compassion, I destroy the darkness that arises from ignorance with the blazing torch of knowledge.

These four verses mark the end of this phase of the Bhagavad-gita's discourse, and we now begin to move in a new direction, which culminates in the great revelation of Chapter 11. There is nothing that is particularly new here; nonetheless, these verses are remarkably dense and reassert a number of important points about the Gita's understanding of God.

What is the next step in spiritual
progression after knowledge of God?

Iti matva bhajante mam. When one has knowledge of the Deity as the origin of the world, one then begins to worship him. The verb *bhaj* used here is the root of the word *bhakti*, meaning 'devotion'. Again, we have the suggestion that *jñana*, or realised knowledge, is not the final stage in the progressive path but is the basis for devotion to God.

What devotional activities are referred to here?

In earlier chapters, the Bhagavad-gita referred to singing devotional songs, bowing down with reverence and making offerings of different types. Here, we are told that the devotees take pleasure in discussing the attributes and activities of the Deity. This reflects the idea referred to earlier in Chapter 4 (v. 9), and we might note that still today in India, assemblies are held in which the stories about Krishna taken from the *Bhagavata Purana* are discussed. So, we have a clear link here between the specific teachings of the Gita and contemporary Hindu practice.

Krishna's response to the devotees' worship

Here, also, we encounter the idea of divine grace as the best means of attaining *moksha*, which was mentioned earlier in Chapter 7 (v. 14). Liberation from rebirth can be attained by means of self-mastery and control of the mind, as Chapter 6 reveals, but it can also be gained as a gift of grace granted by God. Christians often proclaim 'Jesus saves!', and here, we find Krishna expressing a similar idea in relation to those who are his devotees. The word used here, *dadami*, means 'I give', and it indicates very clearly that the Deity has the power to grant *moksha* to those he loves. The precise wording here is *dadami buddhi-yogam tam*, which means 'I give that *buddhi-yoga*', *yena mam upayanti te*, 'through which they reach me'. It is hard to be definite here about the precise meaning of *buddhi-yoga*, although earlier in the Gita, it was used as a synonym for *karma-yoga*. But the main point is that this higher consciousness is attained not by hard effort but as a gift from a merciful, loving God.

The answer to the question of what it is that motivates Krishna to act in this way is given in verse 11, where Krishna says *anukampa artham*, 'due to compassion'. Krishna has a loving relationship with his devotees, and so he feels compassion for their plight in this world. Therefore, he delivers them by bestowing upon them the consciousness that brings liberation from rebirth.

Where is Krishna located according to this passage?

Here, we find a clear statement of the location of the Deity within the core of our being. Krishna is *atma-bhava-stha*, which means he is situated in the existence of the *atman*. The precise meaning of this phrase is a little hard to determine. Shankara and other Advaitins would argue that it confirms the Upanishadic view of the oneness of the *atman* and Brahman, but Vaishnavas suggest that the Deity expands himself as an *antaryamin* manifestation that accompanies the soul and guides it as it transmigrates through different lives. This latter idea finds some confirmation in 18.61. In either case, the point here is that Krishna is situated not only as an aloof, transcendent God looking down on us, but he is present here as well within the very core of our being.

At this point, the flow of the discourse changes abruptly and Arjuna comes to the fore once more. Here, we see that he firstly confesses his acceptance of Krishna's identity as the Supreme Deity, and then asks an important question concerning how a person in this world can constantly think of Krishna.

ARJUNA ACCEPTS
KRISHNA'S DIVINE STATUS

12. Arjuna said: You are the Supreme Brahman, the supreme abode, and the supreme purifier. You are the eternal divine *purusha*, the primordial Deity, unborn and all-pervading.

13. All the *rishis* speak of you in this way, including Narada the divine *rishi*, Asita, Devala, and Vyasa. Now, you yourself are declaring it to me.

14. I accept everything you have said to me as true, O Keshava. Neither the gods nor the Danavas (*asuras*) can understand your manifestation, O Lord.

15. You alone can understand your own Self by your own power, O Supreme Person, for you are the source of all living beings. You are the Lord of all beings, the god of gods, the Lord of the world.

Here, Arjuna accepts that Krishna is indeed the Deity who has been spoken of in these chapters as the creator and controller of the world. Each of the terms Arjuna uses here could be analysed in more detail, for each of them is filled with profound meaning – the Supreme Brahman, the Supreme Abode, the eternal divine person, etc.

It seems that Arjuna had earlier heard about Krishna's divine nature from sages such as Narada, Devala, Asita, and Vyasa. In the *Mahabharata*, we frequently hear of encounters between the Pandavas and various holy men, some of whom refer to Krishna in these terms. However, Krishna is Arjuna's friend and cousin, and so perhaps we should not be too surprised to learn that it is only at this point that Arjuna has fully accepted the fact that Krishna is an *avatar* of Narayana. In verses 14 and 15, we again encounter the idea that the cause knows the effect, the creator knows the creation, but the flow of knowledge cannot move in the opposite direction. Hence, as the creator of all things, Krishna knows all things, but concomitantly, there is nothing that can have knowledge of Krishna. As it is said of Brahman in the *Upanishads*, he is beyond the range of conception even for the gods and celestial *rishis*.

How Can One Conceive of Krishna?

16. You should now fully explain your own divine glories. Tell me about those glorious attributes through which you pervade these worlds and remain present within them.
17. How can I come to know you, O *yogin*, and constantly fix my mind upon you? In what forms of existence can I conceive of you, O Lord?
18. Speak to me again at length, Janardana, about this yoga of yours and your glorious power (*vibhuti*). I am never fully satiated when hearing these ambrosial words.

Now, Arjuna makes his request which will carry the discussion forward into its next phase. He accepts Krishna's divine nature, but it is interesting to note that he now asks about the Deity's presence not in some heaven in the sky but here in this world. He asks about the glories of God as they are manifest in the world around us. Again, this reminds us of Krishna's words at the beginning of Chapter 7, 'As jewels are strung upon a thread, so the whole world is strung upon me', and at the beginning of Chapter 9, 'This whole world is pervaded by me in my non-manifest form'. Krishna is all around us, and yet we do not perceive him, so now Arjuna is asking for help with this problem. How can we come to perceive Krishna's invisible presence within the world? The reply that Krishna gives is both poetic and surprising.

KRISHNA'S PRESENCE
WITHIN THIS WORLD

19. The Lord said: Very well, I will speak about my own divine attributes, but only those that are most prominent, O best of the Kurus, for there is no limit to the extent of my manifestation.

20. I am the *atman*, Gudakesha, situated in the hearts of all beings. I am the beginning of the living beings, and I am their middle and end as well.

21. Amongst the Adityas I am Vishnu; amongst luminous objects I am the radiant sun. Amongst the Maruts I am Marichi, and amongst stars I am the moon.

22. Of the Vedas I am the Sama Veda; amongst the gods I am Vasava (Indra). Amongst the senses I am the mind, and amongst living beings I am consciousness.

23. Amongst the Rudras I am Shankara; amongst the Yakshas and Rakshasas I am Vittesha. Amongst the Vasus I am fire (Agni), and amongst high-peaked mountain I am Meru.

24. Amongst priests I am Brihaspati, the foremost amongst them. Amongst generals I am Skanda, and amongst bodies of water I am the ocean.

25. Amongst the great *rishis* I am Bhrigu; amongst utterances I am the one syllable (*om*). Amongst *yajñas* I am the Japa Yajña, and of things that move not, I am Himalaya.

26. Amongst all the trees I am the Ashvattha (fig) tree; amongst the divine *rishis* I am Narada. Amongst the Gandharvas I am Chitraratha, and amongst those who have achieved perfection I am the sage Kapila.

27. Amongst horses, I am Ucchaihshravas, who appeared from the nectar. Amongst the lords of the elephants I am Airavata, and amongst men I am the sovereign.

28. Amongst weapons I am the thunderbolt; amongst cows I am the *kamadhuk*. Amongst progenitors I am Kandarpa, and amongst serpents I am Vasuki.

29. Amongst the Nagas I am Ananta; amongst those who inhabit the waters I am Varuna. Amongst the ancestors I am Aryaman, and amongst those who exert control I am Yama.

30. Amongst the Daityas I am Prahlada; amongst those who calculate I am time. Amongst beasts I am the lion, the king of the beasts, and amongst birds I am Vainateya (Garuda).

31. Of purifiers I am the wind; amongst those who bear weapons I am Rama. Amongst fishes I am the Makara, and amongst rivers I am Jahnavi (Ganga).

32. Amongst created objects I am the beginning and the end, and I am the middle as well, Arjuna. Of all forms of knowledge I am knowledge of the *atman*, and in debaters I am the ability to reach the ultimate conclusion.

33. Amongst letters I am the letter 'a'; amongst compound words I am the dual word. I am time that has no end, and I am the Ordainer facing all directions.

34. I am death who devours everyone; I am the origin of all things yet to be. Amongst feminine virtues I am fame, good fortune, speech, memory, intelligence, endurance, and forgiveness.

35. Of the Sama hymns I am the Brihat Sama, and amongst Vedic metres I am the Gayatri. Of the months I am Margashirsha, and of the seasons I am that which brings the flowers.

36. Amongst cheats I am dicing; I am the energy of those who possess energy. I am victory, I am resolution, and I am the existence of all that exists.

37. Amongst the Vrishnis I am Vaasudeva (Krishna); amongst the Pandavas I am Dhanamjaya (Arjuna). Amongst sages I am Vyasa, and amongst seers I am the seer named Ushanas.

38. Amongst those who chastise I am punishment; amongst those who seek victory I am good policy. Amongst secrets I am silence, and I am the wisdom of the wise.

There is, of course, much that could be said here by way of commentary, and one might be curious to discover the identity of the different persons, creatures, and objects referred to in each of the verses. Most of these will be familiar to those well versed in the study of the *Mahabharata*, *Ramayana*, and *Puranas*, and we do not have the scope here to explore each verse in detail. For our purposes, it is sufficient to look at the passage as a whole and to try to establish the broader significance of this poetic exposition. We might note the following points:

Krishna's opening statement, *aham atma* ('I am the *atman* within all beings'), can be regarded as philosophically significant. This identity of Krishna-*atman-brahman* is fundamental to Shankaracharya's understanding of the Bhagavad-gita, for it allows him to interpret teachings on devotion to Krishna to mean dedication to realisation of the true self.

Arjuna's question is *katham vidyam aham* ('How am I to know you' or 'How am I to conceive of you'), and so we might feel that the answer given here is not so much a philosophical exposition as an aid to realisation. The world we live in is filled with awesome phenomena that fill the beholder with wonder, so Krishna is saying that the wonder we experience in relation to the natural world should help us perceive the glory of the creator of that natural world. Moreover, that glorious opulence perceived in nature is present there because of the pervasive presence of the glorious Deity. So, our feelings of awe and wonder on seeing mountains, various creatures, or the ocean should help us to appreciate the presence of God within this world.

The point has been made several times before, but again, it is apparent that the Deity is not a purely transcendent entity who exists only in some higher domain. In Hindu monotheism, as expressed here, there is identity between the creator and the creation, and this is a facet of theology that distinguishes Hinduism from other monotheistic faiths.

Perhaps we should not try to overinterpret these verses, but should rather see them as a form of meditation on the glories of God. Even though he is not visible to our present perception, he can be perceived in a reflected form, for the glory of the creation is, in truth, the glory of God and is indicative of the omnipresence of God.

As mentioned above, in the final four verses of the chapter, Krishna himself provides some interpretation of the meaning of the passage.

EXPLANATION OF THE
DIVINE PRESENCE

39. And I am that which is the seed of all living beings, Arjuna. There is no living being, moving or non-moving, which exists without me.

40. There is no end to my divine glories, Paramtapa; what I have revealed is just an indication of the extent of my glory.

41. You should understand that whenever a glorious form of existence displays its opulence or power, this arises from a small part of my splendour.

42. But what is the need for you to understand it to its full extent, Arjuna? It is enough to know that I am present here, sustaining the whole world with just one part of myself.

The main point that we should note here is the distinction between the Bhagavad-gita's teachings and what Christians often refer to as 'natural theology'. The Christian idea is that one can understand the existence of the creator because of the complexity and evidence of design in the created world. It is an argument based on inference. However, the creator is a remote figure who has formed the world whilst remaining separate from it, just as the evidence for the existence of a pot maker can be seen in the pot he has created, although the person himself is no longer visible. Krishna's argument here shares some of those ideas, but the crucial difference is that there is a clear statement of identity between creator and creation. The world is wonderful not just because it was created by a wonderful Deity, but because of the presence of the Deity within the creation. Christians may say that 'God is everywhere', by which they usually mean that the power of God is all-pervasive. For the Gita, it is the actual presence of God that is all-pervasive, although, as yet, we do not have the eyes to see it.

What does Krishna mean when he says that he is the 'seed' of all existence?

One must presume that here, the word 'seed' indicates that Krishna is the primary source from out of which the world emerges and which imbues it with life and consciousness. He is not so much the creator as that from which the world emerges, perhaps like a spider spinning its web. The spider does not use external substances, but emits its creation from out of its own existence. So, Krishna is the creator, the source, and that which gives life to the world.

Following on from verse 39, Krishna explains in verse 40 that he has merely touched upon his divine glories and attributes. In the previous verses, Krishna has not given an exhaustive account of his own glories as they exist in this world. It is just a hint, a small sample, for the full extent of his glory, majesty, and divine potency cannot be described.

Krishna's presence in this world

An important point is made here, which adds to our understanding of the previous teachings on the immanence of the Deity within the manifest world. Here, we see again that the identity of God with the world is asymmetrical. The world is nothing but the Deity, but the world is only a small part of his total existence. The wonders of the world may fill us with awe, but they are not the full potency of God; they are just his *tejomsha*, a small part of his energy (*tejas amsha*). So, when we say that God is present within this world, we must understand that this does not mean that the fullness of his existence is manifest here. He is present in the world, but only in the form of a small part of himself, expanded in order to sustain the order of creation.

CONCLUSION:
A SUMMARY OF CHAPTER 10

Chapter 10 of the Bhagavad-gita can be understood as having four main components. It starts with a reassertion and summation of the principal ideas previously stated about the nature of God and the power of devotion to God. He is to be known as the origin of the world and to be venerated by acts of devotion. This arouses his compassion so that he delivers the devotee from this world and grants liberation from rebirth as a gift of divine grace. In the second phase, Arjuna says that he accepts Krishna's divine identity and asks how the invisible presence of God within the world can be known. Then, in the third phase, the chapter provides illustrations of the glorious features of this world, asserting that their individual majesty should be understood as indicative of the divine presence. The glories of this world abound because of the glorious Lord's pervasive presence here. So, though it is an *avyakta-murti*, a non-manifest presence, it can be perceived in the glory of the world it pervades. This is explained in the final phase of the chapter, in which Krishna states that he is the seed from which the world emerges, and that the wonderful features of this creation represent only one part of his full glory.

If a thousand suns were to rise in the sky at the same time,
each with a blazing effulgence, it might then resemble
the wondrous radiance of that great being. —11.12

CHAPTER 11

At the end of the tenth chapter, Krishna explained that he pervades the world by means of a single part of his energy. Arjuna has already accepted the divinity of Krishna, but in this chapter, he takes the treatise on to its next stage by asking to see directly the *avyakta-murti*, the invisible presence of God that pervades the world. This can only be done when one has acquired a higher perception, and this is granted to Arjuna as a gift of grace. The Gita then moves away from its usual form, in which Krishna presents teachings to Arjuna, and the vision of the divine revelation is described to us through the words of Arjuna himself. So, this chapter of the Bhagavad-gita stands out as being distinct because it contains little by way of direct teachings, and for a short time we are given a descriptive account of the nature of God as it is revealed to Arjuna.

ARJUNA'S REQUEST FOR A VISION OF THE DIVINE PRESENCE

1. Arjuna said: For my benefit, you have explained the ultimate mystery, which is known as the *adhyatma*. Through this explanation, my illusion is now gone.
2. I have heard from you at length about the beginning and end of the living beings, O lotus-eyed one, and about your inexhaustible power.
3. You are certainly what you have described yourself to be, O Parameshvara, and I now wish to behold that glorious form of yours, O Purushottama.

4. If you think it is possible for me to see it, O Lord, then reveal to me your unchanging Self, O Yogeshvara.

Arjuna's request here is straightforward. Krishna has given a theoretical explanation of his identity as the Supreme Deity, referred to here as the supreme mystery known as *adhyatma*. We may recall that this term was earlier defined, at Arjuna's request, as a part of the opening section of Chapter 8. *Adhyatma* means 'in relation to the *atman*', and so one must presume that Arjuna's understanding is that Krishna has revealed himself to be the inner self of all beings. This may give us a further clue to the meaning of the discourse in Chapter 10, for we will recall that Krishna began the revelation of his glories with the words *aham atma gudakesha sarva-bhu-tashaya-sthitah*, 'I am the *atman*, O Gudakesha, situated in the heart of all beings'. Or it may be that *adhyatma* is used in relation to the statement in verse 2 that Arjuna has heard about the beginning and end of all living beings.

The point of Arjuna's request here is that he now wants to directly perceive the philosophical truth about the divine nature that has just been revealed to him. He wants a vision of God!

KRISHNA AGREES TO ARJUNA'S REQUEST

5. The Lord said: Behold, O Partha, hundreds and thousands of my divine forms; they are of various different types, of many colours and configurations.
6. Behold the Adityas, Vasus, Rudras, Ashvins, and Maruts, numerous things that have never before been seen. Behold these wonders, O Bharata.
7. Now, behold the entire world with its moving and non-moving creatures situated as one within my body, O Gudakesha, and whatever else you wish to see.

8. But you cannot see me in this way with your own eyes, and so I give to you divine vision. Now, behold my glorious yoga!

Without hesitation, Krishna agrees to grant Arjuna's request and gives him prior warning of what he is about to see. (In verse 8, the word 'yoga' refers to mystical powers and not religious practice.) It is interesting to note that there is no suggestion here that the divinity of Krishna will be displayed in the form of Vishnu with four arms. It will be a multifaceted form in which all the Vedic gods will be seen as a part of the body of the Supreme Deity along with all the other living beings. Again, one is reminded that Krishna has identified himself as the soul within all beings, and hence, the manifestation of the divine form will include all living beings, past, present, and future.

But of course this is an *avyakta-murti* (9.4) that we do not perceive even though we exist as a part of it. Therefore, as a gift of grace, Krishna bestows upon Arjuna the realised vision, the *divya-chakshus*, which enables him to see the world in a different light, not as the place in which he and other living beings exist but as a manifestation of God himself. Here, one is reminded of Krishna's earlier statement, *dadami buddhi-yogam tam yena mam upayanti te*, 'I give them that *buddhi-yoga* by means of which they come to me' (10.10). The higher, realised knowledge can be obtained by strenuous effort and renunciation, but it is also a gift of divine grace given by God as an expression of his love and compassion.

MANIFESTATION OF THE VISHVA-RUPA

9. Samjaya said: When he had spoken these words, O king, Hari the great lord of yoga revealed to Partha his supreme, glorious form.

10. It had many mouths and eyes and many features wonderful to behold. It had many divine ornaments and many divine weapons, raised aloft.

11. It was adorned with celestial garlands and raiments and was anointed with celestial perfumes. This limitless Deity was wondrous in all ways, with faces on all sides.

12. If a thousand suns were to rise in the sky at the same time, each with a blazing effulgence, it might then resemble the wondrous radiance of that great being.

13. The Pandava then saw the entire world, undivided and yet manifold, situated there in one place within the body of the god of gods.

14. Thereupon, Dhanamjaya became filled with wonder and the hair on his body stood erect. Bowing his head to that Deity and placing his palms together, he then began to speak.

There have been numerous attempts made in art, films, television, and even drama to depict the revelation of the *vishva-rupa* as described here in Chapter 11 of the Bhagavad-gita, but it goes without saying that none of these can come close to capturing the awesome magnificence of the revelation of God described here. The form revealed is inconceivable and indescribable, but let us note a few of the features referred to:

- It is a multifaceted form, manifesting the appearance of many different living beings. The term *vishva-rupa* literally means 'having all things as its form'.
- Thus, it has many faces, mouths, and eyes. If Krishna is the self of all beings, then all beings are a part of his form as displayed here.
- This form gives off a tremendous effulgence as bright as a thousand suns.
- This form contains the entire world. Hence, the world we inhabit is itself a Deity, it is a form of God.

DESCRIPTION OF
THE VISHVA-RUPA

15. Arjuna said: I see all the gods in your body, O Lord, and the entire host of different living beings. I see Brahma, the lord, who remains seated on a lotus, and all the *rishis* and celestial serpents.

16. With so many arms, bellies, mouths, and eyes, I see you with this unlimited form that spreads everywhere. There is no end, no middle, and no beginning as I behold you, for you are the Lord of the world and the world is your body (*vishva rupa*).

17. I see you with a crown, club, and disc, and your fiery effulgence illuminates all directions. I see you everywhere, though you are so difficult to look upon, for the blazing light of fire and sun spreads beyond measure.

18. You are the Supreme Akshara (undeteriorating), that which must be known. You are the ultimate abode of this world. You are unfading (*avyaya*), the guardian of the eternal dharma, and I regard you as the eternal *purusha*.

19. You are without beginning, middle, or end, and have limitless power. You have innumerable arms, and the sun and moon are your eyes. I see you with blazing fire as you heat this entire world with your radiance.

20. From the heavens to the earth, the whole sky is pervaded by you alone, and so are all the directions. After seeing this wonderful and yet terrible form of yours, the three worlds are trembling, O Mahatma.

21. These hosts of celestial beings are entering into you; some are afraid and praise you with folded palms. The hosts of *rishis* and perfect beings (*siddhas*) proclaim the sound *svasti*, and glorify you with hymns and words of praise.

22. The Rudras, Adityas, Vasus, Sadhyas, Vishva-devas, Ash-vins, Maruts, ancestors, Gandharvas, Yakshas, Asuras, and Siddhas are all beholding you in utter astonishment.

23. This great form of yours has many mouths and eyes, O mighty one, and has many arms, thighs, and feet. It has many bellies and many fearsome teeth. After seeing this form, the worlds tremble in fear, and so do I!

24. You are radiant and multicoloured, you touch the limit of the sky, your gaping mouths are wide open, and your wonderful eyes are blazing. Seeing you thus, my inner self is trembling with fear; I cannot maintain my steadiness or composure, O Vishnu.

25. Seeing your mouths with their terrible teeth, which are like the flames at the end of the world, I can no longer recognise the directions or find any peace. Be merciful, O Lord of the gods, abode of the world.

26. All these sons of Dhritarashtra, along with this host of the kings of the earth, as well as Bhishma, Drona, the *suta*'s son, and the great warriors of our army as well

27. Are all rushing forth and entering your mouths with those terrible teeth that are so terrifying. Some of them can be seen caught between those teeth with their heads being crushed.

28. As the many currents of the rivers rush with force and flow towards the ocean, so these heroes amongst men enter your blazing mouths.

29. As moths meet with destruction by rapidly entering a blazing fire, so the people of the world rush forward and meet with destruction by entering your mouths.

30. Devouring the worlds from all sides, you lick them all up with your blazing mouths. Having filled the entire universe with its energy, this terrible effulgence of yours is scorching everything, O Vishnu.

31. Tell me who you are with this fearful form. I bow down to you, be merciful, O greatest of the gods. I wish to know you, the primordial being. I cannot comprehend the acts you are engaged in.

Here, Arjuna describes the vision he is now able to behold and expresses his sense of awe and indeed terror at this dramatic manifestation of divine potency. He is both thrilled and intimidated by what he sees.

The deities who are absent from the vishva-rupa

All the gods are contained within the body of the Deity, including Brahma, who is seen in his usual position seated on a lotus flower; however, there is no mention of either Vishnu or Shiva. In some translations, the word *isham*, 'the Lord', is taken as a reference to Shiva rather than Brahma, but this seems unlikely as the whole phrase reads *brahmanam isham kamalasana-stham*, so that *isham* appears in between 'Brahma' and 'situated on his lotus seat'. We know that Krishna is Vishnu himself (and Arjuna addresses him as such in verses 24 and 30), so Vishnu is outside and beyond the world, but the description here raises questions as to why Shiva is not named as a part of the *vishva-rupa* and indeed about the Bhagavad-gita's awareness of Shiva.

Arjuna's reaction to the vision of the divine

In verses 23–25, Arjuna describes his reaction to the vision he sees before him, and it is nothing like the beatific joy mentioned in Chapter 6 in relation to the *yogin*'s realisation of the *atman*. The form he sees is not benign; rather, it is fearsome, destructive, and terrifying, and Arjuna is overwhelmed by a sense of terror and confusion. His realisation of God is not a blissful experience but a vision of the awesome power and destructive aspect of the divine.

In this sense, the vision he sees is somewhat related to the usual representation of the character of Shiva. It also reflects the true nature of the world, which, on the one hand, provides for the needs of living beings but, at the same time, has a destructive force that takes away the life of every one of us.

> *Does the form described here represent any of*
> *the teachings about the nature of God that*
> *Krishna has delivered previously?*

The form displayed here does indeed correspond to the philosophical or theological descriptions presented at the beginning of Chapter 7 and then again at the start of Chapter 9. In 9.4, it was said, *maya tatam idam sarvam jagad avyakta-murtina*, 'I pervade this whole world through my non-manifest form'. Now, the *avyakta-murti* (non-manifest form) has become a *vyakta-murti* (manifest form), and we see what Krishna was talking about earlier.

A preordained destiny

In verses 26–30, Arjuna particularly notes that his three most dangerous adversaries – Bhishma, Drona, and Karna – are being destroyed by the teeth of the Deity. Hence, he need have no concern about the outcome of the battle, for their fate is already sealed due to the power of God. There is much significance in this part of the vision, for it indicates that the outcome of the battle is even now decided, a point Krishna will refer to when he speaks to Arjuna about his identity.

> *How does Arjuna refer to Karna in verse 26?*

Arjuna refers to Karna as *suta-putra*, 'the son of a *suta*', a rather contemptuous term that refers to Karna's upbringing as the son of a charioteer. In fact, Karna was the son of Kunti and Aditya, the sun god, but the Pandavas were unaware that he was their elder brother and had despised him for his low birth. It is perhaps noteworthy that in verse 34 below, Krishna refers to him by name, though of course this could just be due the requirements of the verse metre.

TIME, THE GREAT DESTROYER OF THE WORLDS

32. The Lord said: I am all-powerful time that brings destruction to the world. My activity here is to put an end to these worlds. Even without you, none of these warriors assembled here in battle array will survive.

33. Therefore, arise and win renown. Defeat your enemies and enjoy a prosperous kingdom. These warriors are already slain by me, and you should merely be my instrument, Savyasachin.

34. Drona, Bhishma, Jayadratha, Karna, and the other heroic warriors have already been killed by me, so you may slay them without hesitation. Fight, and you will defeat your enemies in the battle.

Here, Krishna responds to Arjuna's question by stating that he is time, the great destroyer of worlds (and we might note that Oppenheimer said that he immediately recalled this verse and verse 12 when he witnessed the first explosion of the atomic bomb). Where Krishna says, *kalo 'smi* ('I am time'), we might equally translate it as 'I am destiny'. In other words, the allotted time has arrived for the deaths of all these warriors, and their fate is unavoidable. Arjuna may think of himself as the killer, but in fact he is just the instrument of destiny, which is perhaps another way of saying the instrument of God who takes the form of destiny.

So, this vision and this passage relate back to the very beginning of the Bhagavad-gita, in which Arjuna was lamenting and refusing to kill his friends, respected elders, and close relatives. Now, however, the truth is apparent; whether Arjuna decides to fight or not fight is irrelevant. These warriors will die not because of Arjuna's decision but because it is their destiny, or perhaps because it is the will of God.

Now, this part of the vision raises a very fundamental question about free will and determinism. Do we have any choices about the actions we perform and the results our actions yield, or are the outcomes already determined by the unbreakable force of destiny? This latter view does certainly seem to be the conclusion of this passage, but we should perhaps be a little cautious. Let us not forget that the Battle of Kurukshetra is not an ordinary event, for the Supreme Deity himself has appeared there as an *avatar* in order to ensure that the desired result is achieved. So, it may be that the vision of the outcome reflects these special circumstances rather than indicating a law of universal determinism in which free will is wholly absent.

ARJUNA'S PRAYERS

35. Samjaya said: After hearing Keshava's words, Kiritin joined his palms and paid his respects whilst trembling in fear. He then addressed Krishna again in stuttering tones, bowing down in a mood of awe and fear.

36. Arjuna said: As is appropriate, Hrishikesha, the world is delighted by your glorification and becomes joyful. Whilst the terrified *rakshasas* flee in various directions, the hosts of perfect beings bow down before you.

37. Why should they not bow before you, O Mahatma, for you are greater even than Brahma, the original creator of the world. You are the unlimited lord of the gods, the abode of the world; you are the *aksharam* (that which does not decay); you are being and non-being and that which lies beyond both.

38. You are the original Deity, the primeval *purusha*. You are the ultimate resting place of this world. You are the knower and that which is to be known, the supreme, the abode. This entire world is pervaded by you, O you of limitless form.

39. You are Vayu, Yama, Agni, Varuna, the Moon, Prajapati, and the great-grandfather. I bow to you, I bow to you a thousand times over, and then still, I bow to you once again.

40. I bow to you from the front, I bow from behind, and I bow from all sides, for you are everything. Your power is unlimited and your might cannot be measured. It is you alone who reaches into all things, and therefore, you are that which is all things.

41. Thinking of you as a friend, I spoke presumptuously, saying, 'O Krishna, O Yadava, O my friend'. I was unaware of your greatness, and I did this because I did not understand, or perhaps out of affection.

42. Making jokes, I behaved improperly towards you whilst we were passing time together, resting, sitting, or eating, sometimes when we were alone and sometimes when others were present, Achyuta. Now, I beg your forgiveness, for you are beyond all measure.

43. You are the father of the moving and non-moving beings, you are the object of worship for the world, and you are the greatest teacher. No one is your equal, so how could anyone in the three worlds be greater than you? Your power is unrivalled.

44. Therefore, I bow down to you and prostrate my body. I seek your grace, for you are the worshipful Lord. Please tolerate my conduct, O Lord, as a father to a son, a friend to a friend, or a lover to his beloved.

45. I was thrilled to see this form that was never previously seen, but my mind is disturbed by fear. Now, show me

that other form, O Lord. Show me mercy, O lord of the gods, abode of the world.

46. I now wish to see you with a crown, a club, and a disc in your hand. O thousand-armed one, O Vishvamurti, please now assume once more your four-armed form.

Now, Arjuna is completely overwhelmed by the vision he has seen. It was displayed at his request, but the effect has been altogether too much for him to bear. Krishna is a benign, personal Deity with whom Arjuna had developed a close relationship based on love and affection, but this manifestation of God is something different. Arjuna's response is therefore simply to prostrate himself before the Deity, to beg for His mercy, and then to ask that the form he is beholding be withdrawn. We might note the following points:

Here, again, we see that Arjuna is terrified rather than inspired by the manifestation of the divine he has been granted a vision of. In fact, he is barely able to speak, so great is his terror.

Verse 39 can be regarded as significant. Here, we find Arjuna asserting that the Vedic gods are in fact Krishna himself, presumably because he has seen all of them forming a part of the Deity's *vishva-rupa*. On this basis, one might regard the Vedic hymns that glorify these gods as being dedicated to the one Supreme Deity. Again, the Hindu tradition seems able to reconcile polytheism with monotheism.

Verse 40 contains the words *sarvam samapnoshi tato 'si sarvah*, 'You achieve all things, and therefore, you are all things'. This accords with the Upanishadic statement *sarvam khalv idam brahma*, 'This whole world is Brahman'. We might refer to Brahman as 'that which is all things', and here, we see that the same definition can be applied to the Deity of the Bhagavad-gita. And if we wanted to get technical in our use of language, we might say that the Gita is able to reconcile monotheism with monism.

Perhaps the most significant point here, however, is the way in which Arjuna now regrets his previous intimate behaviour with Krishna. A significant idea in devotional Hinduism, and in the Bhagavata Purana in particular, is the way that a devotee develops this mood of intimate love with God and with Krishna in particular. But here, we see that this mood of intimate love is incompatible with the fear of God that arises from realisation of his full awesome potency. The Bhagavata Purana narrates a story about Krishna as a child in which he is accused by his friends of eating dirt. When his mother, Yashoda, looks inside to Krishna's mouth, she sees the *vishva-rupa* within the child, but the vision is immediately withdrawn, as it threatens the intimacy of the loving relationship between Yashoda and Krishna. In the same way, we see here how the closeness of Arjuna's relationship with Krishna is undermined by this inescapable revelation of the power of God.

In the last two verses, Arjuna asks Krishna to withdraw this form and show him instead the four-armed form with helmet, club, and disc. This clearly refers to the usual iconic representation of the four-armed Vishnu form. The identity of Krishna with Vishnu is not taken any further by the Gita, and indeed, there is nothing to suggest that Krishna responds to this request of Arjuna. However, we have a clear indication here that Krishna is indeed accepted by the Gita as an *avatar* of Vishnu.

KRISHNA REASSUMES HIS HUMAN FORM

47. The Lord said: It was as an act of grace, Arjuna, that I displayed that supreme form to you by means of my own powers of yoga. That form is filled with energy, it is universal, it is unlimited and primeval. I have never displayed it to anyone but yourself.

48. Not through the Veda, *yajña*, recitation, charity, ritual, or harsh austerity can I be seen in this form by anyone other than you in the world of men, O hero of the Kurus.

49. Do not tremble with fear, and do not be bewildered after seeing this form of mine, which is so fearful. Let your fears be dispelled and let your mind be contented; now, behold once more that form of mine.

50. Samjaya said: After speaking to Arjuna in this way, Vasudeva again revealed to him his own form. That great soul consoled the frightened Arjuna by again assuming his benign form.

Here, Krishna accepts Arjuna's request and agrees to withdraw the *vishva-rupa* that has appeared to be so fearful. There are just a few points here we might note:

Where Krishna refers to 'yoga' in verse 47, I think we must take the word as meaning 'mystical powers' rather than 'religious or meditational practice'.

Verse 47 also states that this form had never been displayed before, but it is widely known that Krishna had previously displayed the *vishva-rupa* in the assembly of the Kurus when Duryodhana and his followers were planning to make Krishna a prisoner (Chapter 129 of the *Mahabharata*'s fifth book, the *Udyoga-parvan*). However, the revelation described there is not on the same scale as that perceived by Arjuna, and one must therefore presume that this was only a partial manifestation.

Verse 48 gives a list of the means that are inadequate to allow the practitioner a vision of this form, but it does not say how such a vision may be gained; this, however, is made clear before the end of the chapter.

The two forms of the Deity are referred to as *rupam ghoram* (v. 49), a frightful form, and *saumya-vapu* (v. 50), a benign form. Despite Arjuna's apparent request in verse 46 for a vision of the Vishnu form, the *saumya-vapu* seems to be Krishna in his more usual human appearance. Thus, we can see that the Supreme Deity can be both ferocious (*ugra*) and benign (*saumya*).

Bhakti Is the Key
to Knowledge of God

51. Arjuna said: Seeing this benign human form of yours, Janardana, my mind is now at peace and I have regained my normal condition.

52. The Lord said: It is very hard to gain a vision of this form of mine that you have seen. Even the gods are always longing for a vision of this form.

53. Not through the Vedas, austerity, charity, or sacrificial offerings is it possible to see me in the way that you have seen me here.

54. Only through undivided devotion, Arjuna, is it possible to know me and to see me in this form and indeed to enter into me, Paramtapa.

55. One who performs his deeds for me, regards me as supreme, becomes my devotee, remains free of attachments, and has no hatred for any living being will come to me, Pandava.

In these final verses of the chapter, Krishna tells of the means by which the realisation of God's presence can be obtained.

What form (rupa) is Krishna referring to in verse 52?

It could be that Krishna is here referring to the form Arjuna has described in verse 51, the *manushya-rupa*, the human form that is *saumya*, or benign. This, however, seems unlikely. Almost certainly, Krishna is here discussing the *vishva-rupa*, although after Arjuna's experience we might wonder as to why the gods are so desirous of having that realisation. The point is that what Arjuna has been shown is the presence of God within the world, something which is usually *avyakta*, or invisible to mundane eyes, even those of the gods. But this vision is equivalent to the spiritual realisation that brings liberation from rebirth.

Gaining a vision of the divine form

Verse 53 repeats the point made in verse 48 to the effect that most religious practices are ineffective in leading one to the highest stage of realisation. In verse 54, however, we are told that this vision can be attained through *bhakti*, devotion to the Deity. Here, we might recall verse 3 of the fourth chapter, in which Krishna promised Arjuna that the greatest secret would be revealed to him because he was a devotee of Krishna.

The final phrase of verse 54

Verse 54 is rather unusual in the Gita because of the way in which it describes the attainment of liberation from rebirth. Here, Krishna says that through undeviating devotion, one is able to know him (*jñatum*), to see him (*drashtum*), and to enter him (*praveshtum*). This idea of *moksha* as entering into the Deity is found in other passages of the *Mahabharata*, but in the Gita it is found only in this verse and perhaps in 18.55.

The qualities of a devotee as referred to in verse 55

Four qualities are noted here: (i) performing works for Krishna (*mat-karma-krit*), which, again, equates *karma-yoga* with *bhakti*, (ii) being dedicated to Krishna (*mat-parama*), (iii) being free of attachment (*sanga-varjita*), and (iv) being free of enmity towards any living being (*nirvairah sarva-bhuteshu*); in other words, practising the virtue of *ahimsa* – not harming.

CONCLUSION:
A SUMMARY OF CHAPTER 11

Chapter 11 is very different from the other chapters of the Bhagavad-gita, as it contains little by way of instruction from Krishna to Arjuna. Instead, we have a revelation of Krishna's divine identity, Arjuna's description of the form he sees, and then the prayers he offers to this manifestation of God. The chapter opens with Arjuna asking if he can directly behold the glory of God, which is invisibly present within this world. Krishna agrees to this request and grants Arjuna the higher vision by means of which the presence of God can be directly perceived. Arjuna then describes the awesome vision he sees, with its manifold forms and blazing effulgence. Within that form, he also sees the future outcome of the battle about to take place at Kurukshetra and the deaths of the mighty warriors who are assembled there on both sides. Krishna reveals that he is time or destiny, which takes away the lives of all beings. It is he who controls life and death, and as a warrior, Arjuna is just an instrument in the inevitable progression of time. In a mood of confusion, fear, and awe, Arjuna then offers prayers to Krishna, praising his omnipotence and regretting his previous familiar conduct. At Arjuna's request, Krishna withdraws the *vishva-rupa* and reassumes his benign human form. He concludes by explaining that devotion to God is the only way by which this extraordinary vision of the divine presence can be gained.

Those who venerate with full faith the immortal teaching based on dharma which I have spoken here, who are dedicated to me and are my devotees, are dearly loved by me. —12.20

CHAPTER 12

After the *vishva-rupa* is withdrawn, the Bhagavad-gita's teachings on the nature of God and devotion to God are almost complete, though Krishna does briefly return to this topic in the chapters that follow. In effect, the revelation of the *vishva-rupa* does not amount to a new doctrine but rather a demonstration of the philosophical truths about the nature of God presented in Chapters 7, 9, and 10. We will recall, however, that in the last two verses of Chapter 11, Krishna made the point that the higher vision through which the presence of the Deity can be perceived is obtained only through devotion. At the start of Chapter 12, Arjuna picks up on that point and seeks clarification over the efficacy of the two paths Krishna has been describing, the way of pure *bhakti* and the realisation of spiritual knowledge. We may recall that in Chapter 9, verses 14 and 15, Krishna described these as the two ways by which *mahatmas*, great souls, dedicate themselves to him. And yet, at the end of Chapter 11, Krishna mentioned only *bhakti* as the means of perceiving the *vishva-rupa*. So now, Arjuna wants some clarification of that point and in particular a definitive judgement as to which of the two paths is superior. This question provides the starting point for the final phase of the Bhagavad-gita's instruction on devotion to God, in which the emphasis is placed on the effectiveness of *bhakti* in bringing the highest spiritual goals and also the mood of intimate love that is developed between the Deity and the devotee. And so here, again, we have an important passage that establishes the basis for the devotional spirituality that is such a salient feature of Hinduism today.

BHAKTI OR JÑANA, WHICH IS
THE SUPERIOR PATH?

1. Arjuna said: Between those devotees who dedicate themselves to you, being constantly engaged in the way you have described, and those who revere the non-manifest *akshara* feature, who have the superior understanding of yoga?

2. The Lord said: In My opinion, those who fix their minds on me, who constantly engage in serving me and who possess absolute faith are engaged in the best way possible.

3. But those who dedicate themselves to the non-deteriorating (*akshara*), indeterminate, non-manifest feature, which is present everywhere, is unknowable, and is situated in the transcendent realm, unmoving and constant,

4. Who control their senses and who are equal-minded in all ways, also attain me, delighting as they do in the welfare of all beings.

5. But there is greater difficulty involved for those whose thoughts adhere to the non-manifest feature. For embodied beings, the way to the non-manifest feature is one of suffering.

Looking back over the Bhagavad-gita, we can see that Krishna first emphasised *karma-yoga* and showed how the mood of renunciation it engenders leads to the acquisition of spiritual knowledge, the *jñana* that can be attained through the yoga of meditation. Then, from Chapter 7, Krishna turned to discuss the way of *bhakti*, concluding that this is the means of gaining higher realisation and liberation from rebirth. So now, Arjuna wishes Krishna to state clearly which of these two spiritual paths is superior. He wants a judgement made between them, just as he did at the start of Chapter 5 when he asked about *karma-yoga* and renunciation of action.

*Which of the two paths does
Krishna judge to be superior?*

Krishna is quite clear in the answer he gives to Arjuna's question; it is the devotees referred to at the end of Chapter 11 who are *yuktattama*, engaged in the best form of practice. This verdict is one that might surprise many Hindus, for it is often presumed that *bhakti* is a lesser path to be followed by those who lack the capacity to pursue the higher goal of *jñana*. Here, however, Krishna gives an alternative view. We might note how Shankaracharya comments on these verses. He points out that the *jñanins* have already achieved realised knowledge, and so they do not need to engage in any form of practice or yoga, and it is for this reason that Krishna describes the devotees as the *yuktattama*. This is a brilliant response, but one may have some doubts as to whether it is actually what Krishna means.

*What aspect of the deity is sought by those
who seek the all-pervasive, akshara feature?*

To some extent, the answer here is given in the question. The devotees focus their attention on a personal God who has a specific form and identity, but the *jñanins* seek to realise the formless, inconceivable divinity designated as Brahman in the Upanishads. These two aspects of the divine are frequently referred to as *sa-guna brahman* (*brahman* with qualities) and *nirguna brahman* (*brahman* without qualities), and the commonly held view is that *nirguna brahman* is the higher, ultimate feature of God. It is important to recognise that the Bhagavad-gita accepts that there are two aspects to the divine nature: (1) as the formless, inconceivable, all-pervasive Brahman, and (2) as the personal Deity who is the object of loving devotion for the *bhaktas*. The rather surprising feature of the teachings here is that Krishna insists that worship of a personal

Deity is the superior path, and hence, we must conclude that the Gita is primarily a *bhakti-shastra*.

The equivocal nature of Krishna's answer

In making his verdict, Krishna does not adopt a line of discourse that praises one form of spirituality and simultaneously condemns another. In this sense, the Gita is an archetypal Hindu text that allows and embraces diversity in a manner that is fundamentally tolerant. It accepts that both ways lead to the same the goal, and hence, both are approved of. In verse 5, Krishna seems to explain the reason for the decision he has given. It is not that *bhakti* is inherently superior to *jñana*, it is just that it is easier to practice, and here, we might recall Krishna's words at the start of Chapter 9, when he said that this spiritual path is *su-sukham kartum*, very joyful or very easy to perform. And as Arjuna suggested at the end of Chapter 6, non-devotional forms of spirituality can be very difficult. So it is not that *bhakti* is inherently better than *jñana*, it is just that the highest goal is more easily attained by this means.

The reason why it is easier is now explained in the next two verses.

THE GRACE OF GOD –
KRISHNA SAVES

6. But for those who are devoted to me, who surrender all their actions to me, who worship me and meditate on me through single-pointed yoga,
7. I become without delay the deliverer from the ocean of death and rebirth, Partha, for their consciousness is absorbed in me.

Here, Krishna explains why it is that *bhakti* is a superior religious path to follow. It is more effective in leading the aspirant to liberation from rebirth because it invokes the grace of the Deity, as was explained earlier in Chapter 10, verse 11. It is very hard to achieve this highest goal alone, but for Krishna it is easily done, and he personally intervenes on behalf of the devotees to ensure their liberation. In verse 7, Krishna refers to himself as the *sam-ud-dhartri*, 'the one who lifts up'. Who does he lift up? The devotees described in verse 6. Where does he lift them from? *Mrityu-samsara-sagarat*, from the ocean of death and rebirth. Where does he lift them up to? That is not stated, although we might here refer to verses 54 and 55 of the previous chapter, in which Krishna said that the devotees enter him, *praveshtum mam*, and go to him, *mam eti*. So here, we have a Hindu doctrine of grace, which must sound very familiar to Christians. We often see the words 'Jesus Saves' displayed outside churches, and here, we see the same idea from a Hindu source. With one slight difference, as here, it is 'Krishna saves'.

DIFFERENT TYPES
OF DEVOTION

8. Set your mind on me alone; let your understanding enter into me. You will then dwell in me alone, of this there is no doubt.

9. If you are not able to hold your consciousness steadily upon me, then you should seek to attain me by means of regulated yoga practice, O Dhanamjaya.

10. If you are unable even to undertake this regulated practice, then dedicate yourself to working on my behalf. By performing acts on my behalf, you can still achieve success.

11. And if you are unable to undertake the practice of yoga dedicated to me, then gain self-control and practise the renunciation of the fruits of all action.

12. Knowledge is better than regulated practice, and meditation is superior to knowledge. Renouncing the fruits of action is better than meditation, for from renunciation comes unending peace.

In verse 8, Krishna gives instruction again as to the devotional practices that will invoke the saving grace referred to in 6 and 7. It is all about being constantly absorbed in thinking of Krishna, and this might be through yoga and meditation, as was discussed in Chaper 8, or it might just be a natural part of love of God, for the mind inevitably gravitates towards anyone who is an object of our love. This would seem to be the indication in verse 9 of Chapter 10. And in the later part of this chapter, it is the idea of love of God that is brought to the fore.

The remaining verses of this passage give alternative practices that can be taken up by those who find that they are unable to fix their minds on Krishna as directed by verse 8. Here, we are reminded of Arjuna's objection to *dhyana-yoga* at the end of Chapter 6, and the way in which yoga and *bhakti* are drawn together into one system in Chapter 8. It seems that the fixing of the mind and intellect on Krishna, mentioned in verse 8, are more likely to be a part of the yoga of meditation than absorption based on love. As we have seen, this yoga is very difficult to practice, so here, Krishna offers a list of alternatives in a progressive order. Here they are:

1. Fixing the mind and intellect on Krishna,
2. regulated yoga exercises,
3. dedicating one's work to Krishna,
4. renouncing the results of action as an offering to Krishna.

What we seem to have here is a list that gives a reverse summation of the main points of spiritual practice that Krishna has hitherto presented. The ultimate goal is fixing the mind on Krishna, and this seems very close to the type of yoga practice taught in Chapters

6 and 8, where the final goal is realising the *atman* within one's own being. And because Krishna is the inner self of all beings, this practice is almost identical to *bhakti*. If one finds that one's mind wanders, then one must keep up the practice until it is controlled, as was explained in Chapter 6, verse 36, where Krishna responded to Arjuna's objection. However, if one is unable to engage in this time-consuming regular practice, then there is still the process of *karma-yoga*, which here seems to be divided into two phases. Verse 11 appears to refer to the *karma-yoga* we noted in Chapters 2, 3, and 4, which centres on the renunciation of attachment to the fruits of action. Above that, however, is the practice referred to in verse 10, where *karma-yoga* becomes imbued with a mood of *bhakti* and working without attachment is achieved by dedicating this work to Krishna. Hence, we have a reinforcement of the understanding that the Bhagavad-gita as a whole presents a progressive spiritual path that leads from one step to the next.

Verse 12 is one that has proved to be problematic for both ancient and modern commentators, as it seems to reverse the order of priority given in the previous four verses. Various solutions have been suggested by different commentators, and I do not propose to go into these in detail, as it is the subject for a detailed verse by verse analysis rather than a general study of the Gita's teachings such as this one.

THE QUALITIES
OF THE DEVOTEE

13. He has no hatred for any living being, he shows good-will and compassion; he has no sense of possession and no pride, he remains equal in misery and joy, and he has endurance;

14. He is always contented, he is a *yogin* possessing self-control; he is firm in his commitment and he absorbs his mind and intelligence in me: such a devotee is loved by me.

15. No one in the world has fear of him, and he does not fear anyone in the world; he feels no elation, distress, fear, or passion; such a person is loved by me.

16. He has no hankerings, he is pure, expert, indifferent, free of anxiety, and he has renounced his material endeavours; such a devotee is loved by me.

17. He does not rejoice or hate, lament, or hanker, and he has renounced both pleasing and vile objects; such a devoted one is loved by me.

18. He is equally disposed toward an enemy and a friend, he regards honour and contempt as the same, he has equal regard for heat and cold, and for joy and misery, and he has given up all attachment to the world.

19. He is unmoved by condemnation or praise, he is silent and satisfied with whatever befalls him, he has no permanent abode, and he is steady in his understanding; such a devoted one is loved by me.

20. Those who venerate with full faith the immortal teaching based on dharma which I have spoken here, who are dedicated to me and are my devotees, are dearly loved by me.

The second half of the twelfth chapter provides a description of the devotee whom Krishna delivers from the ocean of death and rebirth. There are a number of questions raised by this passage:

*What can be noticed about the description
of the devotee in these verses?*

The verses here give an extensive list of the qualities to be found in a person designated by Krishna as *mad-bhakta* ('my devotee' or 'one who is devoted to me'), and most, if not all, of these refer to the mood of detachment from the world exhibited by the devotee. Moreover, very little is said about devotional sentiment or devotional practice here; it is all about renunciation of desire, remaining equal despite good and bad fortune, having no enmity towards any living being, and being unmoved by praise or blame. In fact, there is very little to distinguish between the devotee described here and the practitioner of *dhyana-yoga* discussed in Chapter 6. I think this is significant, particularly if we are aware of Shankaracharya's view that devotion to Krishna means dedication to the realisation of the *atman* within one's own being. Now, one might dismiss this interpretation as being just the view of an Advaitin trying to extract from a devotional text a meaning that does not contradict his own preconceptions. There may be some truth in such criticism, but there are certainly indications within the Gita that would support Shankara's view, and the way it describes *dhyana-yogins* and devotees who worship God in almost identical terms is certainly one such indication.

Krishna's attitude towards
the devotee and its significance

The Bhagavad-gita is in many ways a book of paradoxes. We have just discussed how the description of the devotee given here is virtually identical to the representation of the *yogin* who pursues realisation of the inner self, and yet alongside that we have a fundamental difference. Here, we find that Krishna repeatedly uses the words (with minor differences) *yo mad-bhaktah sa me priyah*, 'one who is my devotee is loved by me'. This ties in with the notion of compassion given in 10.11 as the reason why Krishna delivers his devotees. The answer is simple – it is because he loves them. Here, the word *priya* is unequivocal and refers to a relationship of reciprocal love between one individual and another. Hence, this word could not be applied to the *yogin* who attains knowledge of the *atman*, for his joy comes from realisation of his own self-identity. But in this case, there is Krishna as one person and the devotee who is another, and between them there is a relationship of love which motivates the Deity to bestow his grace so that the devotee is freed from death and rebirth. We will find this important idea restated even more emphatically at the end of the Gita, in verse 66 of the Chapter 18. This notion of divine love comes to play a dominant role in later Hinduism, but as is so often the case, we can trace the origins of the different strands of Hindu spirituality back to the Bhagavad-gita.

CONCLUSION:
A SUMMARY OF CHAPTER 12

Chapter 12 draws to a conclusion the teachings that began at the beginning of the seventh chapter focussing on the nature of God, the relationship between God and the world, and the worship of God as a means of achieving liberation from rebirth. At the start of Chapter 13, we encounter another dramatic turn in Krishna's pattern of teaching as he moves abruptly on to a radically different topic. The twelfth chapter began with a question from Arjuna that sought a judgement between the two forms of religion mentioned in verses 14 and 15 of Chapter 9: direct worship of a personal Deity and realisation of the all-pervading presence of God through realised knowledge. Krishna replies that worship of a personal God is a superior practice because realisation through knowledge is a difficult path beset with troubles. Worship is easier because this invokes the grace of God, as he intervenes to liberate his devotee from the ocean of birth and death. Hence, one should fix the mind constantly on Krishna, but if this proves to be impossible, other forms of spiritual practice are recommended that can lead one gradually towards this highest stage. In the final phase of the chapter, Krishna describes the attributes of one who becomes his devotee, placing particular emphasis on renunciation of worldly desires and detachment from the fluctuating fortunes we experience in life. Here, also, he makes the point that the devotee is an object of love for the Deity; it is not just a formal relationship, as between a king and his servant, for there is emotional attachment underlying the devotional mood. Therefore, the point is made, *yo mad-bhaktah sa me priyah*: 'one who is my devotee is an object of my love'.

Whatever a person's state of existence, if he thus understands
purusha *(spirit), as well as* prakriti *(matter)*
with its gunas, he never takes birth again. — 13.23

CHAPTER 13

In the final chapters of the Bhagavad-gita, Krishna branches out from his earlier areas of concern and introduces a number of different topics so that each chapter tends to form a discrete unit of its own rather than there being a consistent line of discussion. Chapter 13 focusses primarily on the distinction between the self and matter, Chapter 14 explores the concept of the three gunas, Chapter 15 turns again to the presence of God within the world, and Chapter 16 looks at the nature and fate of evil-minded persons. Chapters 17 and 18 focus primarily on an analysis of human life in relation to the influence of the three gunas, before Krishna concludes with a brief recapitulation of the main ideas he has sought to emphasise in the text as a whole. All these topics have some connection with the main themes explored previously by the Gita, but they are not exactly central to its primary teachings and so are probably best regarded as 'supplementary observations'. So, let us begin this area of study with a look at Chapter 13 and its discussion of body and soul.

In some versions of the Sanskrit text, Chapter 13 opens with a question from Arjuna about the *kshetra* and *kshetrajña*, the domain (literally, 'field') and the knower of the domain. In Shankaracharya's text, however, and in the Critical Edition of the *Mahabharata*, this verse is omitted and Krishna launches into the topic without any prior prompting. It is perhaps because of the abrupt change of direction that some early editors found it necessary to add a question from Arjuna to give some explanation as to why Krishna should introduce a new and different topic so suddenly. The *kshetra* is the body and the *kshetrajña* is the soul – these terms are found in other passages of the *Mahabharata* in which expositions of Samkhya teaching are to be found. Samkhya literally means 'enumeration' or perhaps 'analysis', and the central idea is to analyse the elements that jointly comprise the material manifestation and then to differentiate them from the soul within the body. Normally in Samkhya texts, the words *prakriti* and *purusha* are used to designate matter and spirit, but *kshetra* and *kshetrajña* are not uncommon synonyms. The ultimate aim of Samkhya is to attain the realisation *anyo 'ham* ('I am different') in the sense that 'my true identity is different from the body and mind that are products of *prakriti*'. Throughout the Gita, Krishna draws repeatedly on Samkhya terminology and concepts in the explanations he gives to Arjuna, but in these final six chapters, the text is particularly influenced by Samkhya ideas. The thirteenth chapter is in some ways quite a complicated one, but it does divide itself up into neatly defined component parts that are given their own headings by the text itself. The first of these sections relates to the domain, the *kshetra* that is our material embodiment. We are then informed about *jñana*, knowledge, and then *jñeya*, that which we must come to know, and finally, we move on to the division between *prakriti* and *purusha* that is the salient feature of Samkhya discourse. Perhaps surprisingly in light of what we have just been reading, there is little suggestion here of any role being played by a Supreme Deity in the overall analysis of existence.

KSHETRA AND KSHETRAJÑA

1. The Lord said: This body, Kaunteya, is referred to as the *kshetra* (field); those who understand such matters speak of he who has knowledge of the field as the *kshetrajña*, the knower of the field.

2. You should also understand that I am the *kshetrajña* present within all the *kshetras*, Bharata. Knowledge of the

>   *kshetra* and *kshetrajña* is knowledge indeed; that is my opinion.
>
> 3. So, listen to me now as I explain briefly about the *kshetra* and what it is like, about the transformations it undergoes, and about which one of them comes from the other. I will also explain who he is and what his powers are.
>
> 4. This subject has been sung about by the *rishis* in many ways in various hymns of the Veda. It has also been explained through reasoned conclusions in the aphorisms of the *Brahma Sutra*.

Here, we see the introduction of the terms *kshetra* and *kshetrajña*, which are used in this chapter (but nowhere else) to designate the body and the soul. There are a couple of interesting points in this introductory passage that we should pay attention to.

In verse 2, Krishna indicates that he himself is the *kshetrajña* in all bodies. This could be taken simply as a reaffirmation of the statement of 10.19, *aham atma* ('I am the *atman*'), in which the Supreme Deity is identified with the self within each person. This would, of course, be very close to the teachings of the Upanishads that identify the individual soul with the Supreme Soul. There is, however, an alternative view that postulates the existence of a manifestation of Krishna alongside the individual soul, the *paramatman* existing alongside the *atman* and guiding it through the process of rebirth, as indicated by 18.61 and other verses. This view is favoured by Madhvacharya and followers of the Dvaita philosophy, who cannot accept any degree of identity between God and the individual soul. The debate between these two interpretations is one we will have to follow as the chapter progresses.

Verse 4 contains an interesting reference to the Brahma Sutra (Vedanta Sutra). The Brahma Sutra is well known as one of the principal texts of the Vedanta school and has been commented upon by all the major *acharyas*, including Shankara, Ramanuja, Madhva, and Vallabha. Most Western scholars believe that this work is a later composition, and reference to it here in the Gita has given rise to some debate. Zaehner comments, 'The Brahma Sutras . . . may not have existed (at the time of Gita) in their present form, but it seems more than likely that collections of aphorisms concerning the nature of *brahman*, that is, the nature of the Absolute, were in circulation already'.

EXPLANATION OF THE KSHETRA

5. The great elements, the sense of ego (*ahamkara*), the intellect (*buddhi*), matter in its non-manifest state (*avyakta*), the eleven senses, and the five objects they perceive,

6. Desire, loathing, joy, misery, the aggregate of all faculties, consciousness, and resolve; this, in short, is what is known as the *kshetra*, along with the transformations it undergoes.

Here, the chapter's topic-by-topic analysis begins with a discussion of the *kshetra*, the field that verse 1 explained was the body, or, in other words, the material component of a living being. We should note the following points here:

At the start of Chapter 7 (v. 4), *prakriti*, or matter, was said to consist of eight component elements: earth, water, fire, air, space, mind, intellect, and *ahamkara* (the sense of ego). In the Samkhya teachings found elsewhere in the *Mahabharata*, the analysis of *prakriti* in terms of its component elements is a typical feature of the discourse. The number of elements referred to does vary between speakers, but the number most usually arrived at is 24, and this is also the number given by the Samkhya Karika, the classical work on Samkhya composed by Ishvarakrishna.

Here, verse 5 gives a breakdown of the elements, and if we count them, we can see that the Bhagavad-gita confirms the existence of 24 elements of matter, as taught in classical Samkhya philosophy. The list is as follows:

- (1–5) the great elements (five in number: earth, water, fire, air, and space),
- (6) ahamkara,
- (7) intellect (*buddhi*),
- (8) the non-manifest state of matter (*avyakta*),
- (9–19) the eleven senses (usually listed as sight, hearing, touch, taste, smell, and mind as the senses of perception, and hands, feet, voice, anus, and genitals as the senses of action),
- (20–24) the five objects perceived by the senses (form/colour, sound, touch sensations, flavour, aroma).

Thus, we can see that the analysis of the *kshetra* given here in the Gita conforms to the usual enumeration of the elements of matter given by Samkhya teachings.

The list given in verse 6 is of the transformations experienced by the body as a result of external stimulation. Hence, this short passage concludes with the words *etat kshetram samasena sa-vikaram*: 'this in brief is the *kshetra* along with its transformations'.

EXPLANATION OF JÑANA

7. Avoiding pride and deceit, not harming, patience, honesty, serving the *acharya*, purity, steadfastness, self-control,

8. Detachment from the objects of the senses, being free of the sense of ego, perceiving the problem inherent in the misery of birth, death, old age, disease, and suffering,

9. Being without attachment and without affection for sons, wife, home, and other such things, always maintaining an equal disposition whatever happens, be it desirable or undesirable,

10. Maintaining undeviating devotion to me through yoga fixed on no other point, living in a deserted place, taking no pleasure in other people's company,

11. Constant dedication to the knowledge designated as *adhyatma* (relating to the *atman*) and perceiving the true object of knowledge; all this is said to be *jñana* (knowledge) and everything else is said to be *ajñana* (ignorance).

In these five verses, Chapter 13 gives us its definition of *jñana*, which is usually taken to mean knowledge or perhaps the realised knowledge that brings liberation from rebirth.

The Bhagavad-gita's definition of knowledge

This definition of *jñana* is probably not the one we would have given if asked, nor what we expected to read. It is unusual because knowledge is defined in terms of a state of detachment from the changing fortunes of the world, and a way of life based on the renunciation of material aspirations rather than an intellectual process. The implication here is that *jñana* is not just about what we know but is about our realisation of the truth and our perception of reality. Knowledge is not just the learning of a series of facts and figures but is reflected in the way we conduct ourselves and our attitude towards the world around us. When we realise the spiritual reality, that *jñana* becomes manifest in a sense of detachment from material things and a mood of indifference to the material manifestation. The lesson here is that *jñana* is not like the knowledge we can acquire from the education system, which may or may not affect the way we live, but is a realisation of the truth that will profoundly affect our whole mode of being.

The sort of person this teaching is aimed at

It would seem that the lifestyle and view of the world indicated here under the heading of *jñana* are for renunciants who have given up their existence in conventional society. In the Ramayana, we find that *dharma* is shown to include a deep sense of loyalty, commitment, and responsibility towards family members, but here, a different notion of proper conduct is indicated by the words *asaktam anabhishvangah putra-dara-grihadishu*, being without attachment or affection for children, wife, and home. One might question whether it is possible to function effectively as a family member if one has no sense of attachment or affection for one's sons and daughters or indeed if such a mood is truly desirable. The point here is that Hindu teachings cover a range of different understandings of *dharma*. In the Ramayana, the *dharma* that is revealed is the *dharma* for life in this world, but what is being discussed here is a *moksha dharma* that takes us wholly beyond this world into the realm of *adhyatma jñana*, absolute knowledge of the spirit and liberation from repeated birth and death.

The significance of verse 10

Verse 10 refers simultaneously to *bhakti*, devotion to the Deity, and yoga practice based on meditation. This link between two apparently divergent forms of Hindu spirituality is a feature of the Gita's discourse we have noted before and can at least partially be resolved by an understanding of the identity between Krishna, the Supreme Deity, and the *atman* that is our own innermost being.

Explanation of Jñeya, 'That Which Must Be Known'

12. I shall now speak about the *jñeya*, the object we must strive to know, for when this is known, one attains immortality. It is without beginning, it is the Supreme Brahman (or it is without beginning and dependent on me); it is said that it is neither existent nor non-existent.

13. Its hands and feet are everywhere, its eyes, heads, and mouths are everywhere, its ears are everywhere in the world; thus it remains, pervading all things.

14. It appears to have the attributes of senses, and yet, in truth, it is devoid of senses. It is without attachment, but it supports all things; it is free of the *gunas*, and yet it experiences the *gunas*.

15. It is both outside and within the living beings; it moves and yet it is unmoving. Because of its subtle nature, it is hard to know; it is far away but very close as well.

16. It appears to be divided up within different living beings, and yet it remains undivided. This sustainer of living beings is the *jñeya*, that which must be known; it devours them, and it brings them into being as well.

17. It is the light of luminous objects and is said to be beyond the darkness. It is knowledge, the object that should be known, and it is accessible through knowledge; it is situated within the heart of all beings.

18. Now, *kshetra*, *jñana*, and *jñeya* have all been briefly explained. After realising this truth, my devotee becomes ready to achieve my state of existence.

We have just been given a definition of the process of knowing that rests on a mood of detachment from the world, or, in other words, a process of knowing that enables us to see the world and our own existence in a wholly different light so that we no longer live and relate to the world around us in the way that we did before. And if our lifestyle and attitude are unchanged, then we may possess learning, but we do not possess knowledge. Now, in this passage, we are instructed about the *jñeyam*, the object on which the knowledge focusses, literally, 'that which is to be known'.

So, what is it that we must know? Here are its characteristics listed:

- It has no beginning
- It is the supreme Brahman
- It is neither existing nor not existing
- Its eyes, ears, etc. are everywhere
- It appears to have senses, but is without senses
- It is not attached to anything
- It is the support of everything
- It is untouched by the *gunas*
- It experiences the *gunas*
- It is within us and outside of us as well
- It is hard to perceive
- It is both far away and very close
- It appears to be divided in different living beings, but is undivided
- It sustains living beings
- It destroys and creates living beings
- It is the origin of light in the world
- It is always beyond the darkness
- It is knowledge and it is the object of knowledge
- It is within the hearts of all beings

The above list shows how close this passage is to the teachings of the Upanishads, and on the basis of Upanishadic doctrine, I think it is reasonable to state that the *jñeya* is the *atman* within each of us, which is identical with Brahman and with Krishna himself. There is also a line of continuity to be detected here with the manifestation of the *vishva-rupa* in Chapter 11.

Let us take each verse in turn in our analysis of this significant and rather difficult passage:

Verse 12: Here, the classical Vedantic idea of *moksha* through realised knowledge is restated. The second line of the verse is problematic because it can be read in two different ways, either *anadimat param brahma*, or *anadi-mat-param brahma*. In the former, the suffix *mat* means 'being, or possessing the quality', and is added to the word *anadi* to mean 'possessing the quality of having no beginning'. *Param brahma* means 'the supreme *brahman*', a phrase used by Arjuna in 10.12 to glorify Krishna. The second reading leaves *anadi* to stand alone as 'without beginning' and then links *mat* to *param* to give the meaning 'dependent on me'. *Brahma* then stands alone as Brahman, which is dependent on Krishna, as is indicated later in the last verse of Chapter 14. Both these interpretations appear equally valid and, as might be expected, Shankaracharya opts for the former, Ramanujacharya for the latter.

Verse 13: This verse is an exact quotation from the Shvetash-vatara Upanishad (3.16). It shows similarities with the revelation of the *vishva-rupa*, and it seems to indicate that the same spiritual manifestation, *atman* or Brahman, is present in every living being.

Verse 14: This verse describes the position of the *atman* within the body. It appears to be in contact with the senses through which it perceives the world and to be in contact with the three *gunas* of which matter is comprised, and yet it is untouched by matter, remaining always transcendent and aloof because of its distinct spiritual identity. The suggestion here is similar to Shankara's notion of illusion; the self appears to be a part of this world, but, as Samkhya teaching emphasises, it is always wholly distinct. The first line continues the quotation from the Shvetashvatara Upanishad (3.17).

Verse 15: This verse seems to be making a similar point to that revealed by verse 5 of the Isha Upanishad, which says that the self moves and yet moves not. This of course is a paradox, but the self is paradoxical because it is not controlled by the rules of time and space that prevail in the material domain. In the second line, we have a further paradox. The topic being discussed is *jñeya*, that which is to be known, but here, it is referred to as *avijñeya*, that which cannot be known. Again, the paradox can be resolved by reference to the Upanishads, for the Kena Upanishad teaches that Brahman cannot be described or conceived of, but it can be known by means of higher realised knowledge, which it refers to as *pratibodha jñana*, literally, 'awakened knowledge'. And the final phrase, a further paradox, seems also to be derived from verse 5 of the Isha Upanishad. According to the Gita, the *atman* is *durastham chantike cha tat*, far away and yet close at hand, whilst the Upanishad states *tad dure tad antike*, which has exactly the same meaning.

Verse 16: Here, the first line seems to confirm the Vedantic view that the individual nature of the *atman* is an illusion. The *jñeya* appears to be divided (*vibhaktam iva*) but is in fact undivided (*avibhaktam*). This is in line with the Upanishadic doctrine of the absolute oneness of Brahman despite the appearance of a multiplicity of individual souls. The final phrase, devouring and manifesting, reminds us again of the *vishva-rupa*, the mouths of which were seen by Arjuna to be devouring the warriors on the battlefield. However, it could also indicate that the life and death of living beings are determined by the presence and absence of the *atman*, and so, in this sense, it manifests and it devours.

Verse 17: The phrase 'light of lights' is taken from the Brihad Aranyaka Upanishad (4.4.16), which discusses the nature of Brahman. There is also a connection here with the statement of 15.6 of the Gita, which indicates that the abode of the Lord is not illuminated by the sun, moon, or fire. In other words, the soul is radiant with its own spiritual effulgence and is not dependent on any other luminous object. In fact, the light of the sun, moon, and fire is merely a reflection of the spiritual radiance that is imperceptible to mundane eyes. Here, again, we may recall how Arjuna was shocked by the blazing effulgence of the *vishva-rupa*, which was compared to the light of a thousand suns. Brahman is knowledge, it is that which must be known, and it can be known, presumably by the *pratibodha jñana* of the Kena Upanishad. And because *atman* and Brahman are one (*ayam atma brahma*), it is located in the heart of every living being, as is stated here.

Verse 18: This is one of the link verses that help to divide the thirteenth chapter into discrete units. This section is ended, and Arjuna is reminded that he has now heard about *kshetra*, *jñana*, and *jñeya*, the material domain (field), the process of knowing, and the object that is to be known. Furthermore, the point is made again that this process of knowledge will elevate the knower to the higher spiritual status in which Krishna himself exists. Here, also we get a brief reminder of the Gita's emphasis on *bhakti*, as we are informed that it is the devotee of Krishna who acquires this liberating knowledge.

PRAKRITI AND PURUSHA

19. You should understand that both *prakriti* (matter) and *purusha* (spirit) have no beginning. You should also know that all transformations and the *gunas* have their origin in *prakriti*.

20. In terms of the enactment of the process of cause and effect, *prakriti* is said to be the ultimate cause, whilst in the experiencing of joy and misery, *purusha* is said to be the cause.

21. Whilst situated within the domain of *prakriti*, the *purusha* experiences the attributes that arise from *prakriti*. Attachment to these attributes is the cause of the *purusha*'s birth in both auspicious and inauspicious wombs.

22. The Supreme *purusha* within the body is the witness and the one who grants permission, the sustainer, the enjoyer,

the great Lord (*maheshvara*). It is he who is spoken of as *paramatman* (the supreme soul).

23. Whatever a person's state of existence, if he thus understands *purusha*, as well as *prakriti* with its *gunas*, he never takes birth again.

A notable feature of the teachings of the Bhagavad-gita is the manner in which it utilises different religious ideas and philosophical systems, and in Chapter 13, we find ideas that appear based on both Samkhya and Vedanta. The previous passage on the *jñeya* is closely related to the Vedanta of the Upanishads, but this next section of the text is based on the Samkhya division between *prakriti* and *purusha*, matter and spirit or body and soul. This dualism and the realised knowledge of our spiritual identity are the key feature of the knowledge taught by Samkhya as the means of gaining liberation from rebirth. As is so often the case, however, the philosophy of the Gita is subtly different from the classical expositions of the system, and this is certainly the case here, where the discourse enters the domain of Samkhya thought. It always seems to be the case that Krishna does not precisely set out the classical expositions of orthodox philosophy, but rather draws on and makes use of different systems in establishing the unique revelation that is the Bhagavad-gita.

Why are both prakriti and purusha
said to be without beginning?

We are familiar with the idea that the soul, the *purusha* or *atman*, is eternal, but we usually assume that matter is temporary. In Christian theology, neither matter nor the human spirit is without beginning, for both are creations of God. Hindu teachings reveal the eternality of the soul but talk of the creation of the world at a specific point in time. Here, the word *prakriti* refers not to the world we see around us, although this is formed from *prakriti*, but to the primal material substance. The world repeatedly comes into being and is then withdrawn, but the primal substance out of which its varieties emerge is eternally existing. It is for this reason that the Gita states that both *prakriti* and *purusha* have no beginning.

The relationship between prakriti and purusha and how they are combined

The Samkhya view is that despite the existence of *purusha* within *prakriti* (as stated here: *purushah prakriti-sthah*), they remain entirely distinct. They are wholly different forms of existence, and hence, it is impossible for them to intermingle in any way. The *purusha* exists as the one who experiences *prakriti*, but it is never truly a part of the *prakriti* existence. There is something of a problem here because, as stated in verses 20 and 21, the *purusha* does experience the effects of joy and misery as a result of attachment to the attributes of *prakriti*, and this in turn suggests a significant degree of involvement. The question arises as to how an entity that is wholly distinct from matter can simultaneously be affected the fluctuations of matter. The Vedantic answer is that ultimately this world is not real, but Samkhya does not share this view. Hence, we must conclude that the relationship between *prakriti* and *purusha* is a very subtle one. They are entirely distinct, but at the same time, there is a close relationship between them.

Who or what is the paramatman mentioned in verse 22?

Various commentators, including Robert Zaehner, have suggested that the *paramatman* of verse 22 is different from the *purusha* of verse 21. This is a view that is in line with the theistic doctrines of the Vaishnavas, but for Shankaracharya and other Advaitins, the distinction is between the self in a state of bondage and the liberated self. It is up to the individual reader to make up his or her own mind on this. There is quite clearly a difference of emphasis between the two verses. In verse 21, we read that the *purusha* experiences the attributes of matter and must undergo rebirth because of attachment to those attributes. But in verse 22, we read about an entity designated as *maheshvara, paramatman,* and *purushah parah,* all of which suggest power and supremacy. However, there is no indication from the text itself that the subject for discussion has changed, and we must be aware that texts such as the Katha Upanishad, which the Gita draws on, refer to the *atman* as the highest principle. For the theist reader, the differences between the two verses will suggest the distinction between God and the living being, but for the non-theist, they show the distinction between the bound and liberated states of existence of the soul.

What previous teaching is hinted at in verse 23?

Here, the phrase 'even though he is active in many different ways' harks back to the earlier teachings on detached action and indeed to Arjuna's preliminary inquiry. The *karma-yoga* teachings are long past by now, but they are not forgotten. It is fascinating to see how, despite its ranging over different topics and its drawing on different sources, the Bhagavad-gita retains its own unique perspective throughout all its different phases and thereby retains a sense of unity despite the diversity of the ideas it sets forth.

KNOWLEDGE AND THE GOAL OF KNOWLEDGE

24. It is by means of the self that some perceive the self within themselves through meditation. Others do this through the yoga based on Samkhya, and others again through *karma-yoga.*
25. Then there are still others who do not gain knowledge by any of these means but devote themselves to the self after

hearing from other people. Dedicating themselves what they have learnt in this way, they too go beyond death.

26. You should understand that every being that has come into existence, moving or non-moving, arises from this combination of *kshetra* and *kshetrajña*, Bharata.

27. The Supreme Lord is equally present in all living beings; when the body is destroyed, he is not destroyed. One who can perceive his presence truly sees.

28. By perceiving the same Lord situated everywhere, a person will not harm the self by means of the self. As a result of this realisation, he goes to the supreme abode.

29. All types of action are performed by *prakriti* (matter) alone. The *atman* is never the performer of action. One who sees this truly sees.

30. When a person sees the manifold existence of living beings situated as one entity and that they expand from out of that one entity, he then attains Brahman.

31. Because it is without beginning and is untouched by the *gunas*, even though it is situated within the body, this unchanging *paramatman* does not act and is not defiled.

32. Just as all-pervasive space is never contaminated due to its subtle nature, so the *atman*, situated within the body in all places, is not contaminated.

33. And just as the sun alone illuminates this whole world, so the *kshetrin* within it illuminates the entire *kshetra*, Bharata.

34. Persons who possess the eye of knowledge can comprehend the distinction between *kshetra* and *kshetrajña*, and the liberation of living beings from *prakriti*. Such persons reach the supreme.

These verses provide the conclusion to the ideas this chapter is seeking to convey, asserting once again the distinction between body and soul and the idea that realisation of this distinction is a means by which *moksha* is attained. This is the fundamental idea on which the Samkhya philosophy rests, and in this sense, the Bhagavad-gita is here confirming the Samkhya *darshan*, though it does so in its own unique manner. Here, we should note the following points:

Verses 24 and 25 again show the Bhagavad-gita's acceptance of the existence of different paths to the same final goal, here designated as perception of the inner self and crossing beyond death. Krishna mentions *dhyana-yoga*, Samkhya, *karma-yoga*, and learning from a teacher as means by which this goal can be attained. The slightly surprising feature here is that *bhakti* is not included. This could be either because meditation on the self is regarded as the same as devotion to Krishna, as other passages of the Gita seem to suggest, or it could be because the way of *bhakti* is regarded as a wholly alternative means of spiritual progress, as indicated by Arjuna's question at the start of Chapter 12.

Verse 26 merely restates the idea that a living being exists in this world as a combination of body and soul, here, again, referred to as *kshetra* and *kshetrajña*, 'field' and 'field-knower'. In verses 27 and 28, however, we again confront the difficulty of how to interpret the word *parameshvara*, which literally means the 'Supreme Controller' or 'Supreme Deity'. We are told that the Lord is equally present in all living beings and that realisation of this presence is the means by which one 'goes to the supreme abode'. Vaishnava commentators, and Madhvacharya in particular, insist that here, *parameshvara* refers to the *antaryamin* expansion of Vishnu who accompanies and guides each individual soul on its passage through the cycle of rebirth. In Madhva's view, *parameshvara* cannot refer to the individual *purusha*, for we have already learned in this chapter that the *purusha*'s attachment to *prakriti* causes it to undergo rebirth. Other commentators, however, will say that *parameshvara* is a perfectly reasonable term to use in relation to the individual soul, for Krishna has earlier identified himself as the *kshetrajña* mentioned in verse 26, and the Upanishads repeatedly assert the absolute identity of *atman* with

Brahman. Again, each individual reader must decide which interpretation seems most reasonable.

In verse 29, the discussion returns to the distinction between matter and spirit, here, *prakriti* and *atman*. The problem with the theistic interpretation of the chapter is that the text would then seem to switch from describing the individual soul to describing the Deity and then back again without indicating that it is now discussing a new topic.

And in verse 30, we have an abrupt switch in emphasis from Samkhya back to Vedanta in a statement that would seem to indicate an Advaitic perspective, although it is more likely a reference to the realisation of the *vishva-rupa* granted to Arjuna as a gift of grace.

The chapter is finally summed up in the last four verses. The *(param)atman* is situated within the body, within *prakriti*, but its spiritual identity remains fundamentally unaffected by this apparent contact. Despite its involvement in the process of transmigration, the inner self remains always distinct from its material embodiment. *Prakriti* is devoid of consciousness, and consciousness only becomes manifest within *prakriti* due to the presence of *purusha*. The sun alone illuminates the whole world with light, and in the same way, the body is pervaded by consciousness that radiates outwards from the soul. One who comprehends this truth about our existence and thereby possesses self-knowledge attains the highest goal.

CONCLUSION:
A SUMMARY OF CHAPTER 13

The thirteenth chapter of the Bhagavad-gita marks an abrupt change in direction away from the discourse on *bhakti* that had marked the previous six chapters (7–12). The main point of emphasis here is the distinction between the soul and the body and the fact that realisation of this distinction will take the adept beyond the cycle of birth and death to the higher domain of the spirit. After its introduction to the teachings and a statement of their credentials, the text gives an analysis of the twenty-four elements of matter that conforms closely to the version presented in classical Samkhya. This Krishna refers to as an explanation of the *kshetra*, or field, a term used here to designate the material body. The Gita then moves on to a subject it refers to as *jñana*, or knowledge, which is here defined in terms of a mood of detachment from the world and the renunciation of material desires. The next passage is entitled *jñeya*, that which is to be known, and here, Krishna draws extensively on the wisdom of the Upanishads in discussing the all-pervasive presence of the *atman*, which is equated with the Deity and with the *vishva-rupa* revealed in Chapter 11. We then have a short discourse on *prakriti* and *purusha*, matter and spirit, which outlines their differing identities and their differing functions in the progression of life in this world. And the final verses discourse further on the transcendence and indeed the supremacy of the soul over matter, stressing again the need to realise this distinction as the means by which liberation from rebirth is attained.

*Transcending these three gunas that cause the body to exist,
the embodied entity is liberated from the misery of birth, death,
and old age, and attains immortality.* —14.20

CHAPTER 14

Chapter 13 gave us instructions primarily focussed on the distinction between body and soul (the *kshetra* and *kshetrajña*, *prakriti* and *purusha*), which reflected the significant influence of Samkhya philosophy on the Bhagavad-gita. It also emphasised the idea that it is knowledge of this distinction which is the key to liberation from rebirth. In the fourteenth chapter, the influence of Samkhya continues as the teaching switches to another of its fundamental concepts, the idea of the three *gunas*: *sattva*, *rajas*, and *tamas*, which pervade every aspect of *prakriti*, the material manifestation. We have already encountered this notion at various points in the Gita as Krishna has used the idea to enhance and illuminate his exposition on other subjects, but it is here in Chapter 14 that we find the *gunas* and their influence explained in full. And the influence of the *gunas* remains a significant feature of the teachings that follow in the subsequent chapters of the text, particularly in Chapter 17 and the first half of Chapter 18, which consist of a threefold analysis of different facets of this world in relation to *sattva*, *rajas*, and *tamas*.

INTRODUCTION TO THE CHAPTER

1. Once more I will speak to you about the highest knowledge, which is supreme amongst all types of knowledge. Comprehending this wisdom, all the sages achieve the highest perfection when they depart from this world.

2. Devoting themselves to this knowledge, they come to my own state of being. Hence, they are not born at the time of creation, and at the time of destruction, they remain undisturbed.

Here, we have the Bhagavad-gita's usual introduction to a new passage of teaching, pointing out that this knowledge is supremely important and that its proper comprehension is a means of achieving the ultimate goal of *moksha*.

CREATION AS THE IMPREGNATION OF THE WOMB OF BRAHMAN

3. My womb is the great Brahman, and I deposit the seed of life therein. Thence arises the origin of all beings, Bharata.
4. Different forms appear in all the various wombs, Kaunteya, but the great Brahman is the womb for them all, and I am the father who bestows the seed.

These two verses stand somewhat apart from the central theme of the chapter, but they are by no means unrelated to it. We might note the following points:

Here, Brahman is described as being the womb that the Deity impregnates in order to create the living beings, and one must presume that here, *mahad brahma*, the great Brahman, refers to *prakriti*. This is a somewhat unusual use of the word *brahman*, but it is also found in the Mundaka Upanishad (3.1.3), which refers to the Deity as *brahma-yoni*, having *brahman* as his womb.

The language employed here, particularly *bija* (seed) and *yoni* (womb), clearly indicates a metaphor of sexual union or even a macrocosmic act of union between the Deity and his *shakti*, as is more typical of Shaiva doctrine.

The idea here is that *prakriti*, which in Shaivism is identified with the Goddess, becomes filled with life and consciousness only when in contact with the male principle in the form of the Supreme Deity. This short passage is therefore a continuation of the ideas found in Chapter 13. *Prakriti* is essentially non-sentient and devoid of the life principle, but it becomes enlivened when it is impregnated with *purusha*, the spiritual element, which represents Krishna himself, as we have heard several times before in the Bhagavad-gita. It is the union of *prakriti* and *purusha* that gives rise to the existence of so many different types of living being, just as at a microcosmic level, a new entity is generated through the union of male and female. Here, however, it is noteworthy that the Gita does not seek to identify the great Brahman with the Supreme Goddess in the manner typical of Shaiva teachings on creation.

A Discourse on the Three Gunas

5. *Sattva, rajas,* and *tamas* are the *gunas* arising from *prakriti.* They bind the changeless, embodied entity within the body, O mighty one.

6. Of these *gunas*, because *sattva* is flawless, it is luminous and has no contamination. It is through attachment to happiness and attachment to knowledge (*jñana*) that it causes bondage, O sinless one.

7. You should understand that *rajas* is of the nature of passion; it gives rise to hankering and attachment. It binds the embodied entity through attachment to action, Kaunteya.

8. And you should know that *tamas*, which is delusion for all embodied beings, appears due to ignorance. It causes bondage through negligence, lethargy, and sleep.

9. *Sattva* causes one to adhere to happiness, whilst *rajas* causes adherence to action, Bharata, and by obscuring a person's wisdom, *tamas* creates adherence to negligence.

10. *Sattva* prevails by subjugating *rajas* and *tamas*, Bharata; *rajas* prevails by subjugating *sattva* and *tamas*, and *tamas* prevails by subjugating *sattva* and *rajas*.

11. When the illumination of knowledge appears in all the doorways in this body, then one should understand that *sattva* has become dominant.

12. Greed, endeavour, engagement in activities, agitation, hankering; these appear when *rajas* becomes dominant, O best of the Bharatas.

13. Dullness, inaction, misunderstanding, delusion; these appear when *tamas* becomes dominant, O child of the Kurus.

Here, we have a succinct explanation of the nature of the three *gunas* and of the ways in which they bind the soul to its existence within the body (the word *guna* can mean 'attribute', 'quality', and also 'rope').

A BRIEF DESCRIPTION OF EACH OF THE GUNAS: SATTVA, RAJAS, AND TAMAS

Sattva is the quality of gentility, good conduct, enlightened understanding, purity, and detachment. It is most usually translated as 'goodness' but also includes cleanliness, wisdom, kindness, and the good life of a contented existence. *Rajas*, on the other hand, is all about passion, activity, endeavour, anxiety, and frustration. People predominated by this *guna* are impelled by their desires and ambitions towards a life of intense action and hard work. But *tamas* falls below the level of *rajas*. Here, there is no intensity, but rather indolence, laziness, and folly. Those predominated by *tamas* are foolish persons who lack the wisdom to see higher truths and also lack the ardour to endeavour to improve their situation.

The relationship between the gunas and prakriti

In verse 5, the *gunas* are described as being *prakriti-sambhavah*, meaning born from or arising out of *prakriti*. This is slightly at odds with the usual view of Samkhya teachings, which state that the *gunas* are inherent qualities of *prakriti*. Because they are a part of its essential nature, the *gunas* are not usually referred to as products of *prakriti*, as seems to be suggested here.

Spiritual and mundane jñana

In the previous chapter and even in the first two verses here, we saw the familiar view that *jñana*, or knowledge, was the means by which the aspirant achieves the goal of liberation from rebirth. Here, both verses 6 and 11 relate *sattva* to *jñana*, but they still regard this *guna* as a cause of bondage rather than liberation. Verse 6 even states *badnati jñana-sangena*, it binds through attachment to knowledge. Shankaracharya explains that as *jñana* is an inherent quality of the *atman*, there cannot be any sense of attachment to it, for that would imply a distinction between *atman* and *jñana*. Hence, the knowledge referred to here cannot be the pure spiritual knowledge but must be mundane learning.

THE GUNAS AND REBIRTH

14. When the embodied soul encounters death whilst *sattva* predominates, it then moves on to the pure worlds obtained by those who possess the highest knowledge.
15. If he meets with death whilst *rajas* predominates, he takes birth amongst those attached to action, and if he dies whilst *tamas* predominates, he is reborn within the wombs of those who are deluded.

16. They say that the fruit of righteous deeds is Sattvic and without blemish. But suffering is the fruit of *rajas*, and ignorance is the fruit of *tamas*.

17. Knowledge arises from *sattva*, and greed arises from *rajas*. Negligence and delusion arise from *tamas*, and ignorance as well.

18. Those who adhere to *sattva* move upwards and those who adhere to *rajas* remain in between, whilst those who adhere to *tamas* and follow, the ways of the lowest *guna* go downwards.

In this passage, the Bhagavad-gita relates the concept of the three *gunas* to the idea of rebirth and karma. Again, the passage is not difficult to follow, but we might note the following points:

In verse 14, the destination attained by persons who adhere to *sattva* is the higher worlds in which the gods reside, or possibly a birth amongst pure-hearted, prosperous, enlightened people in this world. The point here is that *sattva* alone does not lead to *moksha*; all three *gunas* must be transcended.

The indication of verses 15 and 18 is that those predominated by the quality of *rajas* remain in the domain of worldly action, in which people strive for wealth, pleasure, and material goals. However, those who become associated with *tamas* fall from even this position and come to exist amongst the lowest of humanity or even in the animal forms of life.

Verse 17 again associates *sattva* with *jñana*. We are aware that all three of the *gunas* are regarded as causes of bondage, but the indication seems to be that the pursuit of *moksha* must begin from the platform of *sattva*. So, *sattva* is not liberating in itself, but it is the purest of the three *gunas*, and hence, it is the position one must aspire after as a basis for the *moksha dharma*. This point will become more apparent in Chapter 16, in which qualities that are akin to those here connected to *sattva* are indicated as leading to *moksha*. It would not be correct to assert on the basis of this chapter that the human attributes associated with *sattva* are all worthless because they cause bondage and repeated birth and death. Such attributes are to be cultivated but then ultimately transcended.

The basic instruction of this chapter is that those who develop the qualities associated with *sattva* acquire the good karma that leads to a favourable rebirth, those who adhere to *rajas* remain in this world of action, desire, and frustration, and those who cultivate the attributes of *tamas* degrade themselves and gradually slip away from the human state of existence.

MOKSHA:
GOING BEYOND THE GUNAS

19. When the seer observes that there is no agent of action other than the *gunas* and gains knowledge of that which is beyond the *gunas*, he attains my state of being.
20. Transcending these three *gunas* that cause the body to exist, the embodied entity is liberated from the misery of birth, death, and old age, and attains immortality.

This short passage clearly follows on from the previous instruction, which related the *gunas* to the law of karma, and in fact concludes Krishna's teaching on the subject matter of the fourteenth chapter. We have just learned that the particular *guna* with which a person becomes predominantly associated dictates the nature of one's next birth – moving upwards, staying in the same position, or slipping downwards. To gain liberation from rebirth, however, it is necessary to go beyond all three of the *gunas*, for the Samkhya system dictates that *moksha* means 'the absolute separation of *purusha* from *prakriti*'. Here, again, the question arises as to the status of the *sattvaguna*; is it a cause of bondage, or is it a step on the path to liberation? The implication is that it is a part of this world and hence a cause of bondage, but we should be cautious about pressing this conclusion too far, and in Chapter 18, we get clear indications that this is not the whole picture.

The teaching here is a reassertion of the idea found in Chapter 13. The three *gunas* are active in the world, for they are the constituents of *prakriti*, but the soul is merely an observer who is never truly united with *prakriti*. Liberation from rebirth can be attained by realised knowledge of this truth, for one then exists as *purusha* alone and leaves behind the influence of all three *gunas*.

THE CHARACTERISTICS OF ONE WHO HAS TRANSCENDED THE GUNAS

21. Arjuna said: What are the characteristics of one who has transcended these three *gunas*, O Lord? How does he behave? How does he go beyond the three *gunas*?

22. The Lord said: He does not hate illumination, activity, or delusion when they appear, Pandava, and neither does he long for them when they disappear.

23. He remains indifferent, as if undisturbed by the *gunas*, thinking, 'It is the *gunas* alone that are active'. He thus remains steady and does not waver.

24. He is equally disposed in distress and happiness, he is self-contained, and he views a lump of earth, a stone, and gold as the same. He is firmly resolved, and he is equally disposed towards those who are dear to him and those who are not. Likewise he is equally disposed when criticised or glorified.

25. Whether honoured or condemned, he is still the same, and he is equally disposed towards friends and foes. He has abandoned all his worldly endeavours. Such a person is said to be beyond the *gunas*.

Here, we find another passage which describes the characteristics of a person who has attained the highest form of spiritual realisation. And just as in Chapter 2, the description is instigated by a direct question from Arjuna, who seems particularly interested in this subject. If we compare this account to those found in 2.55–72, 6.7–9, and 12.13–19, we will see that Krishna is essentially restating the same ideas regarding the qualities found in one who has attained spiritual perfection. Here are some of the points we might note:

Arjuna's question in verse 21 clearly relates to Krishna's previous discussion of the person who has transcended the *gunas*, and the account that Krishna gives in response to this inquiry relates to a person who is still living in this world. Hence, we can conclude that the Bhagavad-gita regards *moksha* as a state of being that can be attained whilst still undergoing bodily existence – the idea of the *jivan mukta*.

Such a person is wholly indifferent to the fluctuating fortunes that beset us whilst we live in this world.

He exists on the level of the soul alone and as such is witness to the events of the world but is completely detached from them. He never deviates from his understanding: 'It is the *gunas* that constitute *prakriti* which are active here, but in my true identity I am not involved in that action'. His indifference to the world arises from this realisation.

This indifference is apparent in relation to pleasure and pain, to wealth, to other people, to praise and blame, and to friends and enemies. Existing only as the witnessing *purusha*, he observes these as they arise in life, but he is wholly detached and indifferent to them; he feels none of the emotional responses that others will undergo as a result of encounters with different circumstances.

GOING BEYOND THE GUNAS THROUGH BHAKTI

26. And one who reveres me through undeviating *bhakti-yoga* also transcends the *gunas* and becomes fit to attain the state of Brahman.

27. For I am the foundation on which the immortal, unchanging Brahman exists. I am also the foundation of the eternal dharma and of absolute joy.

The chapter concludes rather as it began with a short passage that seems somewhat out of line with its central teachings. Here, again, as in chapters 5 and 6, we have verses appearing at the end of a chapter that emphasise the theistic and devotional strands of the Gita's thought, and again, some might be tempted to regard these as being later additions to the text inserted by a redactor who sought to show that this was its principal doctrine. Any such theory, however, must remain as unsubstantiated conjecture, and it could equally be suggested that Krishna himself might want to remind his audience of the importance of *bhakti*, especially at a point in his discourse where he has moved on to other topics.

Each of these two verses makes a distinctive point:

Verse 26: Verses 19 and 20 stated that liberation from rebirth is attained through knowledge of the distinction between the true self and the material embodiment shaped by the *gunas*. In this verse, we are reminded of the alternative means of attaining this goal through devotion to the Deity, the two paths noted in 9.14–15 and 12.1–5. This way of *bhakti* also takes a person beyond the *gunas* to the realm of Brahman.

Verse 27: Here, Krishna expands upon the phrase *brahma-bhuyaya kalpate*, used at the end of 26, by explaining that he himself is the *pratishtha*, the basis or foundation, of this Brahman, of *dharma*, and of the pure joy of spiritual realisation. Here, we encounter the problem of what exactly is meant by Brahman. We will recall that in the opening verses of this chapter, Brahman was described as the great womb into which the Deity injects the seed of life, which seemed to indicate that Brahman is *prakriti*, or the total material substance. In verse 26, however, Brahman was referred to as the state of existence attained by one who goes beyond the *gunas*, and due to this proximity, one must presume that it is in this sense that Brahman is referred to here. Therefore, the indication is that the Brahman of the Upanishads is not the ultimate form of the divine, above and beyond the personal Deity, but rather that the personal Deity is the basis of Brahman, which represents his pervasive presence within the world. And here, we will recall that the same point was made at the start of Chapter 7, where Krishna compared himself to the thread that acts as the *pratishtha*, the basis, for a string of jewels.

CONCLUSION:
A SUMMARY OF CHAPTER 14

It is the discourse on the nature of the three *gunas* – *sattva*, *rajas*, and *tamas* – that forms the main substance of this chapter as Krishna informs us of their nature and of the influence they have in determining future rebirths. The chapter opens with the revelation that Krishna is the Supreme Deity who impregnates the lifeless *prakriti* with sentient beings, and here, *prakriti* is referred to as the great Brahman that is Krishna's womb. The Gita then reveals the nature of the three *gunas*: *sattva* as purity, goodness, and wisdom; *rajas* as energy, desire, action, and passion; and *tamas* as darkness, ignorance, sloth, and impurity. The extent to which we cultivate and cleave to each of these *gunas* determines the nature of our future rebirth; *sattva* elevates us to a higher state, *rajas* keeps us here in the domain of material endeavour, and *tamas* carries us downwards to lower forms of existence. Only that person who transcends all three of the *gunas* can escape the cycle of rebirth and attain the highest spiritual goal. Arjuna then asks about the qualities by which such a person can be identified, and Krishna explains that it is primarily his indifference to the fluctuating fortunes of the world based on his realisation that his true identity is not a part of this world. This spiritual state of existence can also be attained through devotion to the Supreme Deity, for Krishna himself is the ultimate foundation on which everything rests.

Entering into the earth, I sustain the living beings through my potency. Becoming the moon, which is imbued with liquid potency, I nourish all the plants. —15.13

CHAPTER 15

As we have seen, in this final section of the Gita, each chapter seems to have its own particular theme, and the fifteenth chapter certainly continues this tendency. At the end of Chapter 14, Krishna reminded us again that in addition to realised knowledge, devotion to a personal Deity is another means of achieving spiritual perfection.

It is this idea that is now developed in the fifteenth chapter, as the text again places its focus on the Supreme Deity who is the creator and controller of all things. In Chapters 13 and 14, the teachings were primarily concerned with the nature of *prakriti*, including the three *gunas*, and the spiritual *purusha* that is the transcendent soul in every being. In Chapter 15, a third factor is introduced, the Deity who is shown to be above and beyond both matter and the individual soul.

Here, then, we have what might be referred to as a theistic form of Samkhya philosophy that teaches the eternal existence of three fundamental principles, *prakriti*, *purusha*, and *ishvara*. This idea is not original to the Gita, for it is the main theme of the Shvetashvatara Upanishad, though there, it is Shiva who is named as the Supreme Deity. The structure of the chapter rests on these three principles. It opens with a discussion of the world as an inverted *banyan* tree, and then considers the transcendent nature of the soul before concluding with revelation about the nature of the Deity, who is identified as Krishna himself. So, despite the fact that it has only twenty verses and appears to be apart from the Gita's central discourse, this chapter must be regarded as making a vitally important contribution to the understanding of the nature of God presented by the text as a whole.

The World as an Inverted Tree

1. The Lord said: They speak of an unfading Ashvattha tree with its roots above, its branches below, and the Vedic hymns as its leaves. One who understands this tree has knowledge of the Vedas.

2. Its branches spread out above and below, nourished by the *gunas*. The objects of the senses are its shoots. Its roots also spread down below into the human domain, where they become combined with action.

3. Its form cannot be identified, for it has no end and no beginning and no foundation, either. Using the sharp weapon of detachment, one should cut down this firmly rooted Ashvattha tree.

4. One should then seek that position from which, once attained, there is no return, thinking, 'I surrender to that original being (*purusha*) out of whom flowed forth the primeval creative impulse'.

5. Without pride or folly, overcoming the barrier of attachment, constantly absorbed in knowledge of the *atman*, with desires nullified, free from the duality identified as pleasure and suffering, those who are free of illusion then progress to that changeless state of being.

6. The sun does not illuminate that place; neither does the moon or fire. Having gone there, one does not return; that is my supreme abode.

The arresting metaphor of the inverted banyan tree is taken from Chapter 6 of the Katha Upanishad, and in fact, the whole of the fifteenth chapter displays a thematic similarity to the sixth chapter of the Katha. Here, we might note the following points:

The ashvattha, or banyan tree, symbolises the material domain, which has no identifiable end, middle, or beginning.

The hymns of the Vedas that glorify the gods as a part of the ritual are here included within that material domain. The conclusion, therefore, is that the ritual *karma-kanda* section of the Vedas is not a part of the path to *moksha*, a point that is repeatedly emphasised by Shankaracharya. The statement of the first verse, according to which one who understands this tree understands the Veda as well, perhaps matches the idea expressed in 2.46; in other words, one who has realised knowledge has no need of the Vedic ritual.

The instruction here is that we must try to break free from our entanglement within this world by cultivating a mood of detachment, as was indicated in verses 7–11 of Chapter 13 and verses 22–25 of Chapter 14. Detachment is compared to the axe that must be used to cut down the ashvattha tree that is the locus of our bondage.

Verses 4–6 then discuss the attainment of *moksha* and the nature of that transcendent state of existence. Again, we may note that whilst verses 3 and 5 emphasise detachment and realisation as the means by which one escapes from this world, verse 4 refers to surrendering to the *adyam purusham*, the original person, and so we see how the Gita constantly refers to the two principal paths to *moksha* discussed by Krishna at the start of Chapter 12.

All we learn about the spiritual domain is that once the *atman* reaches that position, it is never again reborn in this world, and that this sphere of existence is illuminated by a spiritual radiance. Here, we will recall the statement of Chapter 13 that the *jñeya*, that which is to be known, is the source of light in all luminaries and that it is beyond all darkness. Verse 6 is not original to the Gita and is taken almost verbatim from the Upanishads (Katha, 5.15; Mundaka, 2.2.11; and Shvetashvatara, 6.14).

THE TRANSMIGRATING SOUL

7. In the world of living beings (*jiva-loka*), the eternal living element is nothing but a part of me. It draws to itself the

five senses and the mind, which is the sixth, all of which reside in *prakriti*.

8. When the Lord (*ishvara*) takes on a body and when he moves out from it, he holds on to these six and moves on in the way the wind carries aromas from their original place.

9. Presiding over the senses of hearing, sight, touch, taste, and smell, as well as the mind, he then experiences the objects of the senses.

10. Whether he is departing or remaining, or whether he is experiencing the world by association with the *gunas*, those who are deluded do not perceive him. Those, however, who possess the eye of knowledge can perceive him.

11. *Yogins* who pursue their endeavours perceive him situated within their own being, but those who are unintelligent and fail to achieve self-mastery are never able to perceive him despite making the endeavour.

After considering the entanglement of the material world and the means of escaping from that entanglement, Krishna now moves on to discuss the second of the three fundamental principles – the individual *atman*. This passage is quite complex and open to a number of different interpretations, so we should think about it quite carefully.

The relationship between the individual soul and the supreme deity

In verse 7, Krishna asserts that the *jiva-bhuta*, the living being, is a part of himself, *mama . . . amsha*. This statement would tend to confirm Ramanuja's view of limited identity between the soul and God (for the part is non-different from the whole and yet there is a distinction between them) and to pose some difficulty for Madhva's theology of absolute difference, the *dvaita-vada*. The statement given here tends to confirm and to elucidate the passages on the relationship between the Deity and the living beings that are to be found at the beginning of Chapter 7 and of Chapter 9.

Who or what does the word ishvara refer to in verse 8?

The ideas contained in verses 8–10 would seem to suggest that here, the word *ishvara*, which is usually used to designate the Deity, refers to the individual soul, the *jiva-bhuta* of verse 7. This is slightly unusual but can probably be explained by the previous statement that the *jiva* is a part of the Deity, and because the soul is the controller of the body. In this role as controller, the *jiva-bhuta* or *atman* utilises the five senses and the mind in order to experience *prakriti*, the domain of matter.

The meaning of the metaphor in verse 8

As the wind moves from one place to another, it carries with it the aroma of its previous association. The presence of flowers can be experienced within a house where no flowers are present because they are growing in a garden outside the window. In the same way, the soul carries the impressions of its previous existence into a new embodiment. This conforms to the idea of a subtle body surrounding the soul as it moves from lifetime to lifetime. The soul itself is entirely spiritual and so is always untouched by its material surroundings, but the subtle body of mind and senses bears the impressions or *vasanas* or previous experiences, and it is by this means that the law of karma is enacted.

How is one able to perceive this ishvara?

In verse 11, Krishna says *pashyanti jñana-chakshushah*, those who have the eye of knowledge can perceive the *atman*, and in verse 12, he states that *yogins* who make the proper endeavour perceive the *atman* within themselves. This would seem to confirm the ideas found in Chapter 6, where it was revealed that control of the mind and effective practice of meditational yoga allows the adept to perceive the spiritual *atman* within the very core of his own being.

THE PRESENCE OF GOD
WITHIN THE WORLD

12. The energy emanating from the sun, which illuminates the entire universe, and that of the moon and fire as well: you should know that energy as mine alone.
13. Entering into the earth, I sustain the living beings through my potency. Becoming the moon, which is imbued with liquid potency, I nourish all the plants.
14. I become the *vaishvanara* energy, the digestive heat, and in this form reside within the bodies of the living beings. By combining with the *prana* and *apana* breaths, I digest the four types of food.

And now the chapter turns its attention to the third of the three principles, the Supreme Deity who is also present within this world. Here, we might note the following points:

Verse 12 confirms what Krishna said in 13.17, *jyotisham api taj jyotis*: he is the radiance of all luminaries, which was itself a quotation from the Brihad Aranyaka Upanishad (4.4.16), and builds on the earlier statement that the abode of the Deity is not illuminated by sun, moon, or fire (15.6). In other words, the radiance that is apparent in this world is a reflection of the glorious radiance of the spirit by which Arjuna was overwhelmed in his vision of the *vishva-rupa*.

It is the Earth that sustains all life, but here, we are told that the Earth is able to do so only because it is permeated by the energy of God. The traditional Indian belief is that plant life is nourished by the rays of the moon. Here, we are informed that as with the earth, the sustaining influence of the moon is a result of the presence there of the divine potency.

The term *vaishvanara* has a number of different meanings, but the context reveals that here, it is used to refer to the fiery element present within the stomach that digests the food we eat by combining with two of the breaths in the body. Again, Krishna suggests that this energy is potent because it is a part of the energy of God, which sustains and empowers the world that exists all around us.

In verses 12 and 13, it is made clear that Krishna's empowering presence in this world is in the form of his divine energy and potency, confirming the statement with which the teachings of the tenth chapter conclude, to the effect that all the glories of this world arise from a small part of his potency. So, when Krishna says that he is present within the body as the *vaishvanara* energy that digests food, we should understand it as reflecting the view that the energetic source is present in the energy it emits. It is the energy of God that sustains the material world and enables it to nurture life, and it is in this sense that God pervades this world.

THE THREE ETERNAL PRINCIPLES

15. And I am situated in the hearts of all; memory, knowledge, and the loss of knowledge arise from me. It is I alone who am to be understood from all the Vedas. I am the creator of Vedanta, and I alone am the knower of the Vedas.

16. In the world, there are these two *purushas*, the *kshara* (decaying), and the *akshara* (non-decaying). The *kshara* is all living beings, whilst that which is situated beyond it is referred to as *akshara*.

17. But the highest *purusha* is different again and is designated as the *paramatman*. This is the immutable Lord who enters the threefold world and sustains it.

18. And because I am beyond the *kshara* and superior to the *akshara* as well, I am therefore celebrated in both general speech and in the Veda as 'Purushottama'.
19. One who is not deluded and knows me thus as *purushottama* knows all things. He then worships me with his entire existence, O Bharata.
20. I have now revealed this most secret of teachings, O sinless one. One who comprehends this doctrine is wise indeed and has fulfilled all his duties, O Bharata.

The final six verses of the chapter refer directly to the three principles discussed above, forming a passage that is very important for our understanding of the Gita's ideas about the nature of God and the relationship between God, the soul, and the material world.

Krishna as situated in the hearts of all beings

Here, Krishna is again identifying himself with the *atman*, as he did in 10.20 and then in 13.2. Where the verse states that he is to be understood from all the Vedas, this must surely mean the Upanishads, which reveal the truth about the *atman* and its identity with Brahman. This view is confirmed by the reference to Vedanta in the final line, for the term Vedanta is often used to indicate the Upanishads. Ramanuja, however, suggests that this means that where the Vedic hymns glorify Indra, Agni, Varuna, or one of the other gods, it is Krishna who is worshipped, for he is present within all the gods. Both Ramanuja and Shankara accept that the verse confirms the identity of Krishna with the *atman*, but other Vaishnava commentators have suggested that here, we have another reference to the *paramatman* form of the Deity who accompanies a living being and guides it through the process of transmigration. There is a sense here that the manifestation of the Deity being referred to is in control of the individual being, whereas the *atman* in this world exists in a state of bondage and subjugation. Hence, this suggestion is not wholly unreasonable and finds confirmation at the end of the Gita in verse 61 of the final chapter.

What is being referred to as the kshara
and the akshara in verse 16?

The word *kshara* literally means 'subject to change and deterioration', whilst *akshara* means the opposite. In other chapters, the word *akshara* has been used to refer to the spiritual domain in contrast to the temporary material manifestations (as for example in 8.11, 8.21, and 12.3). This would suggest that the two *purushas* discussed here are the temporary person who will meet with death and the eternal soul that exists beyond that personality – *kshara* and *akshara*.

The discussion is complicated by the use of the word *purusha*, which, as we have seen, is the usual Samkhya designation for the *atman*, or soul. From this perspective, the *kshara purusha* is the soul in a state of bondage experiencing death, and the *akshara purusha* is the liberated soul that does not experience any material circumstances. Against this view, one must say that *kshara*, decaying, linked to *purusha*, the soul, seems an unusual combination. Shankaracharya regards the *kshara purusha*, which is all living beings, as the material embodiment that is subject to decay and the *akshara purusha* as the eternal *atman*. Ramanujacharya, on the other hand, regards both *kshara* and *akshara* as referring to the *atman*, the former in a state of bondage, the latter in its liberated state. Both interpretations seem equally valid, though one might note here the statement of 7.4–5 regarding the *para* and *apara prakritis* that might be taken as equivalent to this passage. For what it is worth, I think I would favour Shankara's view here, as it seems more consistent with the overall teachings of the chapter.

Who or what is the paramatman referred to in verse 17?

The *paramatman* is specifically mentioned as being 'different' (*anya*) from the *kshara* and the *akshara*, a statement that clearly implies some degree of distinction between the self and God, in contrast to the Advaitic notion of absolute identity. This principle is designated as the *uttama purusha*, so that we now have three *purushas*: the *kshara*, *akshara*, and *uttama*. I would suggest that these three are to be identified as matter, the individual soul, and the Supreme Deity. In verse 18, Krishna identifies himself as this *uttama purusha*, beyond the *kshara* and the *akshara*, and as we are fully aware by now, for the Gita Krishna himself is the Supreme Deity.

The connection between verse 19 and verse 8 of chapter 10

Both verse 19 of this chapter and verse 8 of Chapter 10 point out the connection between spiritual knowledge and religious practice, the practice being contingent upon the knowledge. So, when one understands that Krishna is the Supreme Deity, one then engages in acts of devotion of the type mentioned most specifically in Chapter 9 (vv. 14 and 26).

A brief summary of the teachings presented in this passage

After revealing himself as the indwelling self who controls and guides the living being, Krishna then states that there are two types of *purusha*, one subject to decay and one that is eternally unchanging. This could refer either to the material body and the soul, or else to the soul in a state of bondage and the liberated soul. Beyond these two *purushas* is the supreme, *uttama purusha*, which is Krishna himself, the Supreme Deity. One who understands Krishna's status as the Supreme Being worships him in a mood of loving devotion.

CONCLUSION:
A SUMMARY OF CHAPTER 15

Chapter 15 follows the principal doctrine espoused by the Shvetashvatara Upanishad, which states that there are three eternal principles: matter, the individual soul, and the Supreme Deity. Verses 1–6 speak of the world of matter using the metaphor of the inverted banyan tree; one who seeks liberation from rebirth must use the weapon of detachment to cut through the entanglement of this world and attain the higher domain.

Verses 7–11 speak of the second principle, the individual soul that is a part of the Supreme Deity. The soul is present in this world within various forms of material embodiment and transmigrates from one form to another, carrying with it the latent impressions of its sensual perceptions. The practitioner of yoga is able to perceive the existence of the soul within his own being, but most people remain unaware of its existence.

Verses 12–15 then discuss the third of the three principles, the Supreme Deity who is Krishna himself. It is by means of his potency that the sun, the moon, and fire give out light and heat; it is through him that the earth nourishes and sustains living beings, and he is the internal fire that allows the digestion of food. He is also present as the soul within the heart of every being who is the controller of the passage of life. The final five verses provide a distinctive account of the three elements that comprise the entirety of material and spiritual existence.

There are two *purushas* in this world: (1) the *kshara*, the person who decays and who is all living beings, and (2) the *akshara*, the person who does not decay and is thus in a higher position. Above and beyond these two is the Supreme Being, the Deity who is Krishna himself and who is the sustaining force that allows the world to continue. When one understands this identity of Krishna as the controller and the maintainer of the world, one then follows the path of *bhakti* and worships him with devotion.

*Pursuing insatiable desires and filled with deceit,
pride, and passion, due to delusion they adhere
rigidly to their false conceptions.* —16.10

CHAPTER 16

Again, we find here that a new chapter brings a new topic for discussion, as is typical of this final phase of the Bhagavad-gita. Here, Krishna's theme is the *daivi sampad*, the characteristic qualities of righteous persons, and the *asuri sampad*, the characteristic qualities of the wicked. In fact, most of the chapter deals with the latter topic, explaining the mentality of wicked persons and also the fate that awaits them after death. Literally, *daivi sampad* means 'the nature of the gods', and *asuri sampad* means 'the nature of the *asuras*', who are the evil adversaries of the gods in the tales of the Puranas. However, the teachings appear to refer to persons of this world and their differing mentalities. One's attention is also drawn again to the *Mahabharata* narrative and to the conduct of the righteous Pandavas and the iniquitous Kauravas. In fact, one might interpret the teachings here as being a direct commentary on the two, particularly as the *Mahabharata* reveals that the Kauravas are *asuras* who have been born in this world, whilst the Pandavas are earthly manifestations of the gods.

THE DAIVI SAMPAD
AND THE ASURI SAMPAD

1. Fearlessness, being pure at heart, remaining resolute in the pursuit of knowledge through yoga practice, charity,

self-control, performing sacrifices, study of the Vedas, austerity, honesty;

2. Not harming, truthfulness, avoiding anger, renunciation, tranquillity, never maligning others, compassion for other beings, being free of greed, kindness, modesty, never wavering;

3. Energy, patience, resolve, purity, the absence of malice, and of arrogance; these constitute the qualities of one born with the *daivi sampad*, the godly disposition, Bharata.

4. Deceit, arrogance, pride, anger, harshness, and ignorance are the qualities of one born with the *asuri sampad*, the asuric disposition, Partha.

5. The *daivi sampad* leads to liberation, but the *asuri sampad* is regarded as a cause of bondage. Do not be concerned – you have been born with the *daivi sampad*, Pandava.

6. There are two types of living being in this world, the *daiva* and the *asura*. I have described the *daiva* at some length, so now hear from me about the *asura* disposition, Partha.

Here, the first three verses give a list of the qualities that constitute the *daivi sampad*, whilst verse 4 gives a shorter list of the characteristics of the *asuri sampad*. So, in this passage, the Bhagavad-gita becomes something of a treatise on morality by defining virtue and wickedness under these two headings. The *daivi sampad* is based primarily on the principle of doing what is good to others and avoiding the greed and selfishness that lead a person to injure those around him. The *asuri sampad*, by contrast, rests on intense arrogance, contempt for others, and a harsh, uncaring disposition. The idea here is not unusual and is one that would be shared by most forms of ethical discourse. There are, however, some significant points:

A virtuous and a non-virtuous disposition

Verses 3 and 4 indicate that the qualities a person possesses are inherent from birth rather than something one can aspire towards. There is a certain tension within Hindu thought over the extent of free will, and one may question whether a wicked person truly has the capacity to reform himself. The qualities a person possesses are shaped by the activities performed in previous lives, which predetermine one's inherent nature. The indication here is that the degree of free will a person has in making moral decisions is significantly circumscribed by the inherent nature with which he is born. The suggestion is that one is born good rather than achieves goodness. This, of course, is not the entire picture, and there are numerous examples (Valmiki is perhaps the most of obvious of these) and passages of teaching that place the emphasis on the other side of the debate.

Virtue as a prerequisite for liberation

The account of the *daivi sampad* given in the first three verses is primarily a list of moral attributes that would seem to approximate to the nature of the *sattvaguna* as described in Chapter 14. The difference, however, is that Chapter 14 stated that *sattvaguna* is a cause of bondage, whilst here, we learn that the *daivi sampad* leads to *moksha – daivi sampad vimokshaya*. Again, this is a debate with two sides to it, resting on the question of whether morality and virtue are the way to attain liberation from rebirth or whether the duality of right and wrong is to be wholly transcended. Chapter 14 suggested that virtue was a manifestation of *sattvaguna* and so not a feature of transcendence, but here, an alternative view seems to be presented. We will take up this debate again later in the Gita's discourse, but at this stage one might suggest that whilst virtue alone is not sufficient to grant *moksha*, it is an essential part of the purifying process that allows realised knowledge to appear in one's heart. On the basis of this understanding, it is possible to say that attachment to righteous living can be both a feature of bondage in this world and also a gateway to the enlightenment that brings liberation from rebirth.

THE ASURI SAMPAD, THE NATURE OF WICKED PERSONS

7. Asuric persons know nothing about the performance of ritual action or about the renunciation of action. Neither purity nor good conduct are ever found in them, nor indeed is truthfulness.

8. They say, 'The world has no truth to it, it has no absolute basis and no presiding Deity. It comes into being without any causal factor. What cause for existence can there be apart from sexual desire?'

9. Those who have destroyed their own selves and have little intelligence adhere to views of this type. Inimical to all, they then engage in cruel deeds and bring destruction to the world.

10. Pursuing insatiable desires and filled with deceit, pride, and passion, due to delusion, they adhere rigidly to their false conceptions and proceed on the basis of impure resolve.

11. Right up to the point of death, they are beset by limitless anxieties, devoting themselves to the fulfilment of sensual desires, convinced there is nothing more than that.

12. Bound by hundreds of ropes in the form of their aspirations, dominated by desire and anger, they accumulate wealth by immoral means in order to fulfil their desires.

13. 'I have obtained this much today, and I will obtain more to satisfy my desire. This much wealth is mine now, and this much more will come to me in the future.

14. 'I have slain this enemy, and I will kill the others as well. I am the Lord, I am the enjoyer, I am successful, powerful, and happy.

15. 'I am wealthy and born into a good family. Who is there who can be my equal? I will perform sacrifices, I will give charity, and thus I will rejoice'. Such are the ideas of those deluded by ignorance.

16. Being distracted by so many different notions, entangled in the net of delusion, and addicted to the enjoyment of their sensual desires, they fall down into an impure state of hell.

17. Being full of self-importance, stubborn, and intoxicated by wealth, pride, and passion, they dishonestly perform rituals that are *yajña* in name only, deviating from the prescribed method.

18. Absorbing themselves in egotism, strength, arrogance, desire, and anger, they display hatred and envy towards me, present as I am in their own bodies and in the bodies of others as well.

These verses provide an extended psychological insight into the nature of persons who are prone to act wickedly and who therefore exist within the *asuri sampad*. Here, we might note the following points:

The qualities of those who represent the *asuri sampad* are shaped primarily by pride, ambitious desire for material gain, a lack of compassion or respect for others, and a harsh, cruel disposition. Again, one's mind is drawn back to the *Mahabharata* narrative in which characters such as Duryodhana and Duhshasana perfectly represent the type of person being referred to here.

Verses 8–11 seem to indicate that there is a connection between wicked conduct and an atheistic or even nihilistic view of the world. It is suggested that their pride and materialism are based on the view that there is no existence apart from this world, and hence, one should abandon moral restraints and focus exclusively on self-interest. The concomitant conclusion might therefore be that religious believers are more righteous in their conduct because they understand the existence of a higher domain and their attitudes are shaped by a religious morality. This is an interesting point to debate, and some might feel that religious belief is no guarantee of righteous conduct or that atheism leads inevitably to immorality.

In verses 13–15, Krishna uses the first person to express the prevailing attitudes of the wicked adherents of the *asuri sampad*. Here, we see that it is not so much their lack of religious belief that leads to wickedness as their selfish pursuit of material goals. They want to be wealthy, powerful, and admired, and they ignore all moral constraints in the pursuit of these goals, destroying, or harming those who stand in their way without compassion. It is this self-absorption and lack of compassion for others that is the principal feature of such persons.

In verse 17, we see that wickedness can exist side by side with religion, or at least the ritualistic aspect of religiosity. Those of the *asuri sampad* may display an outward commitment to religion and even be givers of charity, but they do so only to enhance their personal prestige. There is no generosity of spirit and no real commitment to spirituality; it is all just a vain show that will allow such a person to enhance his reputation and flatter his vanity.

In verse 18, almost as an aside, Krishna reveals that he is present in the bodies of these wrongdoers and in the bodies of others as well. Again, we might presume that here, Krishna is talking about characters from the *Mahabharata*. In different passages, we read of how Duryodhana and his party treat Krishna as an enemy, and on one occasion try to imprison him, and yet philosophically, we are also aware that he is their own self. The point is that their ardent materialism and cruel pursuit of self-interest blinds them to their own true identity.

THE FATE OF THE WICKED
AND THE GODLY

19. Those cruel persons are filled with hatred and are the lowest of men. Within the cycle of rebirth, I cast such impure beings into *asura* wombs, where they stay forever.

20. Entering an asuric womb birth after birth, such fools never attain me, Kaunteya, and so they fall down to the lowest state of existence.

21. This doorway to hell that destroys the soul is threefold, consisting of desire, anger, and greed. You should therefore renounce these three.

22. A man who frees himself from these three gateways of *tamas*, Kaunteya, can act for his own welfare and then proceed to the highest abode.

23. One who abandons the rules ordained by scripture and acts according to his own desire can never attain perfection, happiness, or the highest abode.

24. Therefore, scripture should be your authority in establishing what should and should not be done. When you understand the rules revealed by scripture, you can then act in accordance with your duty.

Here, the discourse moves away from a description of the nature of those who fall under the *asuri sampad* to an account of the fate they will undergo in the world to come. Most, if not all, of the world's religions contain some teaching to the effect that good conduct will be rewarded in the afterlife, while the wicked will have to suffer some form of retribution for their misdeeds. Indian religion usually expresses this in the form of the doctrine of karma, and it is this idea that is being referred to here.

Krishna as the righteous judge

In this passage, one is able to notice some differences from the doctrine of karma as it is more usually expressed. The main point I would note is the role of the Supreme Deity in the suffering that comes to those who act wickedly. As it is proclaimed in the Upanishads and elsewhere, the law of karma is usually presented as an automatic process by which a person creates his or her own destiny through thoughts, words, and deeds. The thoughts we think, the words we speak, and the deeds we perform all reshape the subtle, psychic identity through which the process of rebirth takes place. We become whatever we have made ourselves to be. The idea here, however, is rather closer to that of the western religions, in which a righteous God acts as judge and jury and bestows punishment and reward on all people. Here, Krishna seems to speak of himself in a similar manner as the one who casts (*kshipami*) the wicked ones down into the degraded forms of life.

The word used here for hell is naraka. What does this mean?

Christianity and Islam have both traditionally taught the idea of an eternal hell in which sinners (and non-believers) are tortured perpetually for all time. This vision naturally raises questions about the nature of the God who demands such violent and cruel forms of retribution, and many Hindus would feel that their own beliefs do not include ideas of this type. As we see here, however, Hinduism does indeed contain the idea of hell, and the same is true of Buddhism and Jainism. In the *Mahabharata* and the *Puranas*, we find descriptive accounts of various types of hell in which wrongdoers are punished in horrific ways for their misdeeds, usually with Yama as the presiding deity who oversees these torments. One important difference is that Hindu teachings insist that existence in hell is not eternal and that after some time, the wrongdoer will be reborn in this world. It is also the case that many Hindus do not feel obliged to accept every word of their scripture as literal truth, and it is often said that hell and heaven are both part of our existence on this earth, where we suffer great misery. Hence, hell is to be taken not as worlds of torment but as the sufferings we must endure in the here and now as a result of previous actions.

Righteous conduct as based on one's dharma

In verses 23 and 24, it is interesting to note that Krishna defines wickedness as breaking the rules prescribed by scripture, the *shas-tra-vidhi*, although elsewhere in the *Mahabharata*, he states that *dharma* cannot be defined in terms of shastric rules. Here, we must accept that good and bad conduct is defined in terms of adherence to the rules presented in the Vedic *dharma-shastras*. Arvind Sharma makes a good point in his introduction to *The Hindu Gita* when he points out that Krishna's teachings are first and foremost designed to persuade Arjuna that he should fight. By throwing down his bow and refus-ing to wage war, Arjuna stands in breach of the *kshatriya-dharma* as defined by *shastra*; therefore, it is natural that Krishna should refer to these rules when trying to persuade Arjuna to act. This connection between the teachings of the scriptures and Arjuna's duty to act is pointed out very clearly in the final verse of the chapter.

CONCLUSION:
A SUMMARY OF CHAPTER 16

As is usual in this final section of the Bhagavad-gita, Chapter 16 introduces a subject that is not directly linked to the princi-pal lines of discussion followed by the text as a whole. Here, we have a more or less discrete consideration of the righteous and the wicked, with the focus primarily on the characteristics of the latter and the fate they will suffer as a result of their misdeeds. The chapter opens with a list of most of the qualities we would expect to find in a righteous person. This is referred to as the *daivi sampad*, the position of those who are like the gods. This covers only the first three verses, and from this point onwards, the chapter is devoted to a consideration of the *asuri sampad*, the nature of those who are wicked and devoid of virtue. It is explained that such persons are predominated by a sense of pride, aggression towards others, and a total lack of compassion or moral sensitivity. Although they may involve themselves in religiosity, they have no spiritual sensibilities and their lives are focussed exclusively on the selfish acquisition of power, prestige, and wealth. They have no consideration for the welfare of others, and if anyone becomes their rival or opponent, they respond with hatred, scorn, and violence. Such persons disregard the moral teachings of the scriptures and act on the basis of their own whims and desires. We are then informed that despite the success they may achieve in materialistic terms, such persons are destined to suffer in the world to come as the law of karma inexorably takes effect under the direction of Krishna who is the Supreme Deity. Thus, the wicked will be cast down into the region of hell, where they will endure suffering as a result of their evil deeds, which brought pain, strife, and misery to the world.

For all beings, the faith they have
corresponds to their nature. —17.3

CHAPTER 17

The seventeenth chapter offers a rather curious mixture of ideas but is predominated by the analysis of different aspects of life and religious ritual in accordance with the three *gunas* – *sattva*, *rajas*, and *tamas*. Chapter 17 opens with a question from Arjuna, which is really a response to Krishna's previous assertion that proper action is that which is in accordance with scriptural injunction. Arjuna now asks whether one can pursue a form of spirituality that is not regulated by such injunction, but Krishna does not really give a direct answer. Rather, he refers the issue to the inherent nature of a living being as it is shaped by the predominance of one or other of the three *gunas*. This initial response to the question gives rise to the main line of discussion in the chapter as Krishna describes different types of worship, food, Vedic ritual, religious austerity, and charity in relation to the three *gunas*; and this line of instruction is continued well into the eighteenth chapter. In Chapter 17, however, we have a pause after verse 22, and a short passage of six verses that deals with the religious usage of the three sacred words: *om*, *tat*, and *sat*. This passage is perhaps comparable to that at the end of Chapter 8, as it seems to come out of nowhere and is not obviously connected to the progress of the teaching. But for this chapter, the main emphasis is on the threefold analysis based on our understanding of the *gunas*.

THE SIGNIFICANCE OF FAITH

1. Arjuna said: There are some people who faithfully make offerings but ignore scriptural rules. What is their status, Krishna? Is it said to be in *sattva*, *rajas*, or *tamas*?

2. The Lord said: The faith of embodied beings arises from their inherent nature and is of three types. It can be based on *sattva*, *rajas*, or *tamas*. Now, hear about this.

3. For all beings, the faith they have corresponds to their nature, Bharata. A person is formed by his faith, for the nature of that faith shapes what he is.

4. Those who are sattvic make offerings to the gods, those dominated by *rajas* worship *yakshas* and *rakshasas*, whilst other persons under the influence of *tamas* worship spirits and ghosts.

Arjuna's question here is a very obvious response to Krishna's concluding words in Chapter 16, where he pointed out that a person situated in the *daivi sampad* must adhere to the teachings of the scripture and must therefore perform his prescribed dharmic duty, something which Arjuna has shown himself unwilling to do. So now, Arjuna is asking whether it is acceptable to pursue a spiritual path whilst ignoring these rules and regulations relating to social order.

What, then, are we to make of Krishna's response? It is an interesting question that Arjuna asks, but there does not appear to be a direct answer in the verses that follow. Arjuna has referred to the people he is asking about as being 'endowed with faith', and it is this point in particular that Krishna responds to. He is stating that faith alone does not guarantee spiritual progression, for faith itself is shaped by the *guna* that predominates a person's character. So, the answer Krishna gives is really a negative one that confirms the point he made at the end of Chapter 16. This hypothetical person may have faith in the path he follows, which ignores scriptural injunction, but we should know that faith alone is inadequate, for the faith we have is a product of own inner nature, and that nature is a product of material tendencies.

I think the point that Krishna is making here is that if we select or shape our own spiritual path, then the form of religion we create will not be truly spiritual because it will arise from a form of faith that is related to *gunas*. On the other hand, the religion prescribed by scripture comes from a higher source untouched by the *gunas*. The latter point is not stated overtly, but I think it is implicit in what the Gita is saying here. And we might go on to suggest that a logical inference from this teaching is that the many forms of religion exist not because God or the sages present different ideas but because people are predominated by different material qualities and that material identity shapes the type of religion they adhere to.

EXCESSIVE ASCETICISM CONDEMNED

5. Some people who undertake acts of austerity perform ferocious deeds not sanctioned by scripture. They are motivated by hypocrisy and egotism, and are beset by the power of desire and passion.

6. They simply cause the elements of the body to waste away, and they afflict me as well, for I am also present in the body. You should understand them as having the conviction of the *asura* nature.

These two verses seem to serve as an example of the point that Krishna has just made. Through his question, Arjuna appeared to suggest that the presence of faith legitimated a religion even though it was not based on scripture, but Krishna replied that faith alone is not a suitable criterion because faith comes in different forms and arises from the material qualities inherent in a person's nature. Here is an example: Some people base their religion on

extreme asceticism and the mortification of the flesh in a manner
that ignores the teaching of scripture. Such people certainly have
faith in their spiritual path, but that factor alone does not make
it legitimate. It is in fact a form of *adharma* because they are predominated by the lower *gunas* of *rajas* and *tamas*, and the style of
religion they adhere to reflects their inherent nature because it is
not regulated by the test of scripture.

FOOD IN RELATION
TO THE GUNAS

7. Now, the food all beings find pleasing is also of three
types, as is *yajña*, austerity, and charity. Listen to this
analysis of those categories.
8. The foods liked by sattvic persons are those that bring
long life, vigour, strength, and health, and which cause
happiness and delight. Such foods are very tasty, juicy,
crisp, and pleasing.
9. Foods liked by persons predominated by *rajas* are bitter,
sour, salty, very hot, pungent, strong-tasting, and burning. Such foods cause suffering, sorrow, and ill-health.
10. The foods liked by those predominated by *tamas* are generally stale, tasteless, rotten, left by others, dirty, and
foul.

Having answered Arjuna's question by making reference to the
three *gunas*, Krishna then rather cleverly uses this as a link to a
further passage of teaching in which he shows how the various
facets of our lives are all influenced by these *gunas*, starting with
the food we eat. It is significant to note that this does not take the
form of lists of foods that can be eaten and forbidden foods, as is
found in the Islamic Shariah or the Jewish law. Rather, Krishna
talks about types of food and leaves it up to the individual to

make his or her choices. And it is significant that here, there is no direct prohibition on the eating of meat or even of beef.

The sattvic food is what we might today call the 'healthy option'. It is food that prolongs life and brings good health as well as making the body fit, active, and invigorated. The science of *ayurveda* contains a detailed analysis of food types, but on the basis of what Krishna says here, we must presume that fresh fruit and vegetables, whole grains, and other forms of light, nutritious food can be taken as sattvic. Rajasic foods seem to be those that are very strong tasting, salty, and pungent; perhaps in the modern supermarket, they would be the heavily processed foods that contain unsaturated fats and are hard to fully digest. And finally, the tamasic foods are those which are really unfit for consumption – leftovers and stale or rotten food. The point here, I think, is that these are the sort of foods that are eaten by people who are negligent and have no concern over what they are putting into their body. It is interesting to note that these different types of food are referred to as *tamasa-priya* or *sattvika-priya*. The type of person you are is shaped by the predominance of one of the *gunas* over the others in your psychological and physical makeup. And the type of person you are dictates the type of food you will find attractive; some people like salty, processed food, whilst others prefer to eat fresh fruit and vegetables. These different predilections are symptomatic of the presence of the different *gunas* within different persons.

YAJÑA IN RELATION TO THE GUNAS

11. When *yajña* is performed by persons who do not desire to gain thereby, in strict accordance with the proper rules, and with the mind absorbed in the thought 'It is my duty to make this offering', then it is of the nature of *sattva*.

12. But when it is performed with some result in mind or out of vanity, O best of the Bharatas, that *yajña* is of the nature of *rajas*.

13. And when it is performed without regard for the proper rules, without food offerings, chanting of the hymns, payment to the priests, or any real faith in the process, they say that *yajña* is of the nature of *tamas*.

Now, using the same format, the discussion moves on to a consideration of the Vedic ritual. Here, there is an important point to note, which gives further insight into our earlier discussion of whether the *sattvaguna* is a cause of bondage or a platform for the pusuit of *moksha*.

What can be seen in these verses that connects them to the previous teachings of the Bhagavad-gita?

Here, we find that the performance of *karma-yoga*, as outlined in the early chapters of the Gita, is associated with the *sattvaguna*. In verse 11, we read that the *yajña* is sattvic when it is performed without any desire for personal gain, simply because it is one's religious duty to do so. And in verse 12, the ritual performed with a desire for personal gain is designated as being 'of the nature of *rajas*'. So, it seems that *karma-yoga* is closely associated with the quality of *sattva*, and as we have heard it repeatedly said that *karma-yoga* is a means of gaining liberation from rebirth, it seems that *sattva* can be regarded as a part of the path to *moksha*. We will see this pattern emerging again as the text continues to follow this format with *sattva* being equated with desireless action, *rajas* equated with action based on desire, and *tamas* the negligent, heedless, and inappropriate performance of action.

AUSTERITY IN RELATION
TO THE GUNAS

14. Austerity of the body is said to consist of worship of the gods, brahmins, teachers, and wise men, cleanliness, honesty, celibacy, and not harming (*ahimsa*).

15. Austerity of speech is said to consist of speaking words that do not disturb others and which are true, loving, and beneficial, as well as the regular recitation of the Vedas.

16. And austerity of the mind is said to consist of mental serenity, benevolence, silence, self-control, and a pure disposition.

17. When men engaged in yoga undertake this threefold austerity with the highest faith and without desire for any result, that austerity is said to be of the nature of *sattva*.

18. But when the austerity is undertaken for the sake of gaining respect, reputation, and honour, or out of vanity, it is said to be of the nature of *rajas*; this indeed is unstable and impermanent.

19. And that austerity by which one inflicts pain on oneself due to foolish notions, or which is intended to bring destruction to others, is declared to be of the nature of *tamas*.

Here, Krishna moves on to the third of the four topics he reviews in this chapter in relation to the *gunas*. This is *tapas*, or religious austerity, and we might note the following points:

At the beginning of the chapter, Krishna was very critical of persons who undertake harsh austerities that can harm the body, pointing out that this type of religious practice is not recommended in the scriptures. And here, that same theme is continued as *tapas* is first defined in a rather novel manner. In the *Ramayana*, *Mahabharata*, and *Puranas*, we read of *tapas* being performed by holy men living in the forest, and this typically takes the form of some form of severe restraint of eating, drinking, or breathing, or even the adoption of painful bodily postures and exposing oneself to severe heat and cold. Here, however, Krishna defines *tapas* in a rather different manner that makes its practice possible for people in all stages of life.

Tapas is defined in two ways, both of which have three divisions: firstly, in terms of body, speech, and mind, and then in terms of the three *gunas*. Where *tapas* is related to body, speech, and mind, it is quite clear that the practice spoken of here is very different from the harsh mortification of the flesh we read of in the *Puranas*. Bodily *tapas* consists of showing respect to those worthy of it, cleanliness, honesty, sexual restraint, and not harming others. Austerity of speech means to speak only the truth or words that are pleasing, to not cause pain to anyone, and to recite sacred texts. And austerity of the mind means to remain peaceful and to have a kind, gentle, and benevolent attitude towards others. So, apart from anything else, Krishna is offering something of a redefinition of *tapas* that moves it away from the harsh physical austerity more usually associated with the term.

In the second threefold definition of *tapas*, which is based on the *gunas*, we see again how *sattva* is associated with *karma-yoga*, and *rajas* with the pursuit of selfish desire. Furthermore, the statement of verse 17 that the three types of austerity are undertaken by men who are *yukta*, or engaged in yoga, also suggests a connection between *sattva* and the spiritual path that leads to liberation from rebirth.

CHARITY IN RELATION TO THE GUNAS

20. Charity given with the thought 'This should be given', presented to a suitable recipient from whom nothing is expected in return, and at the right time and place, is of the nature of *sattva*.

21. But that charity which is given with the expectation of getting something in return, with the hope of some future reward, or with reluctance is of the nature of *rajas*.

22. And that charity which is given at the wrong place and wrong time, to an unworthy recipient, or which is given without respect and with contempt, is known to be of the nature of *tamas*.

In the final section of this passage, the same threefold analysis is applied to the giving of gifts in charity. Again, we may note the link that is drawn between the absence of selfish desire, *karma-yoga*, and the prevalence of *sattva* in the performance of the action. Apart from the absence of desire for something in return or for personal prestige, in sattvic charity there is also the question of the gift being given to a 'suitable recipient'. Who is this suitable person? Some will suggest that this implies that charity should only be given to brahmins, religious institutions, or persons who are righteous, and not to those who might use the gift to purchase alcohol or drugs. This may well be what Krishna is meaning here, but the statement is not explicit. One might equally regard the 'suitable recipient' as a person who is starving and whose life depends on the gift we might give.

THE SACRED WORDS 'OM TAT SAT'

23. The words *om tat sat* are understood as a threefold designation of Brahman. It was with this *mantra* that the brahmins, Vedas, and *yajñas* were established in ancient times.

24. Therefore, in accordance with the prescribed rule, the followers of the Veda always recite the syllable *om* when they perform ritual acts of *yajña*, charity, and austerity.

25. Without desire for the fruit of their action, persons who seek liberation from rebirth recite the syllable *tat* when

they perform various ritual acts of *yajña*, austerity, and charity.

26. This term *sat* is used to designate both reality and virtue. The word *sat* is also used to denote a righteous act, Partha.

27. Hence, dedication to *yajña*, austerity, or charity is referred to as *sat*; the action by which these are undertaken is also designated as *sat*.

28. However, if an act is performed without faith, be it a sacrificial offering, a gift in charity, or an act of austerity, it is referred to as *a-sat*, Partha. It has no effect either in the world to come or here in this world.

This passage marks a sudden change in the direction of the discourse that is really quite surprising. There is a link, however. The previous verses have reviewed the different types of *yajña*, *tapas*, and *dana*, which are religious acts typically performed within the Hindu tradition. Here, Krishna elaborates further on these rituals by explaining that when they are performed, the sacred words *om*, *tat*, and *sat* are enunciated to enhance their sanctity. Here, we might note the following points:

There is much that could be said here on the Upanishadic references to the words *om*, *tat*, and *sat*, but such a detailed study would be beyond our scope. Suffice to say that here, again, the Bhagavad-gita is closely connected to the religious ideas espoused by the major Upanishads and in particular the statement of the Mandukya Upanishad that *om* is *brahman*, as repeated here in verse 23.

Verses 24–27 seem merely to point out that each of the three words *om*, *tat*, and *sat* is used as an invocation when the rituals of *yajña*, *tapas*, and *dana* are performed.

In verse 28, Krishna returns again to the issue of faith that was raised by Arjuna in the question with which the chapter began. In his initial response, Krishna pointed out that faith is not necessarily a positive quality, for it is of different kinds as shaped by the *gunas,* and a person who is not guided by the scriptures may have faith in a form of religion that is wholly pernicious. Here, however, the other side of the argument is presented as we are told that any religious act must be accompanied by faith if it is to be efficacious. Otherwise, it will be like the rajasic and tamasic rituals referred to above that are undertaken just to enhance a person's prestige, or negligently, and without any real commitment.

CONCLUSION:
A SUMMARY OF CHAPTER 17

Chapter 17 of the Bhagavad-gita opens with Arjuna's question as to whether religious actions that ignore scriptural injunction are still valid if they are performed with faith. To this, Krishna replies that faith alone is not enough, for one's faith is shaped by one's inner nature and can in fact lead one to follow pernicious forms of religion. The discussion was then extended to reflect firstly on food, and then on three types of religious action, Vedic ritual, religious austerity, and charity – *yajña, tapas,* and *dana.* Krishna pointed out that these can be undertaken in different ways depending upon the predominance of a particular *guna: sattva, rajas,* or *tamas.* The idea implied here is that a ritual act may be performed with faith, but if that faith is a product of *rajas* or *tamas,* then the ritual will be characterised by the flaws referred to in these verses. The chapter concludes with a brief discussion of the sacred words, or *mantras,* enunciated whilst the ritual acts of *yajña, tapas,* and *dana* are performed, and a statement that although faith alone may be not be enough, it is still an essential requirement if the ritual is to be properly executed.

Wherever there is Krishna, the master of yoga,
and wherever there is Arjuna, who bears the bow,
there will also be good fortune, victory, success,
and good judgment. —18.78

CHAPTER 18

Chapter 18 is the final chapter of the Bhagavad-gita, and it is also the longest, containing a total of 78 verses. The content of the chapter can be divided into three parts. The first phase of the teaching extends from verse 1 to verse 39 and continues and expands upon the discussion begun in Chapter 17. Here, we find further reflection on the ritual performance of *yajña*, *tapas*, and *dana* and in particular the question of when and if such acts are to be given up so that the aspirant can seek the ultimate goal of *moksha*.

After a detailed consideration of the nature of action and its results, the Gita then resumes its analysis of different aspects of our existence in relation to the three *gunas*. Here, the discussion focuses on six topics to add to the four covered in Chapter 17. These are knowledge, action, the performer of action, intelligence, resolve, and happiness. This discourse continues up to verse 39, and at this point, Krishna begins to conclude his instructions by recapitulating and summarising the main points he has sought to convey to Arjuna, and it is notable that the three topics he particularly highlights are *karma-yoga*, the realisation of spiritual knowledge, and finally the path of *bhakti* (which is particularly emphasised here).

The third and final part of the chapter forms a conclusion to the Bhagavad-gita as a whole. Krishna warns that this teaching should not be given to an unsuitable person but to those who are receptive. Arjuna then confirms that his mind has been changed by the words Krishna has spoken, and the vision he has seen. He will now take up his bow once more and fight in the battle. The final verses return to the original setting in Chapter 1, with Samjaya emphasising to Dhritarashtra that the presence of Arjuna and Krishna means that victory is certain for the Pandava cause.

SAMNYASA AND TYAGA– TWO TYPES OF RENUNCIATION

1. Arjuna said: I wish now to learn about the subject of *samnyasa*, O mighty Hrishikesha, and about the distinction between *samnyasa* and *tyaga*, O slayer of Keshin.

2. The Lord said: Learned men understand *samnyasa* to be the giving up of any action motivated by selfish desire. The wise further define *tyaga* as the renunciation of the fruits of all action.

3. Some of those endowed with wisdom assert that all action must be abandoned because it is inherently flawed. But others say that ritual acts of *yajña*, charity, and austerity must not be abandoned.

4. Now, hear my verdict on this debate over renunciation, O best of the Bharatas. It has been asserted that renunciation is of three types, O tiger amongst men.

5. The ritual acts of *yajña*, charity, and austerity must not be abandoned. Rather, they should be performed, for *yajña*, charity, and austerity can purify even men of wisdom.

6. But even these types of action should be performed only after renouncing attachment to them and the reward they bring. This is my ultimate conclusion, Partha.

Arjuna's question here might seem to be a complete change of subject, for the words *samnyasa* and *tyaga* both mean 'giving up' or 'renunciation', and are often used in relation to the renunciation of the world by sages and *sadhus* who wish to live as monks in pursuit of exclusively spiritual goals. The question arises, however, from the previous discussion of religious action – *yajña*, *tapas*, and *dana* – for renunciation includes the giving up of these ritualised forms of religion. Hence, Arjuna is asking here whether the practices considered in Chapter 17 are just preliminary forms of religious action that are to be given up when a person progresses to the higher levels of spiritual realisation. Krishna concedes that even amongst the wise, there are different opinions on this subject, but then gives his own decision that corresponds with his earlier insistence that Arjuna must fulfil his dharmic duty.

The words samnyasa and tyaga are often taken as being virtually synonymous. How does Krishna define the distinction?

Krishna defines *samnyasa* as the complete renunciation of ritual action, and here, one must presume he is referring to the ancient institution by which a brahmin renounces the world in later life to become a *samnyasin*. For most of his life, the brahmin is a performer of rituals, but when he takes the vows of *samnyasa*, he gives up these practices, living apart from society and seeking only spiritual realisation. *Tyaga* is here equated with the *karma-yoga* that Krishna discussed in the earlier chapters of the Bhagavad-gita. Here, ritual action is still performed, but there is a process of *buddhi-yoga*, the internal renunciation of attachment to the result of the action. So here, complete renunciation of action is designated as *samnyasa*, and the renunciation of selfish desire whilst one continues to perform action as a duty is referred to as *tyaga*, seemingly a synonym for *karma-yoga*. The distinction between the two terms made here seems to be unique to the Bhagavad-gita and is not replicated (as far as I am aware) in the use of the terms in other Sanskrit texts.

What decision does Krishna give on whether ritual action is to be given up?

As is to be expected, Krishna gives the decision that *tyaga*, renunciation of attachment to results, is superior to *samnyasa*, the complete renunciation of ritual action. This corresponds with the teachings given at the start of Chapter 3, in which complete renunciation of action was condemned as being impossible to achieve and useless without internal renunciation of desire.

The reason Krishna gives for this verdict is, however, rather different to that stated in Chapter 3. In verse 5, Krishna states that the ritual performance of *yajña, tapas,* and *dana* (as described in the previous chapter) is effective in purifying a person, and the implication seems to be that spiritual realisation can only appear in the heart of one who has attained this position of purity. For this reason, ritualised forms of religious practice are not to be given up; *karma-yoga* is again given precedence over the complete renunciation of the world.

RENUNCIATION IN RELATION TO THE GUNAS

7. The renunciation of prescribed action is improper. The renunciation of such action due to ignorance is proclaimed to be of the nature of *tamas.*

8. If action is given up as painful and because of fear of the suffering it might cause to one's body, that renunciation is of the nature of *rajas*; one will not gain the fruit of renunciation in that way.

9. But if one thinks, 'This must be performed' and then discharges his prescribed duty whilst renouncing attachment and the fruits of action, Arjuna, that renunciation is known to be of the nature of *sattva.*

10. The renouncer who is predominated by *sattva* never loathes action when it is not pleasing and is not attached to pleasant action. He is a wise man, and his doubts are dispelled.

11. It is impossible for any being who has a body to completely give up action, but one who renounces the fruits of action is said to be *tyagin,* a true renouncer.

12. Undesirable, desirable, and mixed are the three types of result that come from action. After death, these befall those who are not renouncers, but never those who are renounced (*tyagins*).

This passage gives further discussion of the subject of renunciation, and here, Krishna employs his usual tool of analysis by looking at the subject in terms of the three *gunas*. Renunciation, like faith, is not necessarily something positive, for it can be a result of the lower *gunas, rajas,* and *tamas.* Where *tamas* prevails, renunciation may occur as a result of laziness, stupidity, or confusion, and where *rajas* prevails, a person may follow the path of renunciation because he finds his dharmic duty difficult or painful – an assertion that has resonance with Arjuna's current position.

In verses 9 and 10, we have the by now familiar equation of the *sattvaguna* with *karma-yoga,* for when action is performed purely as a matter of duty without any selfish intent, then this is the sattvic form of renunciation. Verse 11 repeats the point made in 3.5 that the complete renunciation of all action is an impossibility, for to live is to act. Hence, real renunciation is not so much about physical action but is an internal state of consciousness. And according to verse 12, one who attains this state of renounced consciousness whilst continuing to perform action is not afflicted by the effects of action in accordance with the law of karma. So here, again, we see an equation made between the *sattvaguna* and the *karma-yoga* and then between *karma-yoga* and liberation from the bondage of karma.

FIVE CAUSES OF
THE RESULTS OF ACTION

13. Now, learn from me about these five causal factors, O mighty one, established by the Samkhya system as determining the results of all actions.
14. These are the situation, the performer, the various instruments employed, and the different motions enacted. Destiny is, then, the fifth factor.
15. Whatever action is undertaken with body, words, or mind, be it proper or perverse, these five are its causes.
16. As this is the case, anyone who, due to an undeveloped understanding, sees himself alone as the performer of action has the wrong idea and does not see at all.
17. If a person has no sense of being the performer of action, and if his consciousness is not absorbed in the action, then, even if he kills all these people, he does not kill and he is not bound.
18. Knowledge, the object of knowledge, and the knower represent the threefold impulse for action. The instrument, the deed, and the performer represent the three constituents of an action.

These six verses contain a succinct discourse on the nature and performance of action, and despite their brevity, they offer a number of important insights into a variety of subjects. The opening passages of this chapter have been focused on the issue of whether ritual action is to be performed or whether it should be renounced by one seeking to escape from the bondage of karma, and these verses continue to explore the same subject. Here, we might note the following points:

Five factors are here identified as being instrumental in determining the outcome of any action. These are the place, the performer, the instruments, the exertion made, and, finally, destiny.

It is interesting to note here that this teaching does not accept a doctrine of absolute determinism, as sometimes appears to be the case in Hindu religious thought. It might be argued that because the course of our life is predetermined on the basis of the law of karma, our personal endeavours are not important in determining success or failure. Here, however, a different view is expressed, for four of the five factors listed are to do with the way we perform an action – in other words, personal endeavor – and destiny, shaped by past action – is only one factor of five. Hence, we might conclude that the outcome of any undertaking will be determined by a subtle combination of the efficacy of the endeavour and the destiny imposed upon us by our previous acts.

The main idea in this passage, however, is related, again, to *karma-yoga*, and here, a direct link is drawn between *karma-yoga* and realisation of the true self. The detachment from selfish desire that is the central feature of *karma-yoga* becomes possible as a result of the realisation that the true self is not affected by action and is not the performer of action. Here, five factors were listed, but the *atman*, our own true identity, is not one of them. Hence, realised knowledge and detachment from the fruits of action are concomitant factors in the progress of spiritual awakening.

Verse 17 has given rise to some controversy because it seems to suggest that if one's motive is pure or is unselfish, then even an action that appears overtly wicked does not leave one morally culpable or subject to negative karma. There is no doubt that the Bhagavad-gita moves the focus of moral judgement away from the nature of the action itself and on to the motive which prompts one to perform the action. That is not to say, however, that the Gita is indifferent to the nature of the action itself, for *karma-yoga* insists that it should be action in accordance with *dharma* that is performed without desire. However, because it is very difficult to determine what a person's motive is, this verse could give support to the type of political or religious fanaticism that produces acts of extreme violence and claims a moral basis for them on the grounds that they are not selfishly motivated. This could even be applied to any doctrine of a 'just war'; in the case of nations that engage in violent confrontations, it is typically difficult to demonstrate the falsity of such a claim. It is more or less on this basis that some modern writers have been critical of the morality of the Gita and have accused the text of giving ideological support to warmongers. Here, however, Gandhi's comments on the Bhagavad-gita provide a useful sense of balance, for he argues that the Gita only gives legitimacy to acts of violence when they are performed by one who is wholly free of selfish desire and has no sense of enmity towards any other being. Now, some may abuse this doctrine to justify their acts of cruelty, but such misuse of an idea does not necessarily invalidate a doctrine or teaching. The point is that this verse and similar ideas found in the Gita must be understood strictly within the context of the teachings of the text as a whole, and not extracted from it without wider understanding.

Knowledge in Relation to the Gunas

19. Knowledge, action, and the performer of action are all threefold, according to the *gunas*. This can be shown by analysis in relation to the *gunas*, so now listen to the way these are arranged.
20. When one changeless existence is seen in all beings, undivided in their diverse forms, you should know that knowledge to be of the nature of *sattva*.
21. But when knowledge displays an understanding based on distinction, and recognises varying types of existence in different living beings, you should know that knowledge to be of the nature of *rajas*.
22. And that knowledge which is not based on reason, which attaches itself to a single causal factor as if it were

everything, which is unaware of the truth and thus limited in scope, is regarded as being of the nature of *tamas*.

After the extended consideration of the nature of action, which
arose from Arjuna's question about the renunciation of action,
Krishna now returns to the pattern of teaching he began in Chapter
17, using the three *gunas* as a basis for analysing different aspects
of human life. Here, he moves beyond the three types of religious
ritual discussed above (*yajña, tapas,* and *dana*) and considers firstly
knowledge, then action itself, and then the performer of action.

THREE TYPES OF KNOWLEDGE

Sattvic knowledge is that which perceives the single reality existing
within every being rather than the diversity of existence in terms
of the material forms. There is more than a hint of Advaita in this
verse, but this is not the only possible explanation, for it could be
that the sattvic knowledge perceives an identical *atman* in every
being without seeing each *atman* as identical with Brahman. And
once again, we see the direct relationship that exists between the
quality of *sattva* and spiritual realisation.

Rajasic knowledge does not perceive the spiritual reality existing within each being but sees only the external mundane world. In
other words, knowledge related to *sattva* is equated with spiritual
insight, whilst rajasic knowledge is confined to that which can be
perceived through the senses.

Knowledge related to *tamas* appears to be the sort of mindless
fanaticism that is beyond the call of reason, or else just plain stupidity. Unfortunately, this type of knowledge seems to be quite
widespread in contemporary society.

ACTION IN RELATION TO THE GUNAS

23. Action that is ordained, performed without attachment, and undertaken without passionate endeavour, hatred, or desire for the fruits is said to be of the nature of *sattva*.
24. But action performed due to hankering for a desired object, with a sense of pride, or with excessive endeavour is regarded as being of the nature of *rajas*.
25. And action undertaken due to delusion and without regard for consequences, damage, harm, and ability is said to be of the nature of *tamas*.

Verse 18 above pointed out that knowledge, its object, and the knower provide the impulse for action, for action is usually predicated by thought and perception. So, different types of knowledge give rise to different types of action in accordance with the *gunas*, and these three types of action are delineated here.

Three types of action

Sattvic action is, again, clearly equated with the Gita's doctrine of *karma-yoga*. When action is in accordance with *dharma*, and when it is performed dispassionately, as a duty, then it is of the nature of *sattva*. Action performed on the basis of personal desire or out of a sense of pride is of the nature of *rajas*, and tamasic action is the sort of stupid, callous, or cruel action that is frequently seen to occur simply because of the degraded nature of the person who performs it. In all three instances, we can certainly think of examples in the world today when action of this type is seen to be performed.

THE PERFORMER OF ACTION
IN RELATION TO THE GUNAS

26. When he is free of attachment, never speaks with any sense of 'I', is endowed with resolve and fortitude, and is unmoved by success or failure, the performer of action is said to be of the nature of *sattva*.

27. But if he is desirous and seeks the fruit of action, is greedy, violent by nature, and impure, and is beset by feelings of delight and sorrow, that performer of action is regarded as being of the nature of *rajas*.

28. And that performer of action who is negligent, vulgar, obstinate, deceitful, vicious, indolent, uninspired, and procrastinating is said to be of the nature of *tamas*.

In the third of this set of passages, Krishna considers the nature of the performer of action in relation to the three *gunas*, and here, the pattern is very similar to that noted above in relation to the action itself, with a further affirmation of the close link between *karma-yoga* and *sattvaguna*.

Three types of actor

When the performer of action is influenced by *sattva*, he acts without attachment to the results, with firm resolve and with no sense of pride in his achievements. When the performer is influenced by *rajas*, he is aggressive and passionate and has an ardent desire for personal gain through his endeavours. But where *tamas* predominates, the performer of action is lazy, stupid, obstinate, and unmotivated.

Intelligence in Relation to the Gunas

29. Now, hear about the threefold divisions of intelligence and of resolve in relation to the *gunas*, which I shall fully explain to show the differences between them, Dhanamjaya.

30. That which understands prescribed action and the renunciation of action, what should be done and what should not be done, what is to be feared and what is not to be feared, as well as bondage and liberation, is intelligence under the influence of *sattva*.

31. But that by which *dharma* and *adharma* are not clearly understood, nor indeed ordained duty and forbidden action, is intelligence under the influence of *rajas*, Partha.

32. But that understanding which is covered by ignorance and so thinks *adharma* to be *dharma*, and has wrong conceptions on all subjects, is intelligence under the influence of *tamas*.

At this point, the discourse changes direction slightly as Krishna moves his analysis away from the performance of action to consider the nature of our intelligence, or, perhaps more precisely, the way in which we understand the world. The points made here may seem obvious, but if we think about them carefully, they contain some very profound truths. The focus of this passage is on the ways in which people understand *dharma*, and here, I think we should interpret *dharma* in the broadest sense as 'righteous conduct'.

People all over the world claim to be acting righteously, but here, the Bhagavad-gita points out that understandings of *dharma* are shaped by the predominance of a particular *guna*. So, if a person is dominated by the quality of *rajas*, he may claim to be acting on the basis of virtue, or *dharma*, but his inherently rajasic nature means that his intelligence is incapable of understanding what virtue truly

is. At a less philosophical level, we might say that people motivated by strong personal desires frequently construct a definition
of virtue that is, in fact, no more than a justification for their own
self-interest, and they are often deluded by their own moral inven-
tions. It is only the sattvic person who is able to withdraw from the
predominance of self-interest and thereby perceive the true nature
of virtue and of *dharma*.

Three types of understanding

Where the intelligence is predominated by *sattva*, a person has a
clear understanding of the world and can distinguish between right
and wrong, and between proper and improper conduct. He also
possesses the spiritual insight to determine how liberation can be
attained, as well as the root causes of our bondage in this world.
By contrast, where *rajas* prevails, a person cannot understand what
is *dharma* and what is *adharma*, or what course of action is moral
and what is immoral. Here, one may note that the rajasic person is
dominated by his selfish desires, and it is this ardour for personal
gain that obscures his understanding of *dharma*. Where the intellect
is under the sway of *tamas*, a person regards wickedness as virtue
and virtue as wickedness. We might think that this must be an
extreme circumstance, but again, if we consider the world around
us, we will see that this type of tamasic understanding is depress-
ingly prevalent.

RESOLVE IN RELATION
TO THE GUNAS

33. That resolve by means of which one holds the activities of
the mind, breath, and senses in undeviating yoga practice
is of the nature of *sattva*.

34. But that resolve by which a person adheres to the goals of dharma, *kama*, and *artha*, seeking results from each of these attachments, is of the nature of *rajas*.

35. And that resolve due to which a man with perverse ideas does not give up sleep, fear, grief, depression, and vanity is of the nature of *tamas*.

In the fifth of these six passages, Krishna turns his attention to the subject of *dhriti*, which can be translated as 'resolve', 'commitment', or 'determination'. As with faith, all people display some form of resolve, but here, we are shown that the object of that commitment is determined by the way in which the *gunas* shape our inherent nature.

Three types of resolve

Although the point has probably been overemphasised by now, it is still noteworthy that the analysis here, again, links *sattva* with the spiritual quest for liberation. Hindu teachings typically refer to four goals of life, *dharma*, *artha*, *kama*, and *moksha* – religion or virtue, wealth, fulfilment of desire, and liberation from rebirth – and these are used here for the purposes of analysis. The pursuit of *moksha* is found where one's *dhriti* is applied to the regulation of the mind through yoga practice, the techniques Krishna revealed in Chapter 6 as a means of acquiring realised knowledge. *Dharma*, *artha*, and *kama* are the goals sought where *dhriti* is predominated by the quality of *rajas*, and where a person has no clear goal to pursue, but is under the control of indolence, misery, and intoxication, the *dhriti* is regarded as being tamasic.

Happiness in Relation
to the Gunas

36. Happiness is also of three types. Now, hear from me, O
best of the Bharatas, about the happiness a person finds
due to his repeated practice, which puts an end to sorrow.

37. That which is like poison in the beginning but at the end
is like nectar is said to be happiness of the nature of *sattva*. It arises due to the serenity of one's intellect.

38. But that happiness which is obtained through the contact
of the senses with their objects, and is like nectar in the
beginning but like poison in the end, is understood to be
of the nature of *rajas*.

39. And that happiness which simply deludes the self in both
the beginning and the end, being based on sleep, indolence, and stupidity, is of the nature of *tamas*.

In the last of the six passages, Krishna turns his attention to the
pursuit of happiness, which is also defined in relation to *sattva*,
rajas, and *tamas*.

Three types of happiness

Where *sattva* prevails, it is understood that true happiness can
only be gained through considerable endeavour and sacrifice,
whilst the happiness of *rajas* is instant gratification of the type that
ultimately leads to suffering. It is fairly easy to infer here that the
notion of sattvic happiness relates to the spiritual joy that is ultimately achieved after extensive practice and the renunciation of
sensual pleasures. This is the joy referred to earlier when the Gita
discussed the yoga practices that lead to realisation of the inner
self; verse 21 of Chapter 6 speaks of *sukham atyantikam*, the highest
happiness that is *atindriyam*, beyond the grasp of the senses. The
rajasic happiness, by contrast, is the pleasure we enjoy through

satisfaction of the senses. Here, the pleasure is immediate, but in the long term it leads only to distress as old age, death, and disease bring us to a state of sensory deprivation and despair. One might also suggest that there is a certain emptiness in life where one's happiness is obtained purely through the senses and, furthermore, that this sense of emptiness and *ennui* is a symptom of modern culture predominated by the capitalist ethos. And finally, the happiness shaped by *tamas* comes from the fulfilment of neither spiritual nor material goals. It is a form of happiness based on foolishness, indolence, and intoxication and, again, is something that is not unfamiliar in the modern world.

From this point on, the teachings of the chapter change direction, and Krishna begins his summary and conclusion of the teachings he has previously imparted, although verse 40 does provide something of a link and a lead in to this new direction. The analysis of life and the world based on the three *gunas* is now complete, and the Bhagavad-gita is again turning its attention back to one of its earlier concerns – the question of how a person can fulfil his social duties whilst simultaneously pursuing the goal of *moksha*.

THE QUALITIES OF
THE FOUR VARNAS

40. Neither on earth nor in heaven amongst the gods is there any form of existence that is free of these three *gunas,* which are born of *prakriti.*

41. The duties of brahmins, kshatriyas, *vaishyas,* and *shudras,* O scorcher of the foe, are designated in accordance with the *gunas* and which arise from the inherent nature of each.

42. Tranquillity, restraint, austerity, purity, patience, honesty, theoretical knowledge, practical knowledge, and faith in the Vedic revelation are the duties of a brahmin, born of his inherent nature.

43. Heroism, energy, resolve, expertise, never fleeing from battle, charity, and displaying a lordly disposition are the duties of a *kshatriya*, born of his inherent nature.

44. Agriculture, tending cows, and trade are the duties of a *vaishya*, born of his inherent nature, whilst work consisting of service to others is the duty of a *shudra*, born of his inherent nature.

The intention here is to lead the discussion back towards the idea of *karma-yoga* by drawing our attention to the question of social obligation. However, we are first given an interesting account of the duties of the four *varnas*, the four original social divisions that are often regarded as the origins of the Hindu caste system. In recent years, the caste system has become a controversial feature of the Hindu traditions, and many modern Hindus feel that it should be regarded as a social phenomenon unconnected with the practice of religion. The Bhagavad-gita has a significant role to play in this discussion, as it provides important insights into the relationship between social duty and the inherent nature of a living being as determined by the presence of the three *gunas*.

The relationship between the gunas and the varnas

The relationship is not overtly stated here, but in verses 40 and 41, we read firstly that all forms of life in this world are influenced by the *gunas* and then that the duties of the four social classes are designated in accordance with the *gunas* that arise from inherent nature. Hence, the implication is that the four *varnas* have different duties to perform reflecting the prevalence of *sattva*, *rajas*, or *tamas* in each of the social classes.

The qualities of a brahmin as discussed in verse 42

Although verse 42 refers to *brahma-karma*, the duties of a brahmin, the list given here really refers to the character required for one who is a member of the highest social class. Essentially, the brahmin is one who displays the characteristics of the *sattvaguna*: self-control, purity, honesty, and lack of material desire. The interesting point arises here as to whether one is therefore a brahmin by birth or by qualities. The suggestion of the Gita is that one is born with a certain inherent nature that naturally gives rise to these qualities, but does that occur only when a person is born into a brahmin family? We might also consider that the Hindu caste system has been the subject of much criticism from both within and without, and in many cases this criticism is fully justified. However, we might also note that in the social order recommended by the Bhagavad-gita, the social elite worthy of most respect does not consist of those who are wealthy, powerful, or ostentatious, but of those who display intellectual, spiritual, and moral qualities and have a certain disdain for wealth and reputation. This view is one that stands in marked contrast to the way in which elites are generally formed in contemporary society.

In each of verses 42–44, the phrase 'karma sva-bhava-jam'
is used, meaning 'action arising from inherent nature'.
How can that phrase be understood?

This is quite a complex question, but I would suggest that the view of the Bhagavad-gita is that previous actions shape the subtle body that surrounds the changeless *atman* so that one is born again under the influence of a specific combination of the three *gunas*. It is the influence of the *gunas* present from birth that determines the inherent nature of an individual; in other words, we are all born with different characters and personalities. That inherent nature determines the character of a person, and this in turn makes a particular type of duty or action most suitable for a person. Therefore, the phrase 'action arising from inherent nature' refers to the type of duty and lifestyle most suitable for a person who possesses those particular qualities.

KARMA-YOGA

45. A man can attain perfection by devoting himself to his own particular duty. Now, hear how a man who dedicates himself to his specific duty achieves that perfect state.
46. He is the one out of whom all beings have evolved, and he pervades this whole world. It is by worshipping the Deity through the performance of his proper duty that a man achieves that perfect state.
47. Even though it may have faults, one's own dharma is still superior to accepting the dharma of another, even if that dharma is perfectly observed. By performing the action prescribed in accordance with his inherent nature, a person never incurs any sin.
48. Even if it be beset by faults, a person should never give up the type of action he is born to perform, Kaunteya. All endeavours are tainted by some fault, as fire is tainted by smoke.
49. His mind is detached from everything, he has conquered his own self, and he is free from hankering; it is by means of such renunciation that a person attains the supreme state, free from the results of action.

The discussion of *varna* and the *dharma*, or action, associated with *varna* leads naturally to a recapitulation of the topic of *karma-yoga* that was covered in some detail in Chapters 2–5 of the text. The fact that this is a recapitulation of previous ideas is made even clearer by the fact that verse 47 is almost identical to verse 35 of the third chapter.

It seems apparent that Krishna is now concluding his teachings in an appropriate manner by summarising the main points he has been seeking to convey, starting with the idea of *karma-yoga* that dominated the opening phases of the Gita. There is, however, a very interesting feature here that was less apparent when *karma-yoga* was discussed earlier in the text.

It is significant to note here how the Gita overtly links its previous idea of *karma-yoga* with its later emphasis on *bhakti*, something that was much less apparent in the earlier chapters. The point made here is that *dharma* is an inherent feature of the creation generated by the Supreme Deity, and therefore, adherence to *dharma* is an act of worship dedicated to the Deity. Previously, *karma-yoga* was advocated because it changed the motive behind the action from selfish gain to performance of social duty, but now, we find that action is to be performed because it as an act of worship. What we are seeing in this summary is that Krishna wants to confirm that his treatise is primarily about devotion to a personal God, and in this final chapter, he shows that his previous teachings on *karma-yoga* and then on the acquisition of knowledge of the self also form a part of the major theme of the discourse, which is the nature of God and worship of God.

One further point we might note here in relation to our previous discussion of *varna* arises from the phrase *saha-jam karma* in verse 48. *Saha-jam* literally means 'born along with', and so the indication is that one is born to perform a particular type of action. This is not quite the same as meaning that one's *varna* is determined by birth, but it does appear to be an indication in that direction.

THE PATH OF KNOWLEDGE

50. Now, learn from me in brief, Kaunteya, how one who has achieved this success then attains Brahman, which is the culmination of realised knowledge.

51. It is by properly engaging his purified intellect, controlling himself by his resolve, renouncing the objects of the senses such as sound, and setting aside both desire and hate;

52. Living in a deserted place, eating only a small amount, regulating his speech, body, and mind, constantly dedicating himself to the yoga of meditation and maintaining a mood of detachment;

53. Giving up egotism, physical power, pride, desire, anger, and any sense of possession, having no conception of 'mine', and remaining always at peace; it is thus that he becomes fit to attain the state of being that is Brahman.

Here, the process of summary and conclusion is continued, as Krishna now refers again to the yoga practice that leads to the acquisition of knowledge of the true self. This in itself provides us with a valuable insight into how the Bhagavad-gita regards its own central teachings as being based first on *karma-yoga*, then on the acquisition of spiritual knowledge and finally devotion to the Supreme Deity. It is also significant that here, verse 50 appears to suggest a progression on the spiritual path from the *karma-yoga* just discussed towards the realisation of knowledge considered here. Perfection in *karma-yoga* provides a basis from which one can proceed to the next step, which involves regulation of the senses and the practice of the yoga of meditation, the *dhyana-yoga* that brings the *yogin* to the Brahman state of being – *brahma-bhuyaya kalpate*. In these three verses, 51–53, we seem to have a succinct restatement of the truths revealed in the sixth chapter, which followed on from the previous discussion of *karma-yoga*, the same order of teachings as is presented here in summary form.

THE WAY OF BHAKTI

54. Existing as Brahman, with his mind made tranquil, he neither laments nor hankers for anything. He is equal to all living beings. Such a person achieves the highest state of devotion to me.

55. And it is through this devotion that he gains knowledge of me, of what and who I am. When he thus properly understands me, he then immediately enters my being.

56. Though he always performs his prescribed duties, he remains dependent upon me, and through my grace, he attains the eternal, changeless position.

In these three verses, Krishna reminds us of the third of the major ideas the Bhagavad-gita has presented to its readers and hearers, devotion to the Supreme Deity. The sequence given here is an interesting one. In verse 54, it seems that the ultimate level of knowledge, existing as Brahman, is the point from which one is able to move on to the stage of *bhakti*. This would seem to suggest that just as *karma-yoga* leads to realised knowledge of the Brahman identity, so this knowledge leads on to the higher state of devotion to God. However, this understanding is complicated by the statement of verse 55, where we read that *bhakti* in turn leads to knowledge of Krishna – *bhaktya mam abhijanati* – and that it is this knowledge of Krishna that is the true gateway to liberation from rebirth. Then, in verse 56, we find a reassertion of the view that *karma-yoga* is a part of devotional practice, as was stated earlier, in verse 46; and here, it is stated that *moksha* is attained not just through knowledge of Krishna but also through the gift of grace bestowed by the Deity – *mat-prasadad avapnoti shashvatam padam avyayam.*

So, what are we to make of this? It seems that the rather simplistic idea of a linear progression through different phases of spiritual life cannot be sustained. There are not three distinct phases – *karma-yoga*, *jñana*, and *bhakti* – with each stage leading to the next and ultimately to liberation from rebirth, but rather a single all-embracing spirituality that includes these three differing but equally significant component elements. So, persons on the spiritual path may be performing *karma-yoga*, meditation on the *atman* to gain higher knowledge, or devotional worship of the Supreme Deity, but in fact, they are all following the same broad spiritual path. And here, we may recall the words that Krishna spoke in Chapter 5: *ekam samkhyam cha yogam* – Samkhya and yoga are, in essence, the same.

ADVICE TO ARJUNA

57. Mentally renouncing all your actions to me, dedicating yourself to me, and resorting to the *buddhi-yoga*, you should keep your mind always fixed on me.
58. By keeping your mind fixed on me, you will overcome all these difficulties through my grace. But if, through pride, you do not listen, you will surely perish.
59. If you surrender to your sense of ego and think, 'I will not fight', this determination will be of no avail, for your inherent nature will surely exert its control over you.
60. Bound to your specific duty, Kaunteya, which arises from your inherent nature, you will be compelled to perform the action that, because of illusion, you do not wish to perform.

So, now the teachings of the Bhagavad-gita have been summarised and concluded, but there are still a few points to tie up, the first of which takes us back to the original starting point of the discourse, as the full instruction that has been given is now to be applied to Arjuna's specific case. The wisdom has been given, so what should Arjuna do now?

A careful reading of verses 57 and 58 reveals that Krishna is suggesting that Arjuna should employ all three of the paths he has just summarised, *karma-yoga* (renouncing all actions to me), *bhakti* (dedicating yourself to me . . . through my grace), and realised knowledge (keep your mind always fixed on me). If Arjuna accepts these teachings, then he will cross beyond all his difficulties; in other words, the dilemma he expressed in the first chapter will be resolved through the teachings Krishna has given.

No choice but to fight

In verses 59 and 60, Krishna is telling Arjuna that he really has no choice in the matter of whether or not to fight. Why is this? As has already been explained, each person has a specific *sva-bhava*, or inherent nature, formed by a configuration of the three *gunas* and reflected in the *varna* system of classical Indian society. Arjuna is a *kshatriya*, a warrior and a ruler, but this designation is not just because of his birth in a royal family. It reflects his inherent nature, which cannot be changed. Arjuna is a warrior by nature, and he cannot change that identity as a matter of free will. It is what he is. Fire must be hot, the sun must shine, and a *kshatriya* must take part in battle. So, adherence to *varna-dharma* is not just what is right in the sense of moral choice; it is what is natural in terms of the way the world is created.

Is there such a thing as free will?

This passage gives significant support to the determinist view of human nature, suggesting that the actual extent of our free will is very limited. Arjuna saw himself as having the power to make the choice as to whether to fight or not, but here, Krishna is asserting that it is not possible for any person to act against his or her inherent nature. This provides confirmation for an earlier assertion found in verse 33 of Chapter 3. However, we must note here that this is not the whole story, for a few verses later, we have the paradox of

Krishna saying to Arjuna, *yathecchasi tatha kuru*, 'you must act as you see fit'. As is so often the case in studying the Bhagavad-gita, we must be wary of simplistic creeds in matters of doctrine.

THE LORD WITHIN EVERY BEING

61. The Lord is situated in the region of the heart of all beings, and he causes every being to revolve through life, mounted on the machine conducted by his mystical power (*maya*).

62. You should surrender your entire being to him alone, Bharata. Then, by his grace, you will attain that eternal position which is absolute peace.

63. I have now revealed to you this wisdom, which is the deepest of all mysteries. After fully considering what you have heard, you should then act as you see fit.

Here, the Gita expands upon its previous point relating to the control exercised by inherent nature over each individual. From the previous verses, it might have appeared that this was part of a natural process of cause and effect, and hence, just one of the laws of nature that govern the universal order. Here, however, as in Chapter 16, a theistic dimension is added to the equation. It is not just that *svabhava*, inherent nature, exerts its influence over the living being as a natural part of its identity, the whole process is overseen by the 'Lord of all beings' – *ishvarah sarva-bhutanam* – who is situated in the region of the heart, *hrid-deshe . . . tishthati*.

What does this mean? It is not an entirely new idea, for the same assertion is to be found in 15.15, but should we take the 'Lord of all beings' to mean the *atman*, the individual soul, or is this referring to the *antaryamin* or *paramatman*, an expansion of the Deity who sits alongside the individual *atman*? Advaitins will tend to follow the former interpretation (although Shankara accepts that the verse is referring to Vishnu), whilst Vaishnavas such as Ramanuja and

Madhva hold to the second opinion. Both interpretations are certainly possible, but in this case, the active role played by the *ishvara* in controlling the transmigration of the soul does suggest an external Deity rather than the soul itself.

Moreover, the Deity in the heart of every being seems to play the role of the traditional monotheistic God by granting salvation to those who become his devotees. In Chapter 12, Krishna stated that he himself is this saviour who delivers the devotees, and hence, one must presume that the Deity in the heart referred to here is in fact Krishna himself, though the idea is expressed in the third person rather than the first.

And finally, we cannot ignore the instruction given in verse 63, which in many ways seems to typify the Hindu approach to religious authority. Krishna is the Supreme Deity, he is God, and he has given revealed truth to the world, but still, the ultimate choice is left up to us. If we follow the instruction then it will be for our benefit, but we must only do so after carefully considering what has been said and recognising its validity. Does Arjuna have free will in this? Apparently so, for he is told to act as he sees fit, and hence, he is not wholly under the control of his inherent nature. Thus, we are to some extent independent beings who do have the power to make choices, and even where the Hindu God issues a command, he does so with the caveat 'Think about this carefully, and then do as you wish' because ultimately, the scripture is our servant and guide, but it is not our master.

ABSOLUTE DEVOTION TO KRISHNA

64. Now, listen again to the ultimate teaching, which is indeed the deepest mystery. You are very dear to me, this is certain, and therefore, I will reveal this for your benefit.
65. Fix your mind on me, become my devotee, worship me, and bow down to me. Then, you will come to me; this is my certain promise, for you are dear to me.

66. Abandoning all types of dharma, take shelter with me alone. I will deliver you from all sins, so do not grieve.

The Bhagavad-gita is now effectively over. The teachings have been given, they have been summarised and concluded, and then they have been applied to the specific case of Arjuna so that he can see a way out of his predicament. Still, however, Krishna is concerned to ensure that his main point has been heard and understood. And what is that point? Again, it is devotion and surrender to God. 65 and 66 are two famous verses amongst the Vaishnavas, and 66 could be said to encapsulate the entire religious philosophy of Ramanujacharya. It is a doctrine of complete surrender and dependence upon a personal Deity who will reciprocate our devotion by relieving us from the sufferings of life. In verse 66, Krishna utters the famous words *aham tva sarva-papebhyo mokshayishyami*, I will deliver you from all forms of *papa*. The word *papa* is usually understood in the sense of sin and the karmic reaction that results from acts of wickedness, but it can also be taken in the wider sense of difficulty, suffering, and affliction. We face many difficulties in life, but here, Krishna, the Supreme Deity, promises that he himself will intervene in the case of those who are utterly dependent upon him and relieve them from all their difficulties.

Hinduism (for want of a better term) is a remarkable religious tradition that seems to defy any sort of categorisation. Here, in the Gita, and elsewhere in the Upanishads, it has been revealed that the highest reality is one's own self, and that the highest spiritual achievement is knowledge of the self, which is knowledge of all things. But here, we encounter a rather different form of religion, a form of monotheism in which a personal God instructs us to worship him in a mood of love, to become dependent upon him, and promises that he will reciprocate by acting as the saviour who delivers the worshipper from the miseries of the world. So often it seems that every idea that has ever occurred in the history of religiosity is to be found somewhere within the *dharma* of the Hindus.

Teaching the Bhagavad-gita to Others

67. You should not reveal these teachings to anyone who lacks austerity or is bereft of devotion, nor to one who does not wish to hear it or one who is envious of me.

68. But one who imparts this supreme mystery to my devotees, thereby displaying the highest devotion to me, will come to me. There is no doubt about this.

69. There is no one amongst men who can perform a deed more pleasing to me than this, nor will there be any person more dear to me than he.

70. And if anyone studies this conversation between us, which is based on dharma, then he is in fact worshipping me through the *yajña* of knowledge. That is my view.

71. Any man endowed with faith and free of malice who listens to this discourse is liberated thereby and attains the auspicious worlds gained by those of righteous deeds.

Now, the last word really has been spoken and we move on to the sort of passage that is to be found at the end of most Hindu religious texts, pointing out the benefits that can be accrued by one who recites, hears, or studies this revelation. Firstly, however, we are told that the message should not be imparted to one who is not a suitable recipient. Jesus gave a similar instruction to his disciples with the wonderful metaphor, 'Cast not thy pearls before swine'. In other words, there is no point in preaching the highest spiritual truths to those who are more in need of basic moral instruction.

On the other hand, one who passes on this wisdom to those who will receive it in an appropriate manner are blessed by Krishna and become dear to him. Moreover, anyone who studies this conversation and anyone who hears it with humility and respect will also be benefited in their spiritual quest. The point here is that hearing alone is not necessarily beneficial, for some scholars and some adherents of other faiths have studied the Gita in a critical manner seeking only to find grounds for condemnation. It is hardly to be expected that such persons will gain spiritually from their contact with the text.

ARJUNA ACCEPTS
KRISHNA'S INSTRUCTION

72. Have you listened to this instruction with a focused mind, Partha? Is your confusion, based on ignorance, now dispelled, Dhanamjaya?
73. Arjuna said: The confusion is dispelled, and through your grace I have regained my understanding. I am now resolute, my doubts have vanished, and I am ready to act in accordance with your instruction.

Here, then, is the simple and anticipated conclusion to the Bhagavad-gita, at least in terms of its position within the *Mahabharata* narrative. At the start of the Gita, Arjuna was moving towards Yudhishthira's position of condemning warfare as an illegitimate act even where the cause is a just one. Now, after Krishna's speech, he accepts that his previous reluctance was based on a lack of understanding, which has been rectified by the teachings he has absorbed.

This is not quite the end of the story, however, for in the opening encounters of the Kurukshetra War, which are described in the *Mahabharata* chapters that follow on from the Bhagavad-gita, we find that on at least two occasions Arjuna again displays a reluctance to fight, particularly when the flow of battle brings him into conflict with Bhishma. Considering his apparent resolve here, it is a little surprising to find Arjuna relapsing back towards his previous hesitancy after battle has been joined, to the extent that at one point Krishna himself comes close to attacking Bhishma and is only prevented from doing so by Arjuna's promise to fight more vigorously.

SAMJAYA'S CONCLUSION

74. Samjaya said: Thus, I have heard this wonderful conversation between Vasudeva and the high-souled Partha, which makes my hair stand on end.

75. It is through the grace of Vyasa that I have heard this supreme mystery, this doctrine of yoga, as revealed by Krishna himself, who is indeed the master of yoga (*yogeshvara*).

76. O king, as I constantly recall this enthralling and sacred conversation between Keshava and Arjuna, I repeatedly experience this sense of ecstasy.

77. And as I repeatedly recall the magnificent form displayed by Hari, great is my sense of wonder, O King, and again and again I feel a thrill of supreme delight.

78. Wherever there is Krishna, the master of yoga, and wherever there is Partha who bears the bow, there will also be good fortune, victory, success, and good judgement. That is my opinion.

Now, we are once more back with the conversation between Samjaya and Dhritarashtra, as Samjaya expresses his wonder and delight at the words he has heard and the vision he was able to share. The 'grace of Vyasa' refers back to the *Mahabharata* narrative, in which Samjaya was given mystical vision by Vyasa so that he was able to view all the events that occur on the battlefield and then relate them to the blind Dhritarashtra, who remained in his palace in Hastinapura. And it is not just the Bhagavad-gita that is spoken in this form from Samjaya to Dhritarashtra. The whole battle narration, which covers four of the *Mahabharata's* eighteen books, is spoken by Samjaya to Dhritarashtra in the same extended dialogue.

So, the Bhagavad-gita draws to its conclusion with a reminder to Dhritarashtra that despite all his hopes and schemes, he cannot hope for victory in this encounter, because of the presence on the opposing side of both Krishna, who is the lord of all beings, and Arjuna, the unconquerable archer.

CONCLUSION: A SUMMARY OF CHAPTER 18

Chapter 18 passes through a number of different phases in its lengthy course. It starts with a discussion of whether ritual acts are to be given up or continued in a detached state of mind, determining that the latter course is superior, and then proceeds to a more detailed consideration of the nature of action and the transcendent nature of the true self, which is merely a witness. Krishna then resumes his systematic series of analyses based on the three *gunas*, which was begun in Chapter 17 but interrupted by the extended review of the nature of action and renunciation of action. In this chapter, six topics are subjected to scrutiny in terms of *sattva*, *rajas*, and *tamas*: knowledge, action, the performer of action, understanding, resolve, and happiness. And in a number of cases, a connection is to be noted between the quality of *sattva* and the performance of *karma-yoga*. From verse 40 onwards, Krishna begins his summary of the main points he has covered in the Gita as a whole, focussing on *karma-yoga*, realised knowledge, and devotion to the Supreme Deity, revealing that these three are constituent parts of one spiritual path. We then return to Arjuna's dilemma over whether to fight in the battle, as Krishna suggests that the teachings he has given provide an effective resolution to the problem. After a further reminder of the importance of devotion to God in removing life's difficulties, Arjuna states that he is now convinced by Krishna's arguments and that he will fight in the upcoming battle. The chapter and the Gita as a whole conclude with Samjaya telling Dhritarashtra of his sense of delight and wonder at the teachings he has heard and the vision he saw. The presence of Krishna and Arjuna ensures that the Pandava host will gain a great victory over the sons of Dhritarashtra.

NAMES OF
KRISHNA AND ARJUNA

Supplied by Rogier Vrieling and Dr Rembert Lutjeharms.
These names appear in the original Sanskrit text (verse numbers
in parentheses). They are not all referred to in the translated text.

NAMES OF KRISHNA

Acyuta — he who never fails his devotees and who never falls down from his position. (1.21, 11.42, 18.73)

Adhiyajña — the Lord of sacrifice; the Super-soul, the plenary expansion of the Lord in the heart of every living being. (8.2, 8.4)

Adideva — the original Supreme God. (11.38)

Adikarta — the supreme creator. (11.37)

Amitavikrama — having unlimited strength. (11.40)

Ananta — he who is unending; he who has no limit. (11.37)

Ananta-rupa — unlimited form. (11.38) *See also* Vishvamurti, Vishvarupa.

Anantavirya — having unlimited potency. (11.19, 11.40)

Aprameya — who is immeasurable. (11.17, 11.42)

Apratimaprabhava — whose power is immeasurable. (11.43)

Arisudana — killer of the enemies. (2.4)

Bhagavan — who possesses all opulences; the reservoir of all beauty, strength, fame, wealth, knowledge, and renunciation. (10.14, 10.17, (*shri-bhagavan uvaca*: 2.2, 2.11, 2.55, 3.3, 3.37, 4.1, 4.5, 5.2, 6.1, 6.35, 6.40, 7.1, 8.3, 9.1, 10.1, 10.19, 11.5, 11.32, 11.47, 11.52, 12.2, 13.2, 14.1, 14.22, 15.1, 16.1, 17.2, 18.2))

Bhutabhavana — source of all manifestations; origin of everything. (9.5, 10.15)

Bhutabhrt — maintainer of all living entities. (9.5)

Bhutesha — Lord of everything; the supreme controller of everyone. (10.15)

Deva — God. (11.14, 11.15, 11.44, 11.45)

Devadeva — Lord of all demigods; God of gods. (10.15, 11.13)

Devavara — great one amongst the demigods; best of gods. (11.31)

Devesha — Lord of all lords; God of the gods. (11.25, 11.37, 11.45)

Govinda — giver and object of pleasure to the cows and to the senses. (1.32, 2.9)

Hari — who removes all inauspiciousness and steals the hearts of his devotees. (11.9, 18.77)

Hrishikesha — the Lord who directs the senses of the devotees; the master of the senses. (1.15, 1.20, 1.24, 2.9, 2.10, 11.36, 18.1)

Isha — the Supreme Lord. (11.44)

Ishvara — the Supreme Lord; the Supreme Controller. (4.6, 15.17, 18.61)

Jagannivasa — refuge of the universe. (11.25, 11.37, 11.45)

Jagatpati — Lord of the entire universe. (10.15)

Janardana — maintainer of all living entities; chastiser of the enemies. (1.35, 1.38, 1.43, 3.1, 10.18, 11.51)

Kala — time (another form of Krishna). (11.32)

Kamalapatraksha — lotus-petal-eyed one. (11.2)

Keshava — the Supreme Lord, Krishna, who has fine, long black hair; killer of the demon Keshi. (1.30, 2.54, 3.1, 10.14, 11.35, 13.1, 18.76)

Keshinishudana — killer of the Keshi demon. (18.1) *See also* Keshava.

Krishna — 'dark blue'; the two-armed form of the Supreme Lord; the all-attractive person. (1.28, 1.31, 1.40, 5.1, 6.34, 6.37, 6.39, 11.35, 11.41, 17.1, 18.75, 18.78)

Madhava — husband of the goddess of fortune; he who appeared in the Madhu dynasty. (1.14, 1.36)

Madhusudana — killer of the demon Madhu. (1.34, 2.1, 2.4, 6.33, 8.2)

Mahabahu — having mighty arms. (6.38, 11.23, 18.1) *See also* (*Names of Arjuna*) Arjuna, Mahabahu.

Mahatma — the great Lord; the great soul. (11.12, 11.20, 11.37, 11.50, 18.74)

Mahayogeshvara — the most powerful mystic. (11.9)

Parameshvara — the supreme controller. (11.3, 13.28)

Prabhu — the Lord, or the Master. (9.18, 9.24, 11.4, 14.21)

Prajapati — the Lord of creatures (Vishnu). (3.10)

Purushottama — the most exalted person. (8.1, 10.15, 11.3, 15.18, 15.19)

Sahasrabahu — thousand-handed one. (11.46)

Sakha — dear friend. (11.41)

Ugrarupa — whose form is fierce. (11.31)

Varshneya — descendant of Vrishni. (1.40, 3.36)

Vasudeva — son of Vasudeva; proprietor of everything, material and spiritual. (7.19, 11.50, 18.74)

Vishnu — the Personality of Godhead; he who pervades the entire universe. (10.21, 11.24, 11.30)

Vishvamurti — personification of the universe. (11.46)

Vishvarupa — whose form is the universe. (11.16)

Vishveshvara — Lord of the universe; the ultimate controller. (11.16)

Yadava — he who appears in the Yadu dynasty. (11.41)

Yajña — the personification of sacrifice; the goal and enjoyer of all sacrifices. (3.9, 4.23)

Yogeshvara — the supreme master of all mystic powers. (11.4, 18.75, 18.78)

Yogi — supreme mystic. (10.17)

NAMES OF ARJUNA

Anagha — sinless one. (3.3, 14.6, 15.20)

Arjuna — 'silver white'; the third son of Pandu and intimate friend of Lord Krishna. (1.46, 2.2, 2.45, 3.7, 4.5, 4.9, 4.37, 6.16, 6.32, 6.46, 7.16, 7.26, 8.16, 8.27, 9.19, 10.32, 10.39, 10.42, 11.47, 11.50, 11.54, 18.9, 18.34, 18.61, 18.76 (*arjuna uvaca*: 1.4, 1.21, 1.28, 2.4, 2.54, 3.1, 3.36, 4.4, 5.1, 6.33, 6.37, 8.1, 10.12, 11.1, 11.15, 11.36, 11.51, 12.1, 13.1, 14.21, 17.1, 18.1, 18.73))

Bharata — descendant of Bharata. (2.14, 2.18, 2.28, 2.30, 3.25, 4.7, 4.42, 7.27, 11.6, 13.3, 13.34, 14.3, 14.8, 14.9, 14.10, 15.19, 15.20, 16.3, 17.3, 18.62)

Bharatarshabha — chief amongst the descendants of Bharata; best of the Bharatas. (3.41, 7.11, 7.16, 8.23, 13.27, 14.12, 18.36)

Bharatasattama — best of the Bharatas. (18.4)

Bharatasrestha — chief of the Bharatas. (17.12)

Dehabhrtamvara — best of the embodied. (8.4)

Dhananjaya — conqueror of wealth. (1.15, 2.48, 2.49, 4.41, 7.7, 9.9, 10.37, 11.14, 12.9, 18.29, 18.72)

Dhanurdhara — carrier of the bow and arrow; carrier of the Gandiva bow, which can never be defeated in war. (18.78)

Gudakesha — Arjuna, the master of curbing ignorance. (1.24, 2.9, 10.20, 11.7)

Kapidhvaja — he whose flag was marked with Hanuman. (1.20)

Kaunteya — son of Kunti. (1.27, 2.14, 2.37, 2.60, 3.9, 3.39, 5.22, 6.35, 7.8, 8.6, 8.16, 9.7, 9.10, 9.23, 9.27, 9.31, 10.23, 10.27, 10.31, 13.2, 13.32, 14.4, 14.7, 16.20, 16.22, 18.48, 18.50, 18.60)

Kiriti — diademed one. (11.35)

Kurunandana — beloved child of the Kurus. (2.41, 6.43, 14.13)

Kurupravira — best among the Kuru warriors. (11.48)

Kurusattama — best amongst the Kurus. (4.31)

Kurusrestha — best of the Kurus. (10.19)

Mahabahu — having mighty arms. (2.26, 2.68, 3.28, 3.43, 5.3, 5.6, 6.35, 7.5, 10.1, 14.5, 18.13) *See also* (*Names of Krishna*) Mahabahu.

Pandava — the son of Pandu. (1.14, 1.20, 4.35, 6.2, 10.37, 11.13, 11.55, 14.22, 16.5)

Parantapa — chastiser, subduer, conqueror of the enemy. (2.3, 2.9, 4.2, 4.5, 4.33, 7.27, 9.3, 10.40, 11.54, 18.41)

Partha — son of Prtha (Kunti). (1.25, 1.26, 2.3, 2.21, 2.32, 2.39, 2.42, 2.55, 2.72, 3.16, 3.22, 3.23, 4.11, 4.33, 6.40, 7.1, 7.10, 8.8, 8.14, 8.19, 8.22, 8.27, 9.13, 9.32, 10.24, 11.5, 11.9, 12.7, 16.4, 16.6, 17.26, 17.28, 18.6, 18.30, 18.31, 18.32, 18.33, 18.34, 18.35, 18.72, 18.74, 18.78) *See also* Kaunteya, Pandava.

Purusharshabha — best among men. (2.15)

Purushavyaghra — tiger among men. (18.4)

Savyasaci — ambidextrous archer. (11.33)

Tata — My (Krishna's) friend. (6.40)

GLOSSARY OF TERMS

Abhyasa: Regulated practice of a particular discipline.

Acharya: A teacher or interpreter of scripture, typically revered by groups of followers.

Adityas: The twelve most prominent among the Vedic gods; the sons of Aditi.

Advaita: Non-dualism; a strand of Vedanta philosophy that teaches the absolute unity of *atman* and Brahman, the individual self and the absolute reality.

Ahamkara: That part of our psychological makeup that gives us a sense of selfhood. Can also mean 'pride' and 'arrogance'.

Akshara: That which does not decay; term applied to both the individual *atman* and to the Supreme Deity.

Antaryamin: The indweller; a term that can indicate either the *atman* or the expansion of the Deity that is present in every being alongside the *atman*.

Apana: The outward breath.

Asana: A sitting posture, as in yoga practice.

Asura: A group of powerful superhuman beings who are generally vicious in nature and who are the eternal enemies of the gods.

Atman: The spiritual entity that is present within every living being and which brings life to inert matter.

Avatara: One who crosses down; a manifestation of the Supreme Deity appearing in this world to restore the order of dharma set in place by the creation.

Avidya: Ignorance, absence of knowledge.

Avyakta: Non-manifest, invisible; a term applied to the state of existence before creation.

Bhagavan: The exalted one, God; a term used for Krishna in the Bhagavad-gita.

Bhajan: A devotional song performed to glorify a deity.

Bhakti: Devotion; one of the paths advocated by the Bhagavad-gita to achieve spiritual perfection.

Brahma Sutras: An early text compiled by Badarayana that purports to summarise the teachings of the Upanishads. Regarded as an authoritative source by *acharyas* of Vedanta.

Brahmacharya: Celibacy or sexual restraint.

Brahman: The ultimate reality that is the source of the world and is the world. Brahman is considered to be that which is all things, but for some *acharyas*, it is a term that denotes the Supreme Deity. In the Gita, it is also used to mean 'the Vedic scriptures' and 'the basic substance of matter'.

Buddhi: The intellect; that part of a person's mental composition that analyses information and makes decisions based on that information.

Buddhi-yoga: The withdrawal of the intellect from material desires so that action is performed with no aspiration for personal gain.

Dana: Charity.

Deva: A deity; a term that can be applied either to the one Supreme Deity or any of the lesser divine beings.

Dharma: Right action; there are a number of other meanings for the word, but in the Gita it means 'acting properly in accordance with pre-ordained rules or in relation to virtue'.

Dhriti: Resolve, determination.

Dhyana: Meditation; controlling the mind and turning the vision inwards in order to gain direct perception of the *atman*.

Duhkha: Sorrow, misery, suffering.

Dvaita: Dualism; the understanding that the individual *atman* and the Supreme Deity (Brahman) are absolutely and eternally distinct.

Gunas: The three strands that pervade everything material and exert an influence over our lives, our mentality, and the manner in which we conduct ourselves.

Ishvara (*Isha*): The controller; the Supreme Deity. The term is sometimes used for the *atman*.

Japa: Quiet or silent recitation of a prayer or *mantra*.

Jiva, Jiva-bhuta: Another term used for the *atman*, although it tends to apply to the *atman* in its state of bondage in this world.

Jñana: Knowledge; either an understanding of mundane affairs or the realisation that brings enlightenment and liberation.

Jñana-kanda: That portion of the Vedas that contains revelations about the nature of the self and the world. Typically applied to the Upanishads.

Jñanin: One who possesses knowledge; an enlightened person.

Jñeya: That which should be known; typically applied to the *atman*, the object of knowledge.

Kaivalya: Aloneness, separation; a term for liberation used in Samkhya teachings to indicate the separation of the true self from matter.

Kala: Time.

Kali-yuga: In Hindu cosmology, the present age, which is regarded as a period of decline and degradation amongst humanity.

Kalpa: A period of creation from the time of the manifestation of the world until its withdrawal.

Kama: Desire, lust.

Karma: Action and reaction.

Karma-kanda: The portion of the Vedas that gives instruction on ritual acts to worship the Vedic deities.

Karma-yoga: The performance of action without attachment or desire for gain; a part of the path leading to liberation from the world.

Kripa: Compassion.

Krodha: Anger.

Kshara: That which decays; the opposite of *akshara*; usually applied to anything that is material, although not to *prakriti* itself.

Kshatriya: The second of the four *varnas*; the social class that includes warriors and rulers.

Kshetra: The field; a Samkhya term for the body and the material manifestation.

Kshetrajña: The knower of the field; a synonym for *atman* and *purusha*.

Mahabharata: The vast Indian scripture of which the Bhagavad-gita is one short passage.

Mahatma: Great soul; a term of respect used for those who are enlightened.

Manas: The mind; that part of our psychological makeup that receives and categorises perceptions received through the senses.

Mantra: A hymn, prayer, or sacred sound; often used in meditation.

Maya: Illusion or divine power; used to denote the force that keeps living beings in a state of illusion about their own identity and that of the Supreme Deity.

Moksha: Liberation, release; a term used to denote the state of liberation from the cycle of karma and rebirth.

Murti-puja: Worship of a deity in the form of a sacred image.

Nirvana: An equivalent term for *moksha*; liberation from rebirth.

Pandita: A learned scholar, or one who has achieved a state of enlightenment.

Papa: Sin, wicked action that produces unwanted karmic results; may also refer to these results as well.

Paramatman: The Supreme Soul; sometimes used to indicate the individual living entity and sometimes for the expansion of the Deity accompanying the individual *atman* through the cycle of rebirth.

Parvan: A chapter or section of a composition. The eighteen books of the *Mahabharata* are referred to as *parvans*.

Pinda: Offerings made on behalf of departed ancestors to ensure their well-being in the afterlife.

Pradhana: *Prakriti* in its non-differentiated, unevolved form; primal matter.

Prakriti: Matter in both its non-differentiated primeval form and in its evolved variegated form as well. In its non-differentiated state, it is also referred to as *pradhana* and *avyakta*.

Prana: The inward breath; also used to denote life itself or the breath of life.

Pranayama: A part of the yoga system that involves regulation of the breathing process.

Prapatti: Absolute surrender to the will of the Deity and complete dependence upon him.

Priya: Beloved, one who is loved.

Punya: Piety, virtue; forms of action that lead to a favourable karmic result.

Puranas: A group of eighteen Sanskrit works, mostly composed after the Bhagavad-gita, some of which describe the deeds performed by Krishna and other *avataras*.

Purusha: A person, a man; a synonym for *atman* frequently used in Samkhya teachings.

Purushottama: The Supreme Person; a term for the Supreme Deity which Krishna applies to himself.

Rajas: Passion, energy; one of the three *gunas*, indicated by desire, passion, and intense activity for personal gain.

Rakshasa: A type of powerful evil being inimical towards the gods and said to roam the forests at night.

Ramayana: An early Hindu scripture that recounts the life and deeds of the Rama *avatara*.

Rishi: A sage or holy man; the *rishis* were the original recipients or 'hearers' of the Vedas.

Sadhu: A wise and holy person; often, a wandering mendicant who is capable of giving spiritual instruction.

Samadhi: The final state of yogic perfection, when the mind is absolutely tranquil and all thought processes are brought under control.

Samkhya: An early system of Indian thought which emphasises the absolute distinction between *prakriti* and *purusha*, matter and spirit, and liberation through knowledge of that distinction.

Samnyasa: Renunciation of the world; often in relation to individuals who renounce their previous lives in pursuit of spiritual perfection.

Sattva: Truth, goodness, light; the first of the three *gunas*; that which inspires virtue, knowledge, and joy in individuals.

Shaivite: A devotee of Shiva who regards Shiva as the Supreme Deity.

Shanti: Peace, tranquillity; a state of consciousness achieved through yoga practice.

Shastra: A text or scripture that gives instruction.

Shruti: That which is heard; the Vedic texts, including the Upanishads.

Shudra: The fourth of the *varnas*; a member of the social class that is duty bound to perform work in the service of others.

Smriti: Scriptures that do not form a part of the Vedas, being composed by human beings.

Sukha: Happiness, joy.

Suta: A charioteer; considered to be of lower birth.

Svabhava: One's inherent nature that is formed by a particular configuration of the *gunas*; it is shaped by previous actions and exists within an individual from the time of birth.

Tamas: Darkness, ignorance; the lowest of the three *gunas*, promoting indolence, stupidity, impurity, and disregard.

Tapas: Acts of austerity undertaken in the hope of gaining some material or spiritual reward.

Tyaga: Renunciation, as defined by Krishna in Chapter 18 of the Gita.

Upanishads: Sacred texts from the Vedas that reflect on the true nature of the world and the individual.

Vairagya: Detachment from material desires; an important element in the practice of yoga.

Vaishnava: A devotee of Vishnu who regards Vishnu as the one Supreme Deity.

Vaishya: A member of the third of the four social classes who is expected to live by trade and agriculture.

Varnas: The four original social classes, Brahmins, *kshatriyas*, *vaishyas*, and *shudras*.

Veda(s): The original revelation of sacred truth divided into four parts, the *Rig*, the *Sama*, the *Yajur*, and the *Atharva* Veda.

Vedanta: A group of religious and philosophical systems based on the teachings of the Upanishads, the Brahma Sutras, and the Bhagavad-gita.

Vijñana: Practical knowledge, or knowledge that brings a higher form of realisation.

Vishva-rupa: The form of the Deity that embodies the entire universe.

Yajña: The ancient ritual prescribed in the Vedas whereby offerings to the gods are made into the sacred fire.

Yoga: In the Bhagavad-gita, a range of different religious practices. More specifically, the practice of mental restraint and inward meditation.

Yoga-maya: The divine potency by which the order of the universe is held in place and living beings are kept in a state of illusion.

Yoga-sutras: A work composed by Patañjali later than the Bhagavad-gita which discusses the philosophy and practice of the yoga system.

Yogin: A person who successfully engages in yoga practice.

Yuga: One of the four ages in Indian cosmology; in the Bhagavad-gita, the term is also used to indicate the total time period of all four yuga ages combined.

Yukta: Sometimes translated as 'integrated', but more generally successful engagement in yoga practice.

BIBLIOGRAPHY

Brockington, J., *The Sacred Thread*, Edinburgh University Press, 1998.

Edgerton, F., *The Bhagavad Gita Translated and Interpreted,* Harvard University Press, 1997.

Flood, G. (ed.), *The Blackwell Companion to Hinduism*, Blackwell, 2003.

Swami Gambhirananda, *Bhagavad Gita with the Commentary of Sankaracharya*, Nesma Books, 2000.

Gandhi, M.K., *The Bhagavad Gita According to Gandhi,* Berkeley Hills Books, 2000.

Johnson, W., *The Bhagavad Gita,* Oxford Paperbacks, 2004.

Leggett, T., *Realization of the Supreme Self: The Bhagavad Gita Yogas,* New Age Books, 2002.

Mehta, R., *From Mind to Super Mind: A Commentary on the Bhagavad Gita*, Motilal Banarsidass, 2001.

Minor, R., *The Bhagavad Gita: An Exegetical Commentary*, Heritage, 1982.

Prabhupada, A.C. Bhaktivedanta, *Bhagavad Gita As It Is,* BBT, 1983.

Swami Satchidananda, *Bhagavad Gita: Living Gita,* Integral Yoga Publications, 1988.

Sharma, A., *The Hindu Gita*, Open Court, 1986.

Sukthankar, V. S., *On the Meaning of the Mahabharata*, Bombay, 1957.

Sutton, N., *Religious Doctrines in the Mahabharata*, Motilal Banarsidass, 2000.

Zaehner, R.C., *The Bhagavad Gita,* Oxford University Press, 1973.

OXFORD CENTRE FOR HINDU STUDIES MANDALA PUBLISHING SERIES

This short courses series is adapted from online courses run by the Oxford Centre for Hindu Studies (OCHS) and is made available in collaboration with Mandala Publishing.

ABOUT OCHS

The Oxford Centre for Hindu Studies (OCHS) is a Recognized Independent Centre of The University of Oxford. It's an academy for the study of Hindu cultures, societies, philosophies, religions, and languages in all periods and in all parts of the world.

THE YOGA SUTRAS: A NEW TRANSLATION AND STUDY GUIDE

This course gives a detailed understanding of the fundamental ideas on which yoga practice is based and the ways in which it has developed during the ensuing millennia. As part of this short course, you will find an accessible translation and commentary on the Yoga Sutras.

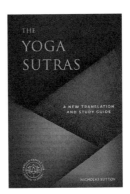

INTRODUCTION TO THE MAHABHARATA AND RAMAYANA: A SHORT COURSE

This course is a broad study of the central narratives, themes, and characters represented in the Mahabharata and the Ramayana and considers the teachings that are imparted by means of direct instruction, instructive incidents, and role models.

HINDUISM PART I— HISTORY, TEXT, AND PHILOSOPHY: A SHORT COURSE

This course provides a broad survey of the scope of Hindu studies, touching briefly on a range of different topics so as to give a comprehensive understanding of the nature and scope of the Hindu religious tradition.

HINDUISM PART II— RITUAL, YOGA, CASTE, AND GENDER: A SHORT COURSE

This course focuses in particular on Hindu religious practice, including temple ritual and the meditational techniques of classical yoga.

MANDALA
PUBLISHING

An Imprint of MandalaEarth
PO Box 3088
San Rafael, CA 94912
www.MandalaEarth.com

Find us on Facebook: www.facebook.com/MandalaEarth
Follow us on Twitter: @MandalaEarth

Library of Congress Cataloging-in-Publication Data available.

ISBN: 978-1-68383-733-6

Publisher: Raoul Goff
Associate Publisher: Phillip Jones
Creative Director: Chrissy Kwasnik
Managing Editor: Lauren LePera
Assistant Editors: Tessa Murphy, Pandita Geary
Senior Production Editor: Rachel Anderson
Senior Production Manager: Greg Steffen

Designed by theBookDesigners

Special thanks to Shaunaka Rishi Das and the entire team at The Oxford Centre for
Hindu Studies

  REPLANTED PAPER

ROOTS of PEACE

Mandala Publishing, in association with Roots of Peace, will plant two trees for each tree
used in the manufacturing of this book. Roots of Peace is an internationally renowned
humanitarian organization dedicated to eradicating land mines worldwide and convert-
ing war-torn lands into productive farms and wildlife habitats. Roots of Peace will plant
two million fruit and nut trees in Afghanistan and provide farmers there with the skills
and support necessary for sustainable land use.

Manufactured in India by Insight Editions

10 9 8 7 6 5 4 3 2 1